To Brian Latham

Blessings & Best

What a Life

Wishes.

Tochi

New Era
International

Go not to the temple to put flowers
upon the feet of God,

First fill your own house with the
fragrance of love...

Go not to the temple to light candles
before the altar of God,

First remove the darkness of sin
from your heart...

Go not to the temple to
bow down your head in prayer,

First learn to bow in humility
before your fellowmen...

Go not to the temple to pray
on bended knees,

First bend down to lift someone
who is down-trodden...

Go not to the temple to ask for
forgiveness for your sins,

First forgive from your heart those who
have sinned against you.

Rabindranath Tagore

What a Life

Dr. Tochi Bhatt
Ph.D, FRSC, FAIC

A **New Era** *International* Imprint

INTERNATIONAL STANDARD BOOK NUMBER (ISBN)

978-81-290-0106-1

What a Life - Dr. Tochi Bhatt

First Published: 2015
This Edition/Reprint: 2015

Printed in India

NEW ERA BOOK AGENCY ®

Publisher • Distributor • Exporter & Orders Supplier
SCO 49-51, SECTOR - 17 C, POST BOX - 52
CHANDIGARH - 160 017 (INDIA)

www.newerainternational.com

EMAIL
neimprint@gmail.com   ₹ 995/-

Dedication

I dedicate this story, of a humble man,
to my daughter Lisa, my son Chris,
my sunshine Amelia
and my daughter-in-law Gillian.
"Guys" thanks for the love and fun you
brought into my life.

To my wonderfully unique,
late, wife Joan.
I thank you for the most fascinating adventure
and turning an Indian born African
wild hunter into a gentleman!!!.
To my current partner,
Pauline for the love, care
and being a wonderful companion.

Last, but not the least to my extraordinary
parents, Sardarni Labh Kaur and
Sardar Naranjan Singh Bhatt,
for their love and endowing me with the genes
to cope with and succeed in this vast world.

One of the lessons I have learned from my father is
that "it's within you to carve out your own future,
create your own destiny." He would say smile, be
polite, and courteous to all.

Glossary - *Indian Words and their Meaning in English*

Ardas— Prayer

Bibiji— Mom (Mother)

Bone-shaker— Buses (Old Public Transport in poor condition)

Diwali— Indian festival of lights

Fauji— Armyman

Gobhi— Cauliflower

Guru— Spiritual teacher/preacher

Guru Granth Sahib— Holy book/Religious text of Sikhism, considered to be the final, sovereign guru.

Jalebi— A sweet made by deep-frying a wheat flour (maida flour) batter in circular shapes, which are then soaked in sugar syrup.

Kirtan— Adoration, or praising, of the divine. In Sikhism, kirtan refers especially to singing of praise as expressed in the hymns and compositions of Sikh scripture.

Loo— Toilet

Manglasutra— A sacred thread of love and goodwill worn by women as a symbol of their marriage in hindu community.

Papaji— Dad (Father)

parathas— Indian Bread (stuffed)

Parsad— Material substance of food that is a religious offering in both Hinduism and Sikhism

Rajnishi Ghost— A special mutton dish served at the Ashoka Hotel, New Delhi

Ras malai— A delicious Indian (Bengali) dessert, white or yellow-coloured balls of paneer (cottage cheese) are served in rich and creamy sugary cream.

Rickshaw (cycle)— A small-scale local means of transport that is human-powered by pedalling.

Rumalla— Square or rectangular piece of silk used to cover the Guru Granth Sahib

Skangvee— Drink made with lime juice in water or soda

Tongas (mechanical) Bone-shaker— Motorcycle rickshaws called the phatphatia. used to be popular and cheap mode to travel short distance in Delhi. But now off the roads.

Vaisakhi— Indian Harvest festival

Preface

This collection of memories is the result of requests by my children, Chris, Lisa, my daughter-in-law Gillian and my nephews Bob and Raj. They were constantly saying to me: "you keep on telling us stories about your and our family's past but unless you put pen to paper we will forget these. Therefore, please scribble something down so the future generations will come to know of our background." In this essay I will make an endeavour to tell all but if I miss anything it is not by design but because of memory lapse. I have tried to live as clean a life as it is possible, in doing so if I have offended any person than I apologise to them and ask for their forgiveness. I have always followed my heart and never given up no matter what life throws at me and hence my moto: *"Pugna non Pavor"* (Fight not Fright).

I can only write about the family up to the time I left Nairobi in early December 1955. The rest of the time will be my own story. In this auto-biography I am not trying to portray myself as an angel or place myself on a pedestal but simply narrating the incidents that occurred during my lifetime. I have probably made more mistakes in life than anybody else in the world, but I have learned from life's path and from observing the talents of others. This is just a story of a man who has, by the grace of God, survived to tell this fascinating tale. Many times I have been asked if I have any regrets in life. My answer has always been the same – no regrets except when my father, God bless his sole, needed me most I wasn't there to help him. Whatever I have achieved has been largely due to my late parents and my late wife, Joan Reed, God bless their souls. My parents worked very hard all their life for all of us.

2015

**Dr. Tarlochan S. Bhatt
(Tochi Bhatt)**
Kimpton
Hertfardshire - U.K.

Index

Descendants of Dr. Tarlochan Singh Bhatt

Pauline Edwina Tarbox
and Bhatt (Griffiths)
born: July. 3, 1944
Berkhampstead,
Hertfordshire

Dr. Tarlochan Singh
Bhatt
born: Jan. 7, 1936
Rattan, (Punjab)
India

Joan Lillian Louise
Bhatt (Reed)
born: May 25, 1932
Islington, London
died: Apr. 2007

Lisa Jane Galia
(Bhatt)
born: Mar. 25, 1967
QE II Hosp. WG City,
Hertfordshire

Christopher John
Bhatt
born: May. 13, 1968
The cottage named
Uplands, Blackmore
End, AL4 8LD

Andre Galia
born: Sept. 16, 1972

Gillian Bhatt (Saward)
born: Feb. 25, 1963

Amelia Jane Bhatt
born: Jan. 31, 2001

Introduction

The voice on the tannoy blared out. "Because of fog we will not be docking at King George the Fifth docks in London instead the Durban Castle will dock at Tilbury." We all sighed with disappointment because we were looking forward to sailing up the Thames. When the ship had docked and the ropes were tied to the cleats on the dockside I walked down the steps of the landing ladder onto English soil on Christmas Eve 1955. The Durban Castle was part of a large ocean going fleet of ships of enormous size that belonged to a company called Union Castle in the days of the Empire. This line used to sail round Africa from Southampton to Cape Town and return home through the Suez Canal. I had spent 25 glorious days on this ship since I embarked on it at the port of Mombasa in Kenya. During this remarkable, beautiful cruise I was lucky to visit Aden, Port Sudan on the Red Sea and then through the Gulf of Suez to Port Suez, the starting point of the wonderful canal. We came through the bitter lake and it was interesting to see arid desert on one side and green country with the railway line and the main trunk road on the other (I believe the word POSH comes from the voyage through the canal. When people went to the East from England they use to say port side out and starboard home). Port Said was the point where we entered The Mediterranean Sea. From here the ship sailed through the Straits of Messina, past Mount Etna where we saws flames spewing into the sky, then to Genoa, Marseille, Gibraltar (where we visited the great siege tunnels, saw the Barbary apes and the key ceremony), the famous Bay of Biscay and finally Tilbury.

There was entertainment each day and evening on the ship, with films on occasions, dances, tombola sessions and special evenings. Special events included cocktail parties, fancy dress parties and dinner dances. As an 18 year old, I did not fully appreciate a lot of the events although I took part in most of them.

On a bleak, cold, foggy December morning I climbed on board the train waiting on platform number 2 at Tilbury station. The train journey from Tilbury to Liverpool Street station, on that winter's morning through the county of Kent was an experience not to be repeated. As the train hurtled through the bleak industrial countryside all I could see-through the windows of my compartment was a panorama of terraced houses with chimneys blowing thick black smoke into an already misty, foggy grey sky. Sitting in a crowded compartment I was saying to myself where are those deep green rolling fields of England that I had read so much about. As the train rattled rat-a-tat, rat-a-tat, through Kent County my thoughts started to drift to the sun drenched Kenya where I had left my parents and siblings behind a month ago.

Growing-up in Kenya

Memories of a childhood spent first in the Sikh colony and then in Eastleigh section1 in Nairobi started to flood back. Sikh colony was a triangular area bounded by Race Course Road, Ngara Road and Desai road, where a large section of the Asian community had settled. Most of the residents, especially Sikhs, had come from Punjab encouraged by the Raj to a newly settled, Kenya colony, part of British East Africa, the other two countries being Uganda and Tanganyika. Tanganyika had been a German colony and at the end of the First World War was given to Britain as a trust territory by the League of Nations. This was the second wave of Indian migrants. The first wave of immigrants from the Indian subcontinent was brought in as indentured labour in 1892 to build the railway line from Mombasa to Lake Victoria in Uganda and there were many Sikhs among them all men of skill, carpenters, blacksmiths and masons. Nairobi was a staging point on this; massive and hazardous construction at that time but eventually became the main centre of trade. My Dad and Mum were among a group of people in the second wave who took up this offer and migrated to the new colony to set up a home and make a new life. By then Nairobi had become a flourishing city.

Dad was a Master Cutter in a factory in Bombay which made garments for the film industry and the Indian army. He took up the offer to try his luck in the new colony and initially worked for a Mrs. Weiss in her shop in Government Road. A few years later he opened his own shop further down the road towards Barclays Bank (DCO) building on the corner of Delamere Avenue and Government Road and was very successful.

In the Sikh Colony we shared a house with three other families. It was a typical house of that period – a single story, stone construction with a courtyard and an access road behind. A room and a kitchen per family, communal wet room with a cold shower and two outside toilets with an Elson tub in each was the accommodation. The Elson tubs were removed and replaced by clean tubs every night through a tin door at the rear of the tubs which sat in a stone construction under the toilet seat. Removal was carried out by what was affectionately known as 'the honey wagon.' If any member of the family needed a hot bath then we had to heat the water in a large tin or a metal pail on top of a charcoal burner and bathed using a mug and Lifebuoy soap. In fact, all the cooking was done on this cooker. Mom who was affectionately known as *Bibiji* used to make biscuits on a similar but larger charcoal cooker which had space for six trays, three for charcoal and three for biscuits. She used to put the cooked biscuits in a large tin with a lid and place the tin on the top shelf in the kitchen. I used to get my brother, Gurmit, to climb on my shoulders so he could reach the tin. Oh!!! To get to all those biscuits was bliss even after the scolding. The father of one of the other families in the house owned an Ariel motor cycle and he use to keep the tank full of petrol. He would say "when the Germans come across the Kenya border I am going south on my bike." He had two boys and two girls we became friends and to this day we are in contact with the surviving members of this family. The father died very young of a large wound on his left leg near the groin. We now know it was a malignant melanoma. Dad helped the family and placed their eldest son Nirmal as an apprentice tailor in a friend's shop in Delamere Avenue so he could support his family. When I attained school age Dad *(Papaji)* took me to the Government Indian School, in Nairobi. This school was later renamed Duke of Gloucester School. I loved school and as I grew older going to school became an adventure, especially on the way home.

A happy time was spent in the Sikh colony in Nagara. All the children played together in the street as there were few vehicles around. I used to say "Let me ask my Labo" (my grandfather had called *Bibiji* by this name from her childhood) when they asked me to come and play with them. We would leave home in the morning and play all day during the holidays. We were never ever bored, and we were allowed freedom all day as long as we were back when our parents told us to come in. Our childhood was one of the best, our love and respect for our parents was second to none and our respect for all our teachers was in our genes. We gladly looked after our younger brothers and sisters without a fuss. We ate what was put in front of us and best of all, there was never any leftovers. We attended temple regularly and in essence enjoyed life. We ran barefoot without thinking about it; if we got cut we used tincture of Iodine on it, which made us jump. We did not wash our hands ten times a day and we were OK. We did not have Play Stations, Nintendos, no video games at all but we had friends, great friends. We made up games with sticks, tennis balls and old bicycle tyres. We had freedom, failure, success and responsibility, and we learned to deal with it all. I think to myself what a wonderful childhood.

I remember going hunting many times with one of *Papaji's* friends who lived at the top end of our street. On one of these hunting trips my sister Meeto sat on a red ant nest. We only realized when we heard an ear-piercing scream. Dad just picked her up and dipped her in the brook that ran past our camp but her bottom was red and sore for weeks. A trip to Charlie's ice cream parlour in River Road every Sunday was a real treat for us children. Once a month, *Papaji* used to take us for a picnic to Ngong Hill. The bus from the city used to terminate here and after alighting the bus we used to walk for a little distance until we found a clear area in the woods. We had to be vigilant because the boundary of Nairobi national park runs very close to Ngong Hill.

In 1941, although I was only 5 years old I can distinctly remember blackout and an occasional dog fight in the sky although we did not witness the war up close. We had many Italian prisoners of war who were interned in the rift valley in Kenya until Italy joined the allies in 1943. They were made to build the road from Kabete to Nakuru through the rift valley in the dangerous and treacherous environment. The compassionate authority allowed them to build a very small Catholic church by the side of the road. It has become famous and people of all faiths go to admire this little church. *(See page P-1, Pic. 1: The Church built by Italian prisoners of war by the side of Nairobi to Nakuru road).*

At the weekend these prisoners were allowed to sell some of the articles, mostly made of wood, they had made during the week in the prisoner of war camp. One of these was a box with inlaid wood of different colours. These boxes were made in such a way that both the key hole and the key were hidden underneath sliding panels so to open one of these boxes you had to first find the key and then had the fun of finding the key hole. Our family bought one of these.

I will always remember Mwangi who looked after us when we were children. He came from a village called Gatundu which lies northeast of Nairobi and had joined the family as house boy. Mwangi stayed with the family for many years. Dad taught him to sew and gave him one of his old Singer sewing machines and he eventually opened his own shop in Gatundu. The village is also famous because the president of Kenya Mr. Jomo Kenyatta came from the area. When I went to Nairobi in 1962, I went to see Mwangi to see how he was and in essence to thank him for looking after us. As children when we had any problem we used to go to him and if we got splinters in our bare feet he would say. "Dudu, we must get it out" and proceed to do that with a needle. He did lot of the daily chores in the house which helped *Bibiji*. What a fantastic fellow?

There are many incidents that occurred while I was growing up in Nairobi. I will mention some of them as we take a walk through this colourful, adventurous life of the Bhatt family as I plough through my essay. A particular one that is vivid in my memory concerns a Sikh family who used to live diagonally opposite the house we lived in. Their daughter killed her father-in-law who, she said, had raped her. She would have been the first woman to be sentenced to death in Kenya. I remember going round collecting signatures for her reprieve. Her sentence was eventually commuted to life imprisonment. Another incident I remember well was the stabbing of Judge Mota Singh's father (Judge Mota Singh is the first person from the ethnic communities to be elevated to this position in England and has chambers in Middle Temple). The Judge's father had come home, a Public Works Department quarters, for lunch and had just sat down when he heard a women's cry for help. He ran out and confronted a black man who had robbed the woman of her gold necklace and as he grappled with the thief he was stabbed in the chest. My Mom (*Bibiji*) who was on her way home from shopping was one of the first people to go to his aid but the poor fellow died, I believe, on his way to the hospital.

A big event in the family's life was when Dad bought our first house in Eastleigh section-1. We moved in the rainy season. The removal lorry, kindly loaned by Mr. Gurbux Singh, got stuck in the mud and had to be towed while we all pushed. Mud was thrown back by the rear spinning wheels. We all got covered with it; to us kids this was fun and adventure. The house was about ten miles from the city centre in a rural area but very close to Eastleigh airport, at that time the only airport in the city. The dirt road we moved into was very close to where the Eastleigh section-1 bus used to terminate. Our house was the second house on the right hand side as you went down the road from the main road, one of the only tarmac roads around the area at that time. For the first time my sister Meeto and I had our own room. We also had a small garden to the right side of the courtyard where we grew vegetables and kept chickens and were rewarded with fresh vegetables and eggs. To this day I can still remember the smell of those fresh tomatoes.

One of *Papaji's* customers, a farmer's wife from the highlands had a pair of magnificent Alsatian dogs. She gave us a puppy from their next litter. *Papaji* let us keep this puppy on the condition that Meeto and I would look after it. We called the dog Tarzan on account of the fact that, at that time, Johnny Weissmuller films of the same name were very popular. The puppy used to urinate and shit in our room and we had to clean up after it. Tarzan grew up to be a large, friendly and affectionate dog and gave the family many years of safety and pleasure. He was a fantastic companion and we all loved him.

Opposite our house was a family where the father was Indian and the mother was a Somali. Their eldest son, a teacher, used to help me with my Urdu homework. Even though they were a very kind and friendly family, they were spurned by most of the neighbours because of the mixed marriage, but Dad was very friendly to them. There was another family about 100 yards diagonally opposite to the left of us where the father was a Sikh, Natha Singh, and the mother was a Kikuyu. They had a very large garden with an orchard full of fruit trees like guavas, pomegranates, bananas and pineapples. We were occasionally allowed in that garden to pick fruit; what a treat and those pomegranates were delicious. At the end of our road in a field was a large property in which lived a haulier by the name of Gurbux Singh and his family. They were very friendly and helpful; in fact it was because of them that we moved to Eastleigh. *Bibiji* was very friendly with the lady of that house, Tej Kaur; they were like sisters. They had four daughters and a son. The youngest one, Charno, came to England for further education before the whole family eventually moved to Southampton. We dated a couple of times but our, out-look on life was unbridgeable at the time. I saw her, a couple of time in the late nineties whenever I went to Southampton to see my sister and her family. Charno had the distinction of being the first person from minority groups to be a headmaster. She eventually became the education officer for the Hampshire County and some years later received an OBE for her services to education in that County. I had the privilege of knowing her and saw her a few months before she died of breast cancer. Unfortunately she did not communicate, to anyone, not even to her family the fact that she was suffering from this dreadful disease.

A few years after our move to Eastleigh *Papaji* converted the front room of our house into a shop and we opened a grocery store called Queens Provision Store. *Papaji* was very patriotic hence the name. It was very successful for a few years until my uncle. Surjeet, and his friends started to interfere. Dad started to lose money and after an agonizing few months decided to close the shop. We were all very sad because to us it was a lot of fun having the shop. It was at Eastleigh that I learned to ride a bike. One day my friends put me on a small bicycle owned by one of them and pushed me down the hill. I was terrified at first but managed to hold on; the rest is history.

The journey to school every morning in a bus with screaming children was also a lot of fun and if we missed the bus which we did deliberately many times, especially on the way home so we could walk and experience all those events on the way. Duke of Gloucester was a great school with many acres of land. There were two hockey pitches, cricket fields and rugby pitches and a running track. The primary school building, the high school building and the hostel for residents were all within one vast area. As I grew older, walking to school and back home was an adventure. When walking home we did not have to think about anything except the smells, the sounds and the texture of nature, the play of light and shadow, the way ahead, and the way home. One day I noticed a plume of black smoke and made a beeline towards it. It turned out to be a tyre dump on fire. I stood behind a fireman and helped to hold the water hose. Somebody must have taken a picture of this young Sikh boy wearing a colourful turban because it appeared in the East African Standard the next day. A copy of that picture and some questions resulted in my getting my Boy Scout fireman's badge.

Another day on my way home I heard cries for help and I ran towards the sound. I looked around and saw a deep ditch filled with water by the roadside in which a young boy submerged up to his neck in water was struggling to get out. I ran around until I found an adult and we both pulled the boy out of the ditch. That evening the boy's parents came to our house to thank me.

One day three of us decided to play truant from school and went fruit picking without permission from the owner of the orchard!!! This was the only time I missed school. I started to climb the guava tree hoping to pick some fruit but on the way about 15 ft from the ground I came across a beehive and realised it too late!!! I was stung about a dozen times in my chest and I slid down –screaming. Thank God I am not allergic to bee stings. When I got home I got a beating for missing school while *Bibiji* pulled the bee stings from my chest. Another time we went to pick guavas from a farm without permission – the farmer, a black women, came at us with a *panga* (machete). I was so terrified that I froze where I stood and urinated in my pants; I was only ten years old at the time.

In 1945 after the unhappy episode of the shop Dad decided to move and we bought a bigger house in Panipat Road, Nagara very close to the Sikh Colony. By this time there were four members in our family. Within a year of moving we built another story on top to make it into a double story house. Gurmit and I had a room upstairs while *Bibiji* and *Papaji* had the unit downstairs. Two Gujarati families also lived in our house; one of them had a son named Madhu who was of my age and we became friends. He had three beautiful sisters and I fancied one of them but nothing could happen because the horrible, I mean disgusting Indian cast system. Madhu and I sat for our Kenya Prelim Examination (equivalent to 11 Plus in UK) in 1947 and the day the results were posted at school Madhu went to check. When he came back he said we had both passed. There was celebration that night in the Bhatt household. Both the junior and high schools were within the same area and I remember being told that when you pass your Kenya Prelim. Exam you walk up those steps to the high school. The steps were visible from our classroom windows. When we started our new class in the high school the following year my English teacher was Narinder Kumar Verma whom I later met in East Africa House in London. He had come to Britain to study law and, I believe, he later became a high court judge in Kenya. Many years later when I went to have my eyes tested at Boots in Welwyn Garden City the Optician was Narinder's cousin.

On the triangular school's sports day one of the sponsors a Sikh gentleman used to watch the proceeding sitting on his shooting stick. I used to look at him and say to myself "I am going to have one of these seats one day." I have one now and use it when I go to see my sunshine, Amelia, setting new school records in 100 meters; she is a beautiful sprinter and a keen hockey player. *(See page P-1, Pic. 2: Amelia - Winner 100 Meter Final; and page P-2, Pic. 3: Amelia the Hockey Wizard).*

Another one of our tenants who worked at a flour mill for a company called Unga Ltd owned a black Ford prefect car which he parked in the front yard. I borrowed it one day, without his permission, and took Gurmit for a ride in it and at the same time honed my driving skills without a driving licence or insurance. He went mad when he found out and of course I got two of the best on my Gluteus Maximus from *Papaji* with his little hockey stick. Tarzan was 160 pounds, and he was thirty-six inches tall measured from his back to the ground, his head higher on a muscular neck. He was a very good guard dog but one day, some bastard poisoned him. His last night on earth he came and sat round each member of the family, as if to say goodbye to each of us. *Papaji's* aid if this dog survives tonight he will be alright, but he died at 2 AM. The worst thing for me was to take the dog to the city's incinerator in a wheel barrow. I vowed that I will never have a dog and to this day I have kept that vow.

I must mention another incident because it left permanent scars on the appendages of my right hand. On Diwali day one year we were sightseeing in an open van. My friend Madhu and I decided to throw lighted fireworks into the crowd. He was igniting them and I was throwing them from the moving van. We had a great laugh as the crowd scattered when the crackers blew up with a loud bang. I picked up a large red banger, my friend lit the fuse and I tried to throw it but it got stuck to my fingers and I could not dislodge it, no matter what I did. To my horror it blew up in my hand with a flash and a loud noise. I dived into *Bibiji's* lap crying with intense pain. They rushed me to the nearest Doctors surgery where the wounds on my thumb, index and middle fingers were washed, stitched, tinctured and bandaged. When we reached home *Papaji* saw my bandaged hand and said he felt sorry for me but then gave me two beauties on my Gluteus with his little hockey stick and said this was for disobeying me because he had told me not to go.

At my suggestion and after a lot of planning in secret I and two friends, Sohan Singh Bains and Gurdev Singh Gill (Gujri), decided to go around the world on our bicycles. The idea was triggered by my encounter in Nairobi with an Englishman who was travelling around the world on a bicycle. Being an adventurer and a dreamer I started to dream about going around the globe visiting various countries without even thinking about the hardships and dangers. I knew we would not get permission from our parents so we decided to leave without telling anyone except I made the mistake of telling my brother Gurmit. We left Nairobi very early one morning and travelled towards Kabete, the start of the Rift Valley, and down towards Gil Gil. This area is Kenya's most fertile region and was known as the white highlands and the scenery is breathtaking. The first night was spent in a grain barn with the blessings of the local farmer who took pity on three young drenched boys. We had rats as companions and they woke us up while playing musical notes on the spokes of our bicycle wheels as they raced to and fro. After the initial fright we got used to our neighbours and anyway we were too tired to do anything and fell sleep. On the road the next day we got a ride to Nyeri in a truck that belonged to a Sikh family and was driven by their son. The town of Nyeri, at the foot of Mount Kenya, is the heartland of Kikuyu homeland. The founder of the Boy Scout movement (Lord Baden Powel) is buried here; also, the Police Training School is nearby in Kiganjo. We were grateful to the Sikh family for their kindness in allowing us to shower and in giving us breakfast (*pranthas,* yogurt and tea). The cycle ride to Nanyoki on the road that goes past Mount Kenya was very pleasant but very tiring. We were able to stop quite a few times especially at the equator, an imaginary line but well posted with signs. Mount Kenya although 200 ft lower than Kilimanjaro (19,340 ft) is technically a difficult climb from the base with a 5.4 rating. When we reached Nanyoki we found out that we could not proceed to Marsabet, a town on the way to Moyale on the Kenya/Ethiopia border without permission from the local police superintendent. When we arrived at the police station we were promptly arrested and locked up. Unknown to us Gurmit had told *Papaji* where we were. *Papaji* got in touch with the police in Nairobi and told them we had run away from home. This was the end of our dream and trip round the world on bicycles.

With a lot of encouragement from *Papaji* I joined the scout movement at the age of seven as a cub scout. The years spent in the movement were adventures and very enjoyable.

Back row, from left: 1st Surinder, 2nd Karam Singh
Next row standing: 1st Inder, 4th Gian
Sitting: 1st Surjeet (T.L), 3rd Raval, K.D. Kapila (Principal),
(contd) Mohan Singh (Scout Master), Ram Murthi
Sitting on floor: 2nd Dushant, Khalid

Pic: I am sitting on the floor on the left at number one. My friend Surjeet is sitting behind me. This was our troop photograph which I found on a web site called "Nostalgic Kenya." The web site was set up by Harjinder Kanwal.

I could write a whole book on these adventures alone, but I will mention only a couple of incidents of which I have a vivid memory. The 13 mile hike, in pairs, for the First Class badge is an overnight stay at a place chosen by the scout leader. We were told to report to a police station in a remote town called Kiambu about 15 miles from Nairobi. The officer in charge told us to camp in the police grounds but to be weary of the wild animals that frequented the area at night. The two of us looked at each other and decided that we were going to climb the nearest tree and sit on one of the branches. That's what we did and stayed there all night without getting any sleep. Itwas just as well because we saw animals like hyenas all around the area.

Much later when I was a senior scout we went to Rowland Park camp ground to carry out tasks for the Venturer's badge working towards achieving our Queens Scouts badge. The three of us reported to the warden and told him what we were there for. He looked at me and said, "I am on fire and running towards you so what are you going to do?" When he got closer to me I tripped him, and when he was on the ground I started to roll him. He got very upset and said, "I just wanted you to tell me and not demonstrate on me."After years of scouting and a great deal of toil and adventure I was awarded the Queens Scout's badge.

The early death of King George VI in 1952 made me the first Queen Scout in Kenya. The certificate and the badge were presented to me by the then Governor of Kenya, Sir Evelyn Bearing in Nairobi Town Hall in August 1952 to the delight of my father. On St George's day the following year, as a member of the colour party, I was asked to carry the Union Flag into the Cathedral at Ngong Hill in Nairobi. The other two members of the colour party were an African scout carrying the scout flag and a European scout carrying the city flag of Nairobi. There are many memories of weekend, summer and training camps at the official campground called The Lord Rowland Camp site at Ngong Hill. I was there with our troop when the camp site was officially opened by Lord Rowland. In fact he was piped from the gate by our Scout Master, Mohan Singh who had learned to play the bagpipe in the Indian army. Mohan Singh was a very keen musician and formed a troop band. I tried to learn to play the bagpipe but found it very difficult. Our troop band played on many marches through the city on various functions and they also competed with other bands. When I came to England I went to the Queens Scouts gathering at Windsor Castle attended by Her Majesty Queen Elizabeth II. I was one of the international scouts who were selected to have their picture taken with Lady Baden Powel for a poster to show the Scout Movements spread across the world. *(See page P-2, Pic. 5: This picture appeared in the East African Standard, hence the Swahili writing).*

I also had the privilege of marching with the London District Scouts in the Remembrance Day Parade, past the Cenotaph in 1957.

Every year two senior boys from schools in the three British East African territories were selected and sent to an outward bound school in a Masai village called Loitokitok for two weeks acclimatization. This village is situated at about 5000 ft on the Kenya side of Mount Kilimanjaro. The first outward bound school was opened by a ship owner called Lawrence Holt in 1941. It included the aspects of fitness, leadership and rescue. I was one of the boys selected from my school to go to Loitikitok. Every morning we woke up at 5.30 AM and assembled on the grassy area surrounded by the Jacaranda, Red Fern and Cedar trees. Here we did our morning exercises and then went for our 5 mile run. On the run we had to contend with dust and heading up we saw the amazing sight of the first rays of sun on the snow peaks of Kilimanjaro. We came back through the indigenous forest and the cawing of the monkeys and the morning dip in the ice cold water of the pool. This went on for two weeks before we started our trek towards the Kibo peak.

We trekked through the rain forest for 6 days spending each night under canvas at various heights and at 11,500 ft the climb became harder due to lack of Oxygen and full load of 40 lbs (tents, sleeping bags, food and stove) in our rucksacks, mostly old army surplus rucks. On the sixth day we started our ascent of Gilman's Point on the rim of the crater at 19,340 ft using ropes and ice axes. On reaching the peak we saw a landscape of giant ice tower spirals with the ice on the floor on inside of the crater. I would like to point out that there are six different routes to ascend and descend Kili and majority of the tourists trek this mountain on the easier routes from the Tanzanian side and they don't usually scale Kibo Peak. When I graduated from school in 1953, I joined the police force and after six months training was posted to the finger print department at the CID Headquarters at Ngong Hill in Nairobi where I spent almost two happy years. I resigned in September 1955 and was told that I had not quite finished my two years. The boss said that if I stayed for two months he would give me a month's holiday. I wrote to Acton Tech College where I had admission to do my A-levels and told them that I was going to miss a term. They were very cooperative and sent me the syllabus for the term. *Papaji* said since I was not in a hurry, instead of flying to England, why don't I travel by boat, and that's how I happened to be a passenger on the Durban Castle by courtesy of *Papaji*.

We were brought up as Sikhs. *Papaji* was the president of the Sikh Temple known as Bazaar Gurudawara for many years. We had to go there every Sunday to observe one of the central dogmas of Sikhism which is *"Seva"* (to serve). Guru Nanak founded the Sikh faith over 500 years ago to create a more humane society on a sub-continent wrecked by centuries of continuous conflict. Sikhism grew out of the basic compassion of Hinduism and essential brotherhood of Islam. But it incurred the wrath of both Hindus and Muslims because it rejected the intolerance of other faiths, the caste system and idol worship. It insisted on treating all people as equals, and enjoined complete equality between men and women. On *Vaisakhi* (Harvest festival) Day in 1699 Guru Gobind Singh (the tenth Guru) founded the fellowship of the *Khalsa* and transformed this movement of peace into a community which placed military values alongside spiritual values. After a great deal of research into Sikhism/Sikh history I decided to cut my hair and not wear a turban anymore. This was a decision not taken very lightly, and only after a great deal of deliberations. Terry, a fellow student, booked an appointment for me with his barber in the Army and Navy Store, Victoria Street at 10 AM on a Saturday in 1957. We walked into the salon on the second floor. I took my turban off and the barber was surprised to see the length of my hair, he asked if it was ok to cut my hair. An hour later we walked out of the shop minus the turban and my long hair. I used to go for a haircut on a Saturday morning every 3 weeks and stayed with the same barber for nearly three years. In my later years I was to spend a lot of time researching Sikhism. My understanding is that Sikhism is an avowedly open and egalitarian creed and the fifth largest religion on earth. Sikhs do not bow to the leader of the service (Sikhism does not have priests) but, instead, to the holy Guru (which means teacher in Sanskrit) Granth Sahib. Given its geographic provenance in 16th century Mughal India and its blending of reincarnation with monotheism, Sikhism is founded on unique and progressive teachings of its founder Guru Nanak. His fundamental teachings are that God is one *(Ik Onkar)* and that the light of God is in every one; therefore, everyone is also one with God. He called for equality of women and rejection of the caste system while calling for all Sikhs, or "seekers of truth" to turn away from traditional religious forms and seek union with God directly. Two hundred years later Guru Gobind Singh a great warrior and a psychologist realized that the Sikhs would need a focal point if another human guru was not appointed. He said the collected texts of all the Gurus and enlightened words of poets of all other religious faiths would be called the Guru Granth Sahib and would be the final and infinite Guru for all the Sikhs forever more. *Kirtan* means" to praise what is exalted," to sing together in adoration of God, and it is an elemental aspect of Sikh devotional practice. If you have faith in God, He will never let you down.

At the age of 15 years I travelled from Kenya to India for the first time to see my grandfather who I had never met. My grandfather was a very frail old man but at the age of 80 took a 15 mile walk in his stride. He had been a wood block printer by profession and, as a young man lost an eye in an accident when someone pocked him with an umbrella. I have an 8 mm film of my uncle demonstrating the art of wood block printing. My grandmother on the other hand was a big, strong woman almost 6ft tall and built like a tank!! She told me that she would place the Singer sewing machine on her shoulder and grab *Papaji*, a 12 year old boy, by the hand and take him to the tailor's shop where he was an apprentice. I was always intrigued by the name Bhatt as it is used by both Hindus and Muslims alike although different variations of it. I decided to research the origin of the name and wrote a treatise on it titled "Bhatt's of Noganwan," which I add here in separate chapter 'Bhatt's of Noganwan (Panjab, India).'

To England

That Christmas Eve in 1955, when I first arrived in England, I caught a taxi from Liverpool Street Station and arrived at East Africa House in Great Cumberland Place (Marble Arch Synagogue stands in its place now). It was a club where students from the three British East African territories could stay until they found accommodation. There, I met many students from Nairobi and other cities in the three territories. I remember my first day in London, learning how to take the tube from Marble Arch, riding an escalator for the first time, and being able to understand that when the paper vendor said pipa it meant paper. After two weeks I found some digs in a nearby street called Sussex Place. The B&B accommodation at number 9 was in a three story Victorian house with a basement. One day when I came to the club the boys asked me if I had found digs. I said yes and when I told them the address they all laughed and said I had moved into a brothel. That would explain the constant movement up and down the stairs practically the whole of the night. My room was on the third floor of this large Victorian house. In the morning when I went for breakfast the dining hall was full of beautiful girls apart from the landlord who looked like an Army Colonel with thick long mustachios. I only stayed there three weeks. On hind sight I think I should have stayed longer and benefitted from the local inhabitants and their enchanting activity. But instead, I found very cheap (thirty shillings per week) digs closer to the college in Acton which I attended for two years.

I passed my GCE, Alevels, in 1957 at Acton Technical College. The college was situated in the High Street and had an extension known as Woodlands at the top of the hill towards Ealing. In fact this was the beginning of Brunel University which is in Uxbridge. The Botany teachers name was Dr. Onions and he later became professor of Botany at Brunel where I met him in 1985.The time spent at Acton Tech was interesting for me because I was introduced into the college life in England and also met a variety of young people of all creeds and colour. The foreign students were invited to talk to the local Rotary Club and some of us were invited by local families to spend Christmas with them. Overall I had a very pleasant time at Acton Tech. One winter's night when I was very late coming home from a party, I was locked out of my digs because we had to be in by 11 PM. I went to the college and opened the small window (all of us knew that the catch of this quarter light was broken) of the gym and slept next to the radiator on a gymnasts training mat where the caretaker found me in the morning. Fortunately for me he did not tell anybody.

I started at Wright Fleming Institute of Molecular Biology, St. Mary's Hospital Medical School at the end of 1957. Initially I worked with A.W. Frankland who was the allergy consultant for the greater London area. He was responsible for developing desensitizing extracts of various ingredients to which people were allergic. I was sent to many places to collect raw materials for these extracts. I remember going to Walls factory at Olympia to collect pig's hair and to the stables in Oxford Mews, near the Hospital, for horse urine. The girl at the stables gave me a bucket and said run when one of the horses urinates. You can imagine the fun I had running around. I did get half a bucket full of urine for my effort. We made extracts of a large number of materials. In the end, we had a large collection of these extracts and they were used in the allergy clinic to desensitize patients. These extracts were eventually bought by Bechams and marketed under the name "Bencard." Dr. Frankland was the president of the Hockey Club and, with his encouragement I played hockey and rugby for the school. I also read for a B.Sc (Hons.) degree in Physiology. Lady Amalia Fleming, Sir Alexander Fleming's widow and a bacteriologist, needed a student to help her. I was asked to help her and I did that for a few months. She was very grateful and gave me an endorsed, gold edged, copy of Alexander Fleming's biography by Andre Moreau, which is one of my treasured possessions. The endorsement reads "To Tochi S. Bhatt, thank you for your help, Amalia Fleming"

The school had many sports and recreation facilities and I managed to play Rugby and Hockey. I went on Easter tours on many occasions and the one I remember most is the Lowestoft Hockey festival because that was close to our president's country house in Suffolk. After the tour the team would go there to relax.

One Saturday I sustained an injury to my back and found myself with traction for few weeks. I was told no more Rugby and asked to swim 40 lengths of the half size swimming pool in the basement of the school to strengthen my back muscles. Jock, the Rugby coach was asked to make sure I did achieve my swimming target every day. After the swimming, Jock used to take me to the squash courts at the back of Wilson House and teach me to play the game. Wilson House was a hostel for students from St. Marys and it occupied practically half of Sussex Gardens on the left side towards Edgware Road. I got hooked on squash by watching an exhibition match between Hashim Khan and Nasrullah Khan (Naz Khan) at St Mary's. I eventually took lessons from Naz Khan at the New Grampions Squash Club, Shepherds Bush. I met Tony Swift, the future Senior National Coach of the Squash Rackets Association at the Grampions, who was also being coached by Naz. I could only afford half a dozen lessons as I was a student with a limited budget. Naz Khan as he was popularly known was "coach extraordinaire" in fact that is his epitaph. I eventually made the team at St. Mary's; I also played for the team at Paddington Squash Club. I achieved a reasonable standard and enjoyed the game very much.

Pic: Mary's Lambs

Pic: Easter Hockey Festival Worthing in 1960

The rugby team from St. Mary's used to train in Hyde Park every afternoon. We used to come out of the front door, turn left and walk under the bridge connecting the Wright Fleming Institute/Medical School to the hospital. We would then go through the gates, cross Praed Street run across Sussex Gardens and through Oxford Mews (which has long since been replaced with a concrete jungle) and enter into the park. The training consisted of a circuit of the park, 25 yard sprints on Rotten Row, ball training, and then back to the gym and finally into the swimming pool. The session used to finish by us diving into the "Fountains Abbey" for a well-earned drink. We trained from Monday to Friday for the match on Saturday. One day when we came out of the school I looked up at the hospital building on our right and saw a pretty young women peering through the window. I waved and, to my surprise she waved back; when I looked behind me the whole team was waving at her, too. It took me two months to build enough courage to ask the young women to come to one of our soirees. The beautiful young women, Joan, became my wife after a lengthy eight-year courtship. She was my English Rose who turned this Indian-born wild African hunter into a sophisticated gentleman!! This was in the early sixties, and there were certain mixed feelings about inter-racial marriages. I admire my English Rose for sticking with me and eventually presenting me with two beautiful and clever children. Joan and I were married on a glorious sunny day in St. Mark's, the parish church of St. Helier in Jersey on New Year's Eve 1966. Our long courtship was not without problems especially in the early sixties. The prejudice that existed was largely due to ignorance and anyway, I did not worry about it. I was lucky to have a very beautiful, brave woman as my companion. In time when Joan's parents realized that we were very serious in our commitment to each other they gave us their blessings. Also it was Joan's younger sister Lillian who insisted that I should be invited home otherwise she would not marry. I distinctly remember that evening. I knocked at their door in Holford Square, Islington. After the usual introductions and a polite chat, Joan's dad said to me "Let us go for a drink," so we went to his Local, The Dirty Dick in Pentonville Road. At closing time we were thrown out and, slightly inebriated, we walked through the front door and were accused of leading each other astray. From that day onwards Mr. Reed treated me like a son he never had.

One day while I was looking for new digs. I met Mrs. Peggy Smith the London organizer of the movement to ban nuclear weapons, popularly known as Campaign for Nuclear Disarmament ("CND"). She was a charming, erudite and helpful lady who offered me a room in the basement of her large Victorian house in Gloucester Road, West London. Members of her organization marched every Sunday from Marble Arch down Oxford Street, lower Regent Street, Piccadilly Circus, to Trafalgar Square carrying anti-nuclear placards. The march would finish at Charing Cross Station and the group would go to J Lyons Corner House for a cup of tea and discussion. I walked with them one Sunday as a polite gesture to Mrs. Smith but hated every minute of it as I did not agree with their views. She expected me to walk with them every Sunday. I made excuses for a couple of weeks. In the end I told her what I thought of the CND movement and she was not pleased. One evening when I got home she asked me to come into her lounge and while we were having a cup of tea she said. "I need the room you are occupying for my nephew who is coming to London from Yorkshire." I lasted a total of 5 weeks in that house. Fortunately for me I found digs in 5, Court field Gardens a stone's throw from Mrs. Smith's house and very close to Earls Court.

University students, at least the majority of them, have always worked during the summer holidays to supplement their meagre education allowance. We use to go to the

National Union of Students offices in Euston Road to look for jobs. My first summer job, which I will never forget, was at Euston Station. I was told to report to the inspector in charge of the night shift. The inspector greeted me with politeness and a broad smile, and said, "Pick that broom and go and sweep platform number 3." When I saw the three foot broom I realised why he was grinning. I started at 00:30 and was still sweeping the platform when the inspector came to ask me how I was getting on at 03:00. It was a never ending task because as you finished one end another train would pull into the station and people would throw more rubbish on to the platform. So, it was a never ending task. The inspector laughed and said "I use this exercise for all new students as an initiation." The rest of my vacation I ended up driving an electric car pulling carts full of parcels, and luggage to be loaded into the trains. I held many summer jobs during my student days. Another time, I worked for "Chequered Flags" in Chiswick as a driver picking up cars from all around the country. I had the pleasure of driving cars like the Jaguar XK120, Austin Healey Sprite, Wolsey, MG, TC and TD series. I remember crashing a TD on the old London Road from Colchester. Just outside of Colchester there was a very sharp bend which I did not know of, and I skidded, and hit the bank, and the car ended up facing the way I had come. It was a frightening experience but I was not hurt and the car was not badly damaged. When I telephoned the boss to tell him that I had damaged his car, his reply was, "Forget the car, are you all right?" I became friendly with the owner. He had a Morris 8 series E 1928 in the back lot which I used to admire. He saw me looking at it and said. "You are interested in that car. I tell you what I will do. I will deduct money from your salary every week and, at the end, you can have that car for £ 50.00." I worked on that car especially the engine out on Longridge Road every evening, come what may, until it was repaired; and I christened it Lulu. At the end of the working session on the car I used to collect all the tools and take them indoors.

In 1959 Joan and I drove Lulu through northern France, to Basle and Altdorf in Switzerland. We drove through St. Gothard pass (there was no tunnel through the Alp's at this point in those days) down to the Italian lakes Maggiore and Garda. We camped near one of the lakes for a well-earned rest. After a couple of days we drove on the Autostrada del Sol to the Italian Riviera via Milan. In Milan we stopped to look at some of the tourist attractions. We saw the city hall in the Pallazo Marino and the Cathedral in Piazzo Duomo. The world's oldest shopping centre, Galleria Vittorio Emanuel II is also in this square. We visited towns like Ventimiglia, Rimini, and San Remo on the Italian Riviera. We especially wanted to stay and visit Ventimiglia as Joan had been there in summer a few years before. The French Riviera and Nice were a real treat and we finally returned to London via Paris after 4 weeks. We camped using a two-man tent, a small stove, two folding chairs, and two inflatable beds. It was fun to camp on the beach on the Riviera and in official camp sites in land. The camp sites in the late fifties were pretty primitive in comparison to the luxurious sites these days. In the bar on the ferry across the channel, a gentleman who looked like an Indian Army Officer came to me and said. "You are the fellow driving the Morris 8 with the little Union Jack pennant on the mudguard. I saw you on the St. Gothard pass. By God you made it, therefore you deserve a pint." So he bought me one.

The following year, Joan and I camped using our primitive camping equipment and took Lulu to Barcelona via Andorra and then back to England via Paris. Lulu behaved perfectly except on the way home. The alternator stopped charging the battery; therefore, we had to get the battery charged every night. I had to remove the battery from the car and carry it to the nearest garage to be charged. Then I had to get it back in the morning and hook it back before the commencement of our journey. It was a fantastic trip. When we reached Paris this time we ran out of money and we decided to go to the British Embassy. At 6 PM I rang the bell and a tall gentleman open the door and asked, "What do you want?" I explained that we were short of money and his prompt response was. "Why don't you go to your embassy?" I said I was standing in front of it. He did smile and then took us in and after some formalities the embassy gave us some money in exchange for our passports. We were issued temporary travelling papers. We got our passports back when we paid the money back to the Home Office in London.

After reading the humorous account of a boating holiday on the Thames in a book titled "Three men in a boat" by Jerome K. Jerome I decided to emulate, as much as possible, their experience. Joan and I hired a boat from Hoseason for a week. We arrived at the boat yard and were given a half hour lesson on cruising, operating locks and general handling of the cruiser. We had a wonderful week cruising past Staines, and stopping at very old pubs for meals. I distinctly remember the railway bridge at Maidenhead because we moored close to it for one night. We never got to Oxford but turned back from Marlow. Nevertheless it was a fantastic week's holiday on the river Thames.

All the students living in and near Earls Court used to congregate in a coffee bar in Earls Court Road. There was one art student who used to sketch portraits of people with pencil or pen. One evening I met an Indian gentleman who introduced himself as Dr. Singh, and his wife, a beautiful German lady. During our talk he said he was from Malaya, which later became Malaysia, and that he was the owner of 62 Longridge Road. Longridge Road was one of the roads that disappeared at the time of widening of the West Way. Dr. Singh said he did not live in the house but wanted someone to look after the house; he was looking at me while talking. As I showed some interest he said I could live there rent free and all I would have to do is collect the rent every week from the other tenants and make sure the place was kept clean. I accepted his proposal and moved into the large front room with the bay window on the ground floor of the large Victorian House. This is where my glamorous but short acting career began. Frank O'Keiff was a student at the Royal Academy of Dramatic Arts and lived on the second floor. We had found a baby grand piano which someone was throwing out and moved it to my room. We used to have parties at the weekend in my room, and as none of us could play the piano except Frank, he used to pretend to be Liberace. We used to put two candelabras on the piano to create the right atmosphere. One evening Frank walked in all excited and said "can you tie a turban?" I said, "Yes, but why?" He said, "If you can, then we have an audition as extras at Pinewood Studios tomorrow. On the morrow we drove to Pinewood Studios where we met Ralph Thomas and Betty Box. They told us to march up and down the stage and I also had to tie a turban to complete our audition. We both ended up with roles in "The Wind Cannot Read," a film with Dirk Bogarde and Yoko Tani. We were told to go to Burmans in Leicester Square to pick up Second-world-war uniforms. I was to play the part of an Indian Air Force pilot with a blue turban.

Pic: Me in the role of an Indian Air Force pilot

Burmans warehouse was an Aladdin's cave full of theatrical costumes and props of all kinds. The actual shooting lasted 6 week sat Pinewood and then a trip to India for two weeks. The set at Pinewood was constructed to look like the inside of the Red Fort in Delhi. In the "class room" the selected officers of the Indian Forces are being taught Japanese so that they can interrogate prisoners during the Second World War. In the picture the General introduces himself and the class to the Japanese tutor.

Some of the extras working on our film also worked on "The Titanic" which was being filmed at night. There was a "sinking model" of the Titanic in the pond at Pinewood. I got invited to have lunch with Dirk Bogarde in the restaurant at Pinewood a couple of times.

Pic: The set at Pinewood was constructed to look like the inside of the Red Fort in Delhi.

I was also cast in a documentary, made by the Shell Company, as a bacteriologist working in the tropics. This was hilarious as it was filmed in December and there was lot of snow around the hospital in Praed Street. They had to use heat lamps to make me sweat.

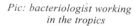

Pic: bacteriologist working in the tropics

In another documentary made by BBC and narrated by Raymond Baxter called The "Unseen Enemies," I played a doctor walking into the hospital through the archway connecting the Wright Fleming Institute and the Hospital. Here ended my short acting carrier for I was too busy studying to take part, as an extra in films.

When I was living in Earls Court I joined the 37th Kensington Scout Troop. They used to meet every Friday in a hall at St Barnabas & St Phillips Church on Earls Court road. The Scout Master was a chap called John Nichollas who had a very dry sense of humour.

THE BOY SCOUTS ASSOCIATION

KENSINGTON

District Commissioner: Brigadier R. C. HALSE, C.B.E. 206, Earls Court Road, S.W.5 (FROmantle 8000-evenings only)	*President:* HIS WORSHIP THE MAYOR OF KENSINGTON *Chairman:* JOSEPH M. WALL, Esq.,	*Hon. Secretary:* Mrs. G. GRAY, 39, Beryl Road, W.6 (RIVerside 3128)

Dear Tochi,

    Please forgive me for not acknowledging your letter of the 20th May; there have been no meetings of the Association until last evening — that is the reason for the delay.

    I put your letter to the meeting of the Scout Sub-Committee last night and we all expressed regret at your decision to hand in your Warrant, especially as you have been in the movement for such a long period.

    Before your resignation is put to the Executive Committee, I have been asked to write to you to know whether you would be prepared to take out a Warrant as A.S.M. in another Group. There are several Groups in the District who would be only too glad of your assistance, and I am sure if you did decide to work with another Group, you would not regret it.

    I, personally, appreciate your reasons for resigning from the 37th, but it seems such a pity that the Scout movement should be deprived of your help because of the incompatibility of one Group. Would you reconsider your decision, or if you would like, surrender your present Warrant and take out one in another Group? Perhaps you will let me hear from you again when you have considered what I have said.

              Yours sincerely,

Pic: D - 1

John had been a Boatswain on a Merchant Navy ship during the war and had spent some time in Egypt. He could speak some Arabic and use to throw Arabic words in his conversation with the scouts and they all use too think it was funny. I resigned from the troop for personal reasons and also I did not want to get involved with the local politics. I stayed friends with John and his family for many years after qualifying and resigning from the troop. I went with the 37th Kensington troop to two summer camps and the one at Boars Hill, Oxford was the most memorable. *(Pic. - D1)*

The best accommodation I had as a student was when in 1959 I moved to Sussex Gardens for the second time. The house belonged to Mrs. Stringer a classy, upper middle class lady from Stoke Poges. The three-story Victorian terraced house with a basement was large and spacious. All of us lived on a full board basis and most worked in the city. In fact, one of them eventually became the Managing Director of Equity and Law Insurance Company and their head office was in Lincoln's Inn Fields. I know this because I met him when I worked in that square with the Imperial Cancer Research fund. Another tenant was a member of the Royal Automobile Club and I played squash with him many times at the RAC in the Mall. It was a very happy house we were like a family. Breakfast and the evening meal were eaten in the very large dining room in the basement. We all sat together with Mrs. Stringer at the head of the table and topics of discussion were the events of the day and what we had been upto. To give Mrs. Stringer a break from cooking during the week we took her out to "Chez Joes" in the mews behind Paddington Station on Sundays, presented her with a bunch of flowers and paid for the meal. This was to thank her for looking after us during the week. A knock at the door one morning as I was getting ready for breakfast jolted me from my thoughts. Mrs. Stringer was at the door looking very pale. I asked her what was the matter? She said, "I think you better come because we cannot wake Jim. Jim Turnbull a retired army major who worked in the city was lying peacefully in his bed. It turned out that he had a myocardial infarction during his sleep. In fact it was Jim who gave me the bowler hat that I wore when I walked to Brighton. I stayed in Mrs. Stringer's house for two years and then moved to Wilson House further up Sussex Gardens towards Edgware

Road. Wilson House was a collection of Victorian terraced interconnected houses, and there was a brick-wall to keep the sexes apart. Therefore, it was quite common to see male students walking on the window ledges to get to the girls accommodation. The warden Dr. Brumfield was very strict and many a student was caught and reprimanded; unfortunately I did not have that privilege.

United Hospitals used to organise an annual walk for students known as The London to Brighton Stroll. It was a very competitive event in which men competed for a shield and the women for a cup. The walk began from the Tower of London with a gun start by the Governor of the Tower and a lone bagpiper walked in front on the old Kent road as far as the Elephant and Castle pub. I took part in this event in 1959 and covered the distance of 58 miles in 15 hours 25 minutes, and of course, wore that bowler hat with my number 308 on it. It was amazing how fast everybody walked and we all reached The Red Lion at Culsdon about the same time. Why the hurry? Because that was the last pub open on the way until we reached Brighton. We were given a rapturous welcome when we reached the finishing post on the sea front, where our numbers were checked and time recorded. Next day when we came back the coach dropped me in front of the house and by the time I crossed the road and got to the front door my landlady had filled the bath for me. She had seen the coach drop me, and that's how slow I had walked because I was tired and my legs were hurting. The reward for completing the walk was a slap up dinner at Guinness Brewery (the sponsors) at Park Royal and a green tie with A23 and a Tuscan embroidered on it. I still have my tie. St Mary's women won the ladies cup and the men came second in the men's section. The event was stopped after three years because of a serious hit and run accident when two students were killed. I was also a member of the sailing club at Mary's and every year we held our annual regatta at Royal Burnham Yacht Club to which the United Hospitals Sailing Club was affiliated and we were encouraged to crew in the RBYC's two 12 meter yachts. The students learned to sail on dinghies on The Brent reservoir popularly known as "The Welsh Harp" named after the pub of the same name which stood nearby. The Welsh Harp was home to many sailing clubs including London University sailing club to which all the Medical Schools in London were affiliated. As we got proficient in sailing we went on to crew the bigger boats on River Crouch and many happy weekends were spent at Burnham sailing on the River Crouch.

Pic: Rigging the dinghy for a sail on River Crouch

One Saturday after our match we were coming back to Paddington in Neville's old car when some bright spark!!! Suggested that we go to the Mall and remove a pennant so that we could add it to the trophies at our sports pavilion in Udney Park Road, Teddington. These were the pennants hung around London for Princess Margaret and Tony Armstrong's wedding on the 6th May 1960. We drove to the Mall, parked the car and all 6 of us trooped off to the flag post close to Green Park and Buckingham Palace. John Reynolds being the

Pic: Threading the sail

lightest was asked to climb the pole and get the pennant. He duly obliged and retrieved a pennant and we went back to the car looking happy and smug. Just when we were ready to leave another bright spark shouted. "Let's get another one." That was a mistake because as JR started to climb the pole he was illuminated by incandescent light from about four torches. All six of us were taken to Bow Street police station and made to spend the night in cells. After breakfast consisting of beans on toast with a mug of tea we were released with a warning. However, a report was sent to the school and Monday morning saw us standing in the Deans office. He was not very pleased but we got away with a severe reprimand.

The sports grounds of the other hospitals and some other teams on our fixtures list were spread all round the greater London area and some were even round the country. One day after our match with The London Hospital Medical School at their grounds at Highams Park one of our player Gaby Williams, a jet-black Ghanaian, said to me, "Let's go to Walthamstow." In the 1960s Walthamstow in East London was a no go area for Asians and blacks. I tried to persuade him that we should not go but to no avail and we landed up at the door of The Sun pub, a very busy pub, on the junction of Forest Road and Chingford Road. As soon as Gaby opened the door the whole place went quiet, you could hear a pin drop. We walked to a large table occupied by quite a few people playing cribbage. Gaby thumped at the table and said. "You don't like us coming to your pub, do you?" Before they had a chance to say anything Gaby said "I am going to ask you three questions and if you answer them correctly, we will buy you drinks all night; but if you are wrong, then you buy us drinks all night." Before they could get their breath, he said "what is the name of your home secretary? Ah ah you don't know. "What is the name of your foreign secretary and what is the name of your Prime Minister? Obviously you do not know, therefore you buy us drinks all night." They were stunned by our audacity in walking into their domain and Gaby's forthright and forceful attack. They relaxed a bit and asked us where we had come from, and what were we doing in Walthamstow. We told them that we were students from St Marys Hospital and were playing Rugby at Highams Park. Those guys bought us drinks and we socialised until closing time when we were all told to go home. I left there that night feeling that their attitude towards Asians and blacks was shear ignorance on their part rather than discrimination. Another time when Mary's beat St. Thomas in the hospitals rugby cup final some of the students from Tommy's were debagged, covered with flour and left in the middle of Piccadilly Circus, all in the name of fun. We also had fixtures with Keeble College and Queens College at Oxford University. Kings College and Jesus College at Cambridge University were also on our fixtures list. When driving to Oxford on the old road, now the A40, for our matches, one always passed through High Wycombe. Just outside the town there are man-made chalk and flint caves in the Chiltern Hills popularly known as Hell Fire Caves. On couple of occasions we visited these caves and learnt that they were used for Pagan practices.

I graduated from St Mary's and also achieved a Hon. Degree in Physiology in 1962 and went home to Nairobi. It was funny and worrying because my family consulted Avtar Singh Rattan, who at that time was considered to be the most erudite person in our community. I think my family didn't believe me- very sad- especially as this is the guy who wanted to make me a cup of tea with water from his hot water bottle when I went to visit him in London a few years later. He had come to England for further studies. He was living in a house in Camden Town and his room was a distance from the water tap. However, I had a very good reunion with the family and I saw my two youngest sisters who were born after I left Nairobi in 1955. I was stunned and still remain in that state at their beauty. They are indeed very beautiful and now very successful in their respective careers. I went to see my sister Meeto in a nursing home in Pangani, owned by Mrs. Dhan Kaur, where she had given premature birth. I said to my parents this baby, wrapped in cotton wool and no incubator, is not going to survive. That tiny little girl is my niece Rachpal Tahim who lives with her husband Inderpal and her three beautiful daughters, Vanita, Priya and Baldeep in Dallas, Texas, USA. *(See page P-2, Pic - 4: Socialising with Rachpal, Inderpal and Chris in Old Dallas).*

It was great to see my parents and my siblings, especially those born after I had left Kenya. I had not been back to Kenya since my arrival in England in1955. I went to see our family physician, Dr. Amin, mainly to thank him for igniting in me an interest in medicine by allowing me to help his Pharmacist

(Mr. Vias) to dispense drugs when I was a young lad. I also visited many school friends especially Joginder and Surgeet Sokhi. My interest in medicine was also compounded by the fact that I came across a book on anatomy at a friend's (Iqbal Singh) house. I am still in contact with Joginder Sokhi who lives in Nairobi and has a successful detective agency. Surjeet Sokhi moved to Bristol recently and I have visited him a few times. I was informed by the family that my brother Gurmit was getting married in India and that I was to attend his wedding. I was to travel to India with East African Airways and when I arrived at Nairobi airport to board my flight I found that they had over booked and given my seat to someone else. Because of my brother Gurmit's intervention I was given a seat in the first class cabin. The Comet flew to India via Aden, Benghazi, Karachi and then Bombay. To my great surprise Deshi was the senior stewardess responsible for the first class cabin. I had known Deshi, the very pretty daughter of a senior civil servant in Nairobi, for a while and was very keen on her. The only other people in the cabin were an Australian family who got off at Aden and for the rest of the trip I was the only one in the cabin. So I ate, drank and got a chance to talk to Deshi. During the conversation she told me that she was serious with an Englishman who was the manager of Coleman Ricketts India Ltd. He worked and lived in Bombay and would meet her at the airport. That was the end of any romantic thoughts I might have had; I felt dejected. In Bombay I stayed at The Natraj Hotel, Marine Drive, for four days. I managed to play very enjoyable couple of games of squash at the Bombay Gymkhana and at Braeburn Stadium. In the Natraj I met a Sikh from Nairobi who was very friendly with Dara Singh an Indian film actor who had been an international wrestler. I had seen/met Dara Singh in the UK when he used to wrestle in the West. Mr. Singh and I were invited to have breakfast with Dara Singh at his apartment one morning. After the breakfast we went to the studiowith Dara Singh where he was filming "Bollywood" version of King Kong. *(See page P-3, Pic. 6: Me, Dara Singh and the person who introduced me to the actor).*

I was allowed to film with my 8 mm cine camera around the busy studio and also the scene they were filming at the time. I was introduced to the heroine of the film, Indira Billi who very kindly posed for me on and around the set. I kept in

touch with the actress and also dated her when she came to London a year later. I didn't get any further than a date!!!!!
(See page P-4, Pic. 8: In deep conversation with Indira Billi)

One of the well-established traditions during the Raj was to have afternoon tea in the Sea Lounge of the Taj Mahal Palace Hotel. I kept that tradition alive by having tea in the sea lounge of the Taj one afternoon with a couple I had met in my hotel. It was an expensive afternoon but the traditional afternoon tea featuring an elaborate buffet spread of classic English delicacies and local favourites complemented with a selection of finest teas made the day. To crown it all the spectacular views of the Arabian Sea was breathtaking to say the least. Walking through the streets in Bombay about lunch time you see many cart's full of stainless steel tiffin carriers. I asked the handler of one of these cart's what was in the containers and where was he taking them? His reply was "I am delivering lunch for the office workers."

Pic: Stainless steel tiffin carriers at Bombay

I left Bombay in the Frontier Mail from Victoria Terminus at 7.20 PM. I had booked my passage on this train with Thomas Cook in London at a total cost of £ 5.00. My companion in the first class compartment was a Sikh Indian Army Officer. That evening we went to the dining car and I ordered roast chicken with all the trimmings, whereas he ordered an Indian meal. When the bill came, my meal cost me three times more than what he paid. He saw the surprise in my face and then said. "Can you speak any of the Indian languages?" I replied Punjabi and Urdu. He said. "From now on you swear in Punjabi a few times and eat Indian food." He was right; things got done quickly and I did not have to pay through the nose for anything after that. After a fast comfortable ride through Maharashtra, Gujarat, Rajasthan, UP, Delhi and Haryana I reached Ambala very early in the morning after 12 hours. The slow train to Sirhind (Punjab) followed by a bus ride to Noganwan was a bit of an anti-climax but an experience. All the landscape was dotted with pairs of oxen and the black buffaloes. The oxen were of the classic Indian breed, small and thin, with brown patches on the head and legs, but with very pale, almost white bodies. They pulled single- furrowed wooden ploughs, or heavy wooden beams that served as clod-breaking harrows. Noganwan a village with about 200 houses and a dozen shops is situated on the main road from Sirhind to Morinda about 7 miles from Fateh Garh Sahib, a Sikh holy place. The brick-built family home is very basic; it is double story with a flat roof. The Ambala to Morinda railway line is just behind the house and it shakes when a train hurtles along. The line is so close that you can touch the train as it passes. By the side of the track on the opposite side to the house is a shrine to a warrior who died at that spot when he fell off his horse. The story is that he, Kheon Singh Bhatt, was a soldier (Major) in Banda Singh Bahadur's army and was badly injured at a famous battle against the Mogul army at a place called Chappar Chiri close to Mani Majra, both places are near Chandigarh. He managed to get back to Noganwan. He is revered by the Bhatt clan and most of the village. The people in the village are very friendly and hospitable. I made an 8 mm movie of Gurmeet's wedding. As the farmers in Punjab at the time were harvesting sugar cane to turn its juice into brown sugar I was allowed to film the whole process. In this ancient process they first extract the juice by inserting sugar cane sticks through a mangle, *'Kohlu.'* Two Bullocks were used to rotate the 2 rollers in the *Kohlu*. The juice was then heated to evaporate the water. The fire needed to heat the juice was provided by dried sugar cane bagarse and the temperature was kept pretty constant. The light brown residue is pure sugar they call gur or jaggery. I wrote a record of my visit to India and titled it "Return to India after 30 years" which is at end of the biography.

After qualifying I worked for a short time with someone who was trying to develop a vaccine for children suffering from Malaria by using a protein from the blood of adult malaria patients. A chance meeting with Maurice Coombs a brilliant organic chemist and a kind man full of ideas got me interested in cancer. He had started a Chemistry department for the Imperial Cancer Research Fund (ICRF) based, at that time, at the Medical Research Council laboratories at Mill Hill. The new laboratories were being constructed in Lincolns Inn Fields next to The Royal College of Surgeons. I liked Maurice's ideas and thoughts about research in cancer. He was thinking on the lines of the prediction by a husband and wife team of American chemists called Fieser and Fieser, who had said that, "if there were endogenous carcinogens then they would be the result of abnormal steroid metabolism." I joined him in the new ICRF labora-tories in Lincoln's Inn Fields in late 1963 and our collaboration and research on compounds collectively called Cyclopenta(a)phenanthrenes (CPP) began. These compounds possess the same carbon ring system as members of the large and important group of natural products, the steroids. Over many years we synthesized about 105 of these compounds. During these complicated seven stage synthesis we dealt with very large quantities of starting materials and hardly took any precautions. I like to call this our German period whenever I delivered a lecture on CPP. We tested many of these compounds for cancer activity using the two stage mouse model and to our horror some of them turned out to be carcinogenic (cancer causing). We also tested CPP using Bacteria and also investigated their biochemistry. This work culminated in 1987 with a commissioned book by Cambridge University Press titled 'Cyclopenta(a)phenen-threnes.' *(See page P-4, Pic. 7: My Book).*

We dedicated this book to our friend and colleague, the late Dr. Cambell Livingston who had passed away at a very young age (42 years) of a heart attack. A great deal of other work emanated in our research during that period, like the discovery of a new tumour promoter, Biogenic Silica Fibres. During this period and through Maurice's encouragement, my interest in Chemistry was ignited. I finished up doing a degree in this subject with National Academic Awards Scheme and have never regretted this fact through my research career. At this stage I had a large number of scientific publications. I decided to register for a Ph.D degree at Brunel University because of my past association with Acton Technical College (Brunel was born at Woodside extension of Acton Technical College where I studied for my A Levels) and also the fact that I knew late Prof. Trevor Slater who held the chair of Biochemistry at Brunel. Both my M.Phil and Ph.D Degrees are from Brunel. So in reality I have two Alma Mater, London University and Brunel University and if I count The Wistar Institute of Anatomy and Physiology/University of Pennsylvania, USA then it's three.

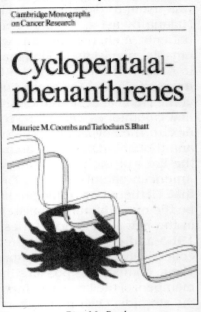

Pic: My Book

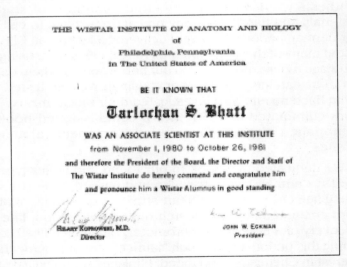

Pic: D - 2 Alma Mater, The Wistar Institute of Anatomy and Physiology/University of Pennsylvania, USA

Some of the staff from the ICRF used to play cricket for

the Royal College of Surgeon's team and I was one of these players. Our home ground was in the field at Down House in Downe village in the County of Kent. Down House is the former home of Charles Darwin and his family. It was in this house and garden that Darwin worked on his theories of evolution by natural selection. Down house is now a museum and is in the guardianship of English Heritage. One summer at the end of the season we had our usual celebration lunch in the garden of Down House. One of the guests arrived late and since there was an empty seat on our table he sat with us. The guest was the distinguished surgeon from St Marys Hospital, Mr. Arthur Dixon Wright. He had Joan and I in hysterics with his impromptu remarks and stories larded with Irish humour. I knew him from my days at St. Mary's and to this day I remember that lunch.

As a result of reorganisation at ICRF the chemistry lab was phased out in 1987. Maurice moved to Surrey University, his Alma Mater, to be the Head of Chemistry and I went to St Bartholomew's Hospital Medical School as a Senior Reader/ Senior Research fellow. My laboratory was in the Joint Academic Unit of Obstetric and Gynaecology. This unit was formed as a result of the merger of the two medical colleges, the Royal London Hospital and St. Bartholomew' Hospital in 1995. I worked on the synthesis of Melatonin and its metabolites also continued my work with Cyclopentaphenanthrenes and Biogenic Silica Fibres. The discovery of Biogenic Silica Fibres as tumour promoter resulted in me receiving the Yamigawa-Yoshida memorial grant from the International Union against Cancer (ICCU) in 1988. This was announced in the Royal Society of Chemistry magazine. I remember Lisa telling me that she was in the university library perusing through scientific journals when she came across my picture and she instantly shouted "Oh that's my Dad" in a very quiet, peaceful surroundings. As part of her course Lisa had to spend a year at a scientific institution. She went for an interview with Smith, Kline & French Research Laboratory at the Frith, Welwyn. The head of the Division of Pharmacology said "are you any relation to Coombs and Bhatt the authors of Cyclopenta(a)phenan-threnes" to this Lisa replied Bhatt is my Dad. A year earlier I had been to that laboratory to advise them on how to handle and dispose of Carcinogenic compounds. At the end of her year at SKF Lisa wrote a Dissertation titled 'Spectroscopic Determination of the Inhibitory Constants of Three Anticholinesterases.'

Pic: D - 3 - Yamigawa-Yoshida memorial award

The prize was to spend three months in the laboratory of my choice in the International Union countries. I named John DiGiovanni's laboratory at the MD Anderson Cancer Centre, (MDACC) Smithville, Texas as I was already collaborating with him. We made the total amount of money given to both of us (money John received for having me in his laboratory and my prize) last for 5 years. I kept going to Texas for three months every year for four years, working mostly on Biogenic Silica Fibres. As the money for our collaboration from the ICCU was coming to an end we managed to secure a grant from NATO in Brussels for two senior investigators in NATO countries and we made the money last for another 3 years. So on and off I was at the MDACC for about 9 very productive years.

INTERNATIONAL UNION AGAINST CANCER

This is to certify that

Dr T.S. Bhatt

is a
FELLOW
of the UICC

having been awarded a

**YAMAGIWA-YOSHIDA MEMORIAL
INTERNATIONAL CANCER STUDY GRANT**

funded by the Japan National Committee for UICC
and the Olympus Optical Company of Tokyo

for a project at

*The University of Texas System Cancer Center
Smithville, U.S.A.*

in 1988

Dr S. Eckhardt
President UICC

Dr G.P. Murphy
Secretary General UICC

Dr J.G. McVie
Chairman UICC
Fellowships Programme

Pic: D - 4 - Yamigawa-Yoshida memorial award

I first came to Texas in 1990 when I was awarded the Yamigawa-Yoshida memorial award by the international Union against Cancer for the work on Silica Fibres. When I landed at Robert Muller Airport at the end of August the temperature in Austin was 105° F and in fact they were having a heat wave.

When we got off the plane the heat came at us like a mortal enemy. It seems to enter through our mouths and nostrils as we grasped for breath. It was so dry it sucked the moisture from our bodies like a thief.

I had met John DiGiovanniin 1980-81 at the Wistar Institute of Anatomy and Biology, University of Pennsylvania. The institute is named after Caspar Wistar Philadelphia Physician and Paleontologist. His great-nephew General IssacWistar housed his great uncle's anatomical collection in the newly established first Biomedical Research facilities in America. It is said that the Botanist Thomas Nuttall named the plant Wisteria after Casper. I went to Leila Diamond's laboratory at the Wistar Institute on a World Health Organisation (WHO) fellowship and John had joined the lab 3 month earlier. We shared an office and a lab for a whole year; we found that we had climbing interest in common and we became friends. We have been very good friends ever since. In the summer of 1994 JohnDiGiovanni telephoned from Texas one afternoon and said "we are going to climb in the Pyrenees and therefore, can you pick me up from Gatwick Airport. He gave me his flight details and then hung up. I did meet him at Gatwick Airport on the appropriate day and time with my climbing gear and apparel. We drove from Gatwick to Dover, boarded the ferry across to Calais. After a short stop at a restaurant we drove to Biarritz where we met up with my friend Roger Barandiarn who had arranged our accommodation in the Pyrenees in a ski chalet. We left our chalet very early one morning and drove across the border into Spain and to the base of our climb. We climbed Pico de Aneto at 3404 meters (11168 ft) the highest peak in the Aragon region of Spain. Two days later we also reached the peak of Vignemale at 3298 meters (10820 ft) the third highest on the French side of the Central Pyrenees. *(See pages P-5 and P-6, Pic. 9: On the glacier of Pico de Aneto; Pic 10: Summit Mt Vignemale 1994, Pyrenees, France)*

In the same year John Di and I attended the International Cancer Congress in Delhi. It was the first time the congress was held in Asia and India was awarded the congress on the basis of their strong cancer programme based at the Tata Memorial Hospital in Bombay. I remember when this was announced at the cancer congress in Hamburg in 1990 when John Di got up and said to me across the hall, "we are going climbing in the Himalayas, you make the arrangements." The congress was held in New Delhi at the Ashoka Hotel and the Taj Mahal Hotel. The evening reception for the delegates was hosted at The Indira Gandhi Memorial Gardens where we were entertained by the singing of Lata Mangashker and Ustad Ala Rakha on the table. In the gardens that evening there were stalls from each state cooking their authentic food. I still remember us lining up for fresh hot *Jalebis.* Immediately after the 5 day meeting we flew to Kathmandu for our climb in the Himalayas. There were 6 of us and we went up to the Annapurna base camp at 4130 meters. This was the camp set up by the British Expedition to the Annapurna in 1976. At this point I attach an account of my visit to attend the cancer congress in Delhi and the climb. I wrote a treatise of this in the form of a diary and produce it here.

International Cancer Congress - Delhi and Himalayan Climb - Nepal. October/November 1994.

The Samovar restaurant in the Ashok Hotel, one of the venues for the Cancer Congress, is a long room with huge windows through which the palm trees and gardens are visible. The room has eight medium size chandeliers, white tables with pale green legs and matching chairs. The floor is pale green marble and the whole place feels very cool but the lunch, *Rajnishi Gosht*, is not. Last night (Sunday the 30th November 1994) we went to a reception at the Indira Gandhi Stadium. It was a very elaborate affair they must have spend a great deal of money. After a musical recital by Lata Mangeshkar (who donated 200,000 Rupee to The Indian Cancer Society) and Tabla and Drum players we were shown a tourist film and after a speech by the Tourism Minister we came out on to the lawns. On the flood lit lawns there were beer trolleys and they were cooking Indian food of every variety available. The longest line was at the Jalebi trolley — oh those hot jalebis, Also there were dancers from six different states. A thoroughly enjoyable evening!

Monday the 31th October 1994, It has been a tiring day attended one lecture and listened to 4 seminars also looked at some of the posters at two different venues. The inter-venue coaches are very comfortable, air-conditioned but I would like a cool beer - not available. There is a talk about Mrs. Gandhi`s contribution to science in India at 5 PM. but I don't feel like going to it. I think I will grab a "bone- shaker" to Janak Puri. One and a half hour later I am still trying to get one of these mechanical *Tongas* - they are all saying that Janak Puri is too far, eventually I get a ride to Janak Puri and experience my first evening rush hour in Delhi. Its hell the pollution is so bad that even a gas mask would be useless. While sitting in the *tonga* I have been looking at the tyres on the lorries and buses and they are all bald (smooth). The evening is spending by visiting my host's friends.

Tuesday the 1st November 1994, Got to the meeting at 9 AM and met up with John. Henry and Ray and found out that John has been afflicted with the Delhi belly. It has been a heavy morning, three sessions on Chemical Carcinogenesis. I must mention the lunch provided by the organisers — each day they lay out a magnificent fayre, huge selection of vegetarian and non-vegetarian dishes, sweets and coffee. Today I had lamb curry with rice and *gobhi* followed by *rasmalai.* The afternoon session was also very heavy. We met up at 4 PM and had a cold beer in Ashoka, collected our tickets to Kathmandu, had a go at the guys at the travel agents for trying to charge the others l00 Rupee each for one telephone call to confirm their already confirmed seats on the Royal Nepal Airlines. I talked to Ray Tennent (NIH) at length about my work with Silica Fibres.

In the evening I attended a reception for the UICC Fellows at the Taj Mahal Hotel. It was a sombre affair, met a few people who were interested in my work. Had difficulty in obtaining a *rickshaw* at 9.30 PM — eventually I get one driven by a young lad who was very good and I gave him an extra 5 Rupee. The fare still only came to 38 Rupee (75p) for a 7 km journey.

Wednesday the 2nd November 1994, As there were no sessions worth attending I decided to go shopping. I had to wait 2 hrs at the Gulf Airlines office to confirm my seat back to England. I visited a market near Connaught Place where I bought a holdall for 150 Rupee. Also went to Palika bazaar where after a lot of haggling I bought two ¾ length leather coats for the price of one i.e. 240 Rupee, The ride back to Janak Puri through the evening rush hours was horrendous and

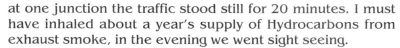

at one junction the traffic stood still for 20 minutes. I must have inhaled about a year's supply of Hydrocarbons from exhaust smoke, in the evening we went sight seeing.

Thursday 3ʳᵈ November 1994, Today is Diwali and a National holiday it's like Christmas in England. The whole thing is much commercialised, shops are full of cheap goods and Indian sweets. Every one gives every one presents. I went to the local market in Janak Puri with Dev and Lata. The whole place was very colourful but dirty, cows wondering around among people. Bought two small locks for 20 Rupee (40p) and four rivets for my case, I should have taken my camera! First sign of stomach problem - my tummy is very unsettled I was introduced to the local General Practitioner (GP) a well spoken and polite person but the surgery is a dump (I suppose by some, I stress some, Indian standards it is very clean). To be fair I must say the area around the Congress Venues in New Delhi is very clean, tree lined boulevards with huge houses hidden behind the trees and well guarded. It appears there are five different standards of life style - very rich, upper middle-class, lower middle-class, poor and miserable wretches — but people are very friendly and courteous. Today was also the day trip to Agra and the coach was leaving the hotel at 5 AM. I keep thinking about the people, who went on it, I did not go as I have been to Agra before. The weather here is mild although this is the start of their winter; it is in fact like spring in England. I have not used my sweater or blazer once. I am eating Indian food three times a day - stuffed prathas for breakfast. *(See pages P-31 & P-32, Pics 76 abcdef and 77 abc-International Cancer Congress - Delhi and Himalayan Climb - Nepal (Oct. Nov. 1994).*

Friday 4ᵗʰ November 1994, morning started with the stomach still in a bad way — no breakfast- had a bad night, those fire works went on half the night, and I was unable to sleep. Also, first sign of a cold developing. To crown it all I had to wait a long time to get a tonga and then had to wait at a level crossing for three trains to pass not a very good way to start the day. Another hard day attended two sessions in the morning and two in the afternoon. The lunch was as usual an elaborate affair. In the evening I had to rush to Tailoo Ram and sons (Army Tailors) in Gopinath Bazaar. I was one hour late as I could not get one of those miserable three-wheelers. From Gopinath we had to go to Raymond's to buy suiting, which cost me 1900 Rupee for a three-meter length. Dinner at Lata's dad place was a feast.

Saturday 5th November 1994, we were up early, attended two sessions in the morning. The closing ceremony was impressive and the moment it finished five of us took two taxi's to Delhi Airport where we passed the two hours drinking bottles of warm beer, not a pleasant experience. The flight to Kathmandu was uneventful except saw corruption at first hand at the airport — a bundle of notes being passed to the immigration officer to allow an Indian family to go through without ID papers. At Kathmandu Airport we were met by the touring company representative who drove us to hotel Mall through the town with running commentary all the way, I tell you! He loves to talk. Mall is a very comfortable 5 star hotel, after shower we walked to the old bazaar had a meal in a Chinese restaurant not much to look at but excellent food.

Sunday 6th November 1994, we were up very early and went back to the old bazaar where we did some shopping. We took a cab to the Swayambhu Stupa, which overlooks the city; it has Buddha's eyes on all four sides supposedly keeping eyes on everybody.

Went to the Durbar Square where we haggled for trinkets and small presents. We had lunch in a little café! In Durbar Square, a genuine Nepalese lunch. After spending most of the day sightseeing we landed up in the Yak and Yeti at about 6 PM. Yak & Yeti is the local pub where all climbers and hikers meet to talk about their adventures - it used to be a lovely old pub and now it has been turned into a 5 star marble complex with a modern bar, what a shame! I forgot to mention that we had a meeting with the touring company staff in the morning in their offices for a briefing. We had our dinner in the hotel restaurant- which was not bad.

Monday 7th November 1994, we were picked by the touring company mini-bus outside our hotel at 7.15 AM and driven to the domestic airport, which is just a shack. The 45 minutes flight to Pokhara was fantastic with impressive views of the Himalayan range on the right side of the plane all the way. At 4000 ft Pokhara airport is just a dirt track with 3 huts and a dozen chairs under a tree as a waiting room.

I had a picture taken of me sitting in one of these chairs to prove that the waiting is outside. *(See page P-32 Pic. 77 a: International Cancer Congress - Delhi and Himalayan Climb - Nepal (Oct. Nov. 1994).* At the airport we were introduced to the leader of the Sherpas (Sardar) and then driven through Pokhara township to the starting point of our Trek/Climb where we met rest of the crew, 14 porters, 3 Sherpa, 2 cook boys. At the starting point we are already 5000 ft high, trekked for 2 hrs stopped for lunch, which lasted one hour. The people are very friendly and they all even 3 year old shout hello! Hello! What is your name? We head upstream on the Modi Khola, cross a tributary and begin a long climb along a remarkable staircase to reach Chandruk (5600 ft).

This is Gurung country where Gurkha soldiers come from. We were told that Gurung dancing and singing could be arranged for trekkers willing to pay. We reached our camp site at an altitude of 6500 ft at 4 PM where we are greeted by tea and cakes, the porters and cook boys walk very fast and get to the camp site ahead of us to set camp and prepare the evening meal which was really interesting, Mutton soup, fried Mutton with carrots, greens and roast potatoes. The view from our camp site is fantastic as the sun is setting we can see Annapurna South (23682 ft), Annapurna I (26545 ft), Machhapuchhare (22942 ft), Annapurna III (24767 ft), and the Peak 29 (25690 ft). We sat outside the tents talking and looking at the peaks and the Milky Way.

Tuesday 8ᵗʰ November 1994, We were woken up at 6 AM (it feels very cold) with a tin mug of tea and after a quick wash we were able to see the sunrise at 6.20 AM. The view when the first rays of the sun strikes the sides of the peaks is incredible and it gets better and better as the sun rises.

We took lots of pictures and after breakfast we were off again by 7 AM. After a steady climb of about 2000 ft we took a brief rest, saw a little girl carrying a bundle on her head which was bigger than her. Another 2 hours and 1000 ft later we stopped for lunch, its getting hot and I am sweating like a pig, the snow goggles Lisa bought for me are a real bonus. Another very good meal, during lunch we talked about our climb and the Sardar (Sherpa Leader) thinks we should reach the peak some time tomorrow about 1500 hr. Pass through a valley full of gigantic rhododendrons covered with moss and pass through two very interesting villages, the region looks very prosperous, we are told that this region is famous for providing Gurkhas soldiers who obviously send their earnings home. We reached our camp site a little earlier then yesterday, many children from the two local villages below us came up to our camp and started to pester us, they were eventually told to go. We camped at 9500 ft and we could see the 'Manasu' range clearly in fact it is on top of us, colder then last night and we had to sleep in two sleeping bags, hat and warm vest.

Wednesday 9th November 1994, We were up at 6.00 AM, very cold and not much Oxygen, saw the sunrise, left camp at 7.30 AM after breakfast walked for about 45 minutes and then started to climb. We had to rest quite a few times in scaling 1500 ft. For the next hour on the trail we saw remains of avalanches, we cross many streams and passed the birch forest along the valley and came to the Inn of Bagara at about 10,825 ft. After another 5 hrs we reach a grassy slope with couple of shops called Machhapuchhare Base Camp (12,150 ft). The face of Machhapuchhare (22,942) looms over us. It is very cold and windy and as we are short of time we are unable to venture across the rubble— covered glacier, therefore, after a short rest and picture session we start our descend back, which is quite rapid. We stop for our night camp on flat portion of a rocky hill, which the porters had cleared by the time we got to it, but in doing so they had disturbed the ants. The hill is a massive ant colony, the buggers bite with a sharp sting. Out came the insect repellent which was applied to the tent door, round our shoes and on our legs, this did the trick and we were not bothered by the critters all night. Also in the cool of the night the ants tend to hide below ground. We celebrated our last evening meal with California Chardonnay (Ray brought it with him from the states) and local beer. We sat telling jokes and stories about climbs-uneventful night.

Thursday, 10th November 1994, We were up at 4 AM in order to get an early start; it`s a cold crisp morning. We start after a breakfast of porridge, eggs on toast and tea. We drop almost 3000 ft in the first hour, its tough going but it is quick— gives me descent any day. Rest and down again, we repeated this all day along with a short break for lunch. The route was

stage I decided that enough is enough and said no. That was the weekend the IRA detonated a bomb in a pub in Guildford. The result was the fact that security became very strict. We were searched every time we went in or out of the camp complex. We took our venture scouts to climb Mount Snowden (3560 ft) in Wales. I went with 4 venture scouts on a 50 mile hike for their Duke of Edinburgh gold award. During this hike over three days we climbed Scafell Pike at 3209 ft the highest peak in England. We also climbed Great gable and its sister mountain Green gables all situated in the Lake District National Park. The Wheathampstead venture Scouts planted a tree on the common at Blackmore End, opposite the Tin Pot pub, as a contribution to the world tree planting year. The tree now stands at 60 ft tall. *(See page P-8, Pic. 20: Tree planting ceremony on the common opposite the "Tin Pot" at Blackmore End).*

During his teenage years Christopher had many friends and among them was a boy called Tim Burland who lived in Wheathampstead. One evening I went to pick Chris from the Burland residence. Tim's dad whom I had met socially a few times opened the door and said "come in I want to introduce you to someone" that someone turned out to be Rev. Desmond Tutu who greeted me with that well known smile. It was a real pleasure to meet and spend a few hours with such a prominent person. I will always be grateful to John for introducing me to Desmond Tutu. John Burland a civil engineer is very well known and is famous for preventing the Leaning Tower of Pisa from toppling over. John studied at Witwaterstrand University in South Africa before he came to England and is currently at Imperial College where he occupies the chair in Civil Engineering.

One day Joan was talking to one of the Mums from Beech Hyde School who owned a long boat on the Grand Union canal. We rented the 58 ft long steel hulled boat from the couple who lived on The Hill at Wheathampstead. We boarded the beautifully decorated boat at Aston Clinton on a sunny Saturday afternoon. Before we sat about circumnavigating the Grand Union Canal we had a comprehensive tour of the boat, its safety features and the rules of the waterways. The owner showed us the ropes (quite literally), the steering, and how to successfully operate a lock (we were already familiar with this task from our trip on the Thames many years past) before leaving us in charge. Not forgetting to leave us a list of daily tasks like filling the tanks with water, checking the oil, water and grease in the engine, and making sure the rudder wasn't fouled. The boat came fully equipped with full size oven, fridge, flushable toilet, very efficient shower. We untied the ropes and proceeded down the GUC towards Milton Keynes, Stoke Brueun and Blisworth tunnel. The engines are set to stay to cruise at 4 miles an hour. In the morning you see a church steeple in a village, walk around the village, cruise all day and find that you are at the other end of the same village in the evening. Our journey took us through some beautiful scenery, past some delightful old pubs and we met some longboat enthusiasts. At Stoke Brueun there is a museum about life on the narrow boats and some very old quaint pubs we moored there for a day and night. Blisworth tunnel is almost 2miles long and you are underground for almost 30 minutes. We turned back at Gayton where the Northampton arm starts. It was a fantastic, relaxing experience and Lisa and Chris loved every minute of it and we talked about it for a long time.

In 1975 I took Joan, Lisa and Chris to Kenya and we stayed with Gurmit who had a house in Southseas. I arrived in Nairobi a day earlier on a 10% concession ticket with Alltalia. The next day Gurmit and I went to the airport to welcome Joan and the children who had travelled by Sudan Airways. We spend a few days visiting various places in the city centre that I used to frequent as a youngster. *(See page P-9, Pic. 21: Joan, Lisa and Chris in Kenyatta Avenue; Pic. 22: Chris and Lisa sitting on one of the Lions guarding the Mcmillan Library); Pic. 23: Chris the news paper vendor).*

I took Joan, Lisa and Chris to the City Park where we used to go for walks and to admire Bougainvillea trees on Sundays when I lived in Nairobi. Joan was amazed at the size of the Bougainvillea trees as she had only seen bushes of this particular flower in Europe. *(See page P-10; Pic. 24: Joann and Lisa in City Park; Pic. 25: Lisa and Dad in City Park).*

We had a wonderful time in Kenya and we went on many safaris. The first safari was to Nairobi National Park where we saw many animals, had tea in the chalet, and had the pleasure of seeing monkeys take cakes and sandwiches out of people's hands. We drove to Kabete and then took the road that runs through the rift valley to Nakuru. This rift is part of the eastern branch that bisects Kenya north-to-south on a line slightly west of Nairobi. It is part of the Great Rift Valley that transcends practically the whole of Africa. Volcanic mountains found along this rift are Mount Kilimanjaro, Mount Kenya, Mount Longonot and Mount Elgon among others. The 100 mile journey to Nakuru on a beautiful tarmac road built by Italian prisoners of war in 1941 took almost three hours. The scenery as you drive through the rift valley is breath-taking. We took a detour to Mt. Longonot, an extinct volcano. I wanted Lisa and Chris to see the crater because as a child I visited this many times as part of our school outings. Nakuru 2004 ft above sea level is a flourishing, cosmopolitan town is situated at one end of a rift valley soda lake named Nakuru. The lake looks like a pink sheet because it is home to a large number of pink flamingos; there are many other species of birds as well. I think this is where Lisa lost her pink ted. *(See page P-11, Pic. 26: With Lisa beside Lake Nakuru; Pic. 27: Lisa and Chris beside Lake Nakuru)*

One of the other lakes we visited in the rift valley is Lake Naivasha. It is a fresh water lake fringed with thick papyrus and has many tourist hotels. We booked into one of farmer Canelli's wooden Bandas and stayed there for three days. Chris and Lisa were playing with two children of their age on the first day and when they came to our Banda we talked to them and asked them to ask their parents to come and have tea with us. We found out that they were Methodist missionary from Luton and were living in Mombasa. They were currently on vacation from their church in the downtown area of that city. They asked us if we would accompany them to search for Lammergeier Eagles; they said there were only two pairs of these Ethiopian eagles that were nesting close by. Next day we walked around the forest without any concern for our safety, even though we were told that there were wild animals around. On the way back we saw an old man with a child who had a plaster cast on his leg sitting by a tree. I asked him where he had come from and where he was going. He said he had carried his son from the dispensary in Naivasha, almost 6 miles, and was going to his village. He pointed out his village about two miles away from where we were. I said to the others that I must give him a lift and so I drove the old man and his son to their house. They were so grateful and thanked me many times. We went to the missionary friend's home in downtown Mombasa, visited their church and had tea with them when we went to Mombasa at the end of our vacation.

We went on many safaris including one to Nanuki where I took pictures of Chris and Lisa straddling the equator sign. *(See page P-11, Pic. 28: At the start of Rift Valley: Pic. 29: Lisa and Chris at the Equator, Kenya).*

The last 10 days of our vacation we went to Mombasa and rented a chalet on Bamburi beach on the Indian Ocean. Our drive from Nairobi to Mombasa took us through Tsavo National Park about two miles from Voi we had a puncture on the near side front wheel. I decided to change the wheel and proceeded to jack the car when Joan reminded me that we were in elephant country. I changed the wheel while Joan, Lisa and Chris were on elephant watch. We spent three days in the National Park and stayed at Voi lodge which had an elephant grid around the stone built bandas. Lisa and Chris found an Elephants Femur lying around the bandas. *(See page P-12, Pic. 30: Chris struggling with an elephant femur).*

In the evening we sat in front of the large window in our banda and observed many wild animals coming to drink from the water hole. The approach of the wildebeest to the waterhole was spectacular as you could see thousands of them coming to drink for a long way. When we reached Mombasa we visited our missionary friends and also the Arab quarter in the old part of the town. We enjoyed our evening walk and the dates, bought from the street seller, through the old town. We also visited Fort Jesus built by the Portuguese around 1590's to guard the port of Mombasa. Between 1630 and 1870 it was conquered 9 times by the Colonial powers and eventually became part of the British Colony of Kenya. The stay in the chalet on Bamburi beach was the best part of our vacation to Kenya. *(See page P-12, Pic. 31: Joan at Bambury chalet on the Indian Ocean, Mombasa).*

For me the highlight of our trip to Kenya was the fact that I coached squash at Parklands Sports Club, a club I was not allowed in when I lived in Kenya. I served as a grade 2 coach, Panel Tutor, member of the management committee and the Council of the Squash Rackets Association for many years. I was asked by the then Senior National Coach, Tony Swift, to get in touch with Mrs. Paul, secretary of the Kenya Squash Rackets Association, when I arrived in Nairobi. She wanted me to coach the National team and also run a week long course for women during the day. Joan and the children used the club facilities and the pool while I coached. By the early seventies the number of people playing squash had increased considerably, and the Squash Rackets Association decided to train top amateurs as coaches to supplement the shortage of professional coaches at the time. These amateurs were allowed to coach for money and yet still retain their amateur status. Through the encouragement of Dick Hawkey, a very good player, administer of the game, and at that time Director of Coaching. I took the coaches course tutored by Dick Hawkey and a year later, in 1973, I took a very tough examination (3 hour written paper and two practical sessions). In fact out of nine people who took the examination only two passed and I was one of them.

The Squash Rackets Association

CERTIFICATE FOR

QUALIFIED AMATEUR COACHES

This is to certify that

T. S.   BHATT.

is a Qualified Amateur Coach of the

Squash Rackets Association

DIRECTOR

Date 16th September, 1973.

SECRETARY, S.R.A.

THIS CERTIFICATE IS THE PROPERTY OF S.R.A. AND IS VALID FOR ONE YEAR ONLY FROM THE DATE OF ISSUE, IT MUST BE SURRENDERED ON DEMAND.

Pic: D - 8

I subsequently went on to coach the Belgian and the French national teams. In October 1978 I was invited by the Belgian National coach to Brussels to coach at a new club near Waterloo (the site of the famous battle). As I was recovering from a sub-arachnoid haemorrhage that year I took two junior International players from England with me for exhibition matches.

As a part 2 Coach and a Panel Tutor of the Squash Rackets Association I used to run week long squash courses for beginners and moderate players at Crystal Palace, Lillishall Hall (Warwickshire), and Bisham Abbey on River Thames. My courses at Lillishall always coincided with that of a fencing course tutored by the Fencing National coach, Tom Norcross. Tom used to teach me fencing and we used to play squash.

Pic: Belgian National Coach and the National Squad

We also took our two groups together for dinner on the last night. Tom and I became friends and when he wrote a book on fencing he gave me a signed copy. In my free time at Bisham Abbey. I used to take the single skull out on the Thames and skull for hours. I also sailed on River Crouch when we went for St. Mary's regatta held every year at the Royal Burnham Yacht Club. At the insistence of Tony Swift, the Senior National Coach, I became the coaching representative for the Eastern Region which included Norfolk, Suffolk, Bedfordshire, Cambridgeshire, Essex and my own county Hertfordshire. This position entitled me a seat on the council and the Management Committee of The Squash Rackets

Association. The management committee met every month at the British Tourist Association offices because the chairman of the committee was the CEO of BTA. The coaching committee held its monthly meeting in the Midlands usually in Daventry. At one of these meetings Tony Swift gave me a letter and said "can you see what this guy wants." The letter was from Roger Barandiaran a Basque who had built a squash club in Biarritz and wanted a SRA coach but not a professional. I telephoned him the next night and we had a long talk he was adamant against having professional coaches because he said they were demanding lot of money. It just happens that we were going to camp in the region of Landes, close to Biarritz, for our vacation the following summer. Roger said why don't you come and coach and we will pay you and provide you with accommodation. When we arrived in Biarritz we were made very welcome and given a flat above the club house. The club is situated very close to Milady beach and has two squash courts which Roger and his wife Angel built. Roger got interested in squash in Bristol where he spent two years working at British Aerospace. I coached for two hours in the morning and two hours in the evening and the rest of the day we were on the beach. The entertainment in the evening and the weekend was fantastic. The pig roast outside the club house, lots of wine and singing were all part of the entertainment. At the end of our two weeks they asked me how much money they should give me for the coaching, and I said I did not need any money because they had given us accommodation. I enjoy coaching, and also we had made many friends. They insisted on paying for the coaching and asked if I could come back next year. We went to Biarritz for many years and the family became friends with Roger, Angel and their two boys, Harvey and Lionel. Roger and I started writing a coaching book for the French players which was published in 1984, after we had come back from the USA and I owned Potters Bar Squash Club. Roger attended one of my part one coaches courses at Wembley and the family stayed with us at Uplands for that week. Two years later with a special dispensation from the Squash Rackets Association I was allowed to examine him. The examination was conducted in Biarritz with two independent players as observers. Roger eventually became the French National coach. As our two clubs were twinned and Paul Carter was a rising star I took him and a female player to Biarritz to play exhibition matches. They played at two clubs in Paris on our way down southwest. The editor of Squash Player Magazine, Brenda Rooney a friend, asked me to compare the Basque game of Pelota with squash for the magazine. I mentioned this to Roger and he fixed a Pelota demonstration for me at the National Stadium in Biarritz. When we arrived at the stadium I was told to get dressed because I was playing with the 1974 World Champion. After some trepidation I found myself on court with a large crowd, including the family, as spectators. It took me a while to get used to the basket but I did not disgrace myself and to cap it all my opponent presented me with the basket he had used to win his world title. I still have the basket and it hangs in my study with my trophies. A copy of the printed article I wrote for the Squash Player in which I compare the two games is attached. *(See page P-12 and 13, Pic. 32: Adjusting the Pelota basket; Pic. 33: Playing Pelota at the National Stadium with the 1974 World champion in Biarritz).*

Another time we were coming back from Biarritz and stopped at a club in Paris and their professional was one of the Khans whose picture was on the front page of the French Squash Magazine that month. When we arrived at the club, Mont Parnas, he was coaching, and when he saw us, he came up and said, "Who is going to play with me." I was recovering from a Sub-Arachnoid Haemorrhage that had occurred a year earlier so I could not play. He then asked Chris to accept his challenge. He was a real gentleman and allowed Chris to beat him and then took the front page of the magazine and signed his picture thus: "To Chris Bhatt who beat me 3-0 in Paris."As the Eastern Area Coaching representative I had a hand in developing Gosling Stadium in Welwyn Garden City as the Eastern Regional Squash Centre in 1979. *(See page P-13, Pic. 35: Discussing the merits of the Regional Centre with the Eastern Area Committee).*

The picture from the Welwyn Hatfield Times shows a picture of Councillor Gordon Ayerst at the official opening ceremony. When I was 16 years old a friend and I sent for a horoscope from an astrologer in India whose advertisement appeared in a magazine for 5 shillings. A couple of months later we received our horoscopes in the form of typed sheets suitably decorated with many Hindu symbols and red ribbon. Mine read that I was going to travel abroad and see the world but my life line has a break. It said if I survive this break at the age of 42, then I will live longer. We thought the whole thing was hilarious and threw the elaborately decorated papers in the trash can.

No, not Dr. Who! How the Chistera basket fits onto the hand.

The Basque connection

Does squash have its roots in Pelota, a game played by the Incas, asks Tochi Bhatt

COULD it be possible that squash and the game of rackets have a common root in the Basque National game of Pelota? it is generally accepted that squash started at Harrow School, where boys started to play 'baby rackets' with a soft ball before graduating to the faster game of rackets.

Rackets is a very fast game played by two or four persons in a large four-walled court, using a small hard ball and a long-handled racket. In 'Pickwick Papers' Dickens describes a late 18th-century open-air court in the Fleet Prison where a form of rackets was played against a single wall by debtors.

I have recently spent some time coaching at a new squash club in Bairritz where I was introduced to *Pelota*. I also played *Trinquet* and *Chistera*, two variations of *Pelota* at the National Stadium in Bairritz and was struck by the many similarities between it and squash and rackets.

The front wall has a tell-tale or tin and you are allowed to use the four walls (in the case of chistera—three walls) of the court. The ball is only allowed to bounce once on the floor (which, incidentally, can be of wood or concrete), and narrow angled shots are also played.

Pelota, which means ball, is the general name for many variations of the game in which two or four players can take part. here I list the three that I came across.

Trinquet, which is well-known in France, is played in a court 30 metres long, 12 metres wide and 15 metres high. It is characterised by the four walls which the ball can touch. Moreover the varieties of shots like 'chilo', 'pan coup' and 'tambour'

make it a spectacular game. It is played with a thick or thin wooden bat (depending on the variation) and a hard rubber ball.

Chistera (Le Frenton 'place Libre') is played on a court 30 metres long, 8.5 metres wide and 10 metres high with three playing walls (back, left and front). The floor is made of wood and the front wall of a special hard stone to take the impact of the hard ball which travels at 300km/hour. The ball is caught in a narrow, scythe-shaped whicker basket, which is secured to the wrist of the player and then thrown with great skill at the front wall.

Le Fronton 'mur a gauche', was another variation I saw being played which seems to have a direct link with the Fleet game. Each village of the Basque country has its church or town hall, in fact any open space.

Tochi demonstrating Chistera.

The court consists of a front wall of characteristic shape and a playing area of part cement and part beaten earth. The dimensions are not laid down but recommended. The construction depends on finance and area available. This is the game that introduces all beginners to the other harder variations of Pelota.

Many forms of Pelota are played in some South American countries. The assumption is that the game was taken to Mexico by the Conquistadors, but history tells us that the Incas and Mayas were playing these games before the Spanish Conquest of Mexico. Could it be that the Basques and Incas are descendants of a common stock as has been suggested by some historians?

The club that I coached at has been built by Roger Barandiaran, a keen, Trinquet-playing Basque and his wife. They spent two years mixing cement mortar and building a two-court complex called 'Squash Biarritz Milady.' It is the only French club that is directly affiliated to the SRA.

The club has a free and relaxed atmosphere. The opening hours are flexible and if you have no partner, Roger or his wife Angel, will fill the gap at short notice.

When I asked Roger why he built the club, he said he got interested in squash while working in Lancashire, and wants to promote squash. The three flags (Olympic, Basque National, Biarritz city) flying outside the club house confirmed the fact that Roger meant what he said.

Squash is beginning to mushroom in France. In 1977 there were 17 courts but today there are 100 courts and they are building at the rate of about a dozen courts per year.

I met Shah Jehan Khan at Montparnasse in Paris. I think the French are very lucky in having such a talented player as their National Coach. He is particularly popular with young people and my 11-year-old son, Chris, took to him immediately. Shah Jehan played three games with him and allowed him to beat him and testified the defeated on a poster of himself which now adorns my sons bedroom wall.

The Basques have a good eye for the ball, especially in the air, and any lose ball is immediately dispatched with accuracy and great speed. The Basques are beginning to take to the game and one can safely say that when ready the Basque will dominate squash in France for a very long time to come.

Squash Monthly February 1980

24

Pic: D - 9

Welwyn and Hatfield Times, Friday, May 19, 1978

New complex puts Gosling Stadium in big league

WITH a ceremonial swipe of the racket, Councillor Gordon Ayers, present chairman of Welwyn Hatfield Council, officially opened the new Eastern Region Squash Centre at the Gosling Stadium, WGC, on Tuesday night.

The £160,000 complex, with its three courts, pre - match room and large spectator gallery, is the first regional centre to be built in the country and more than 100 invited guests were present at its opening.

After top Essex player Paul Wright and Middlesex number one Robbie Robinson had played a few games, guests watched a match between three times former World Squash Champion, Abu Taleb, and World Real Tennis Champion, Howard Angus.

The new facilities are the first phase in a scheme that will make the centre a potential venue for major tournaments. Eventually four more courts will be built, giving the stadium 12 in all.

The courts were built with the co-operation of the Eastern Council for Sport and Recreation, the Squash Rackets Association, Welwyn Hatfield Council and the Welwyn Hatfield Sports Centre Trust Ltd.

Members from all these organisations were among the guests present at Tuesday night's ceremony.

Pic: D - 10

Councillor Gordon Ayres, himself a former squash player, hits the ball that officially opened the new centre.

On Monday the 18th January 1978 I boarded the train at St. Pancras Station with some colleagues to travel home and when the train reached Harpenden Dennis Wang said, "Hey you went to sleep" which was unusual because I normally read the paper or did some work. When we got off the train I felt drowsy as if I had an extra pint of beer, but, in fact, I had had no alcohol. Dennis asked me if I would like to go home with him to rest before I drove to Blackmore End. I replied that I must get home because Joan was taking Chris to music lesson. I walked on the bridge to the car park and remember opening the door of my 1958 Sunbeam Alpine, but, to this day, have no recollection of driving it home. I obviously did because I reached home. Joan was reversing out of the drive to take Lisa to her music lesson. I left my car out on the road, waved to Joan and was greeted by Chris at the front door. He said that Mom had left me a note and, following her instructions I turned on the heat under the two sauce pans on the Hotpoint plates. An hour later, Joan found me unconscious. Chris was trying to raise the neighbours for help and the contents of the saucepans burned to charcoal. She immediately telephoned our GP in Kimpton. Dr. Rushton arrived within 15 minutes and after looking at my condition said. "Subarachnoid Haemorrhage" and started telephoning local hospitals. This was 18th January 1978 and all the beds were occupied with winter casualties. In frustration he telephoned St. Albans City Hospital and told them he had a patient with meningitis knowing full well that they could not refuse to admit a patient with a communicable disease. I was rushed to the city hospital and admitted into the isolation ward and when they discovered blood in my spinal fluid during a lumbar puncture procedure they realised that I had a brain haemorrhage. Joan found herself following the ambulance on the M1 in pouring rain as I was being taken to Royal Free Hospital in Hampstead, where I was in an intensive care unit for 10 days. Mr. McCall the consultant Neuro-surgeon told Joan to expect the worst, but she, the family and the congregation at St. Helens in Wheathampstead prayed for me and with God's help I pulled through. I was transferred back to St Albans City Hospital where I stayed for further six weeks, lying on my back, not allowed to move, blanket baths, bed pans and the lot. Joan stayed alert and did everything that needed to done, but on the 12th day of my illness she collapsed in our local Pharmacy in Wheathampstead, where Mr. Smith and the staff looked after her. Now this was 1978 and I was 42 years old. Was the Horoscope that I had read in 1950 right? I will leave the readers to decide. In hind sight I now wish I had not been so hasty to trash it. Joan told me afterwords that both Lisa and Chris kept saying that nothing is going to happen to their Dad because he is strong. Dr. Rushton (God bless his soul) also told me that he lied to get me into the hospital; in fact it was quick thinking on his part that probably saved my life. It took a whole year for me to recover fully. Joan was convinced that my brain bleed was due to my hauling car engines etc. I had spent the previous two years restoring a Sunbeam Alpine 1958 model with the Daimler Dart rear wings which I had acquired from a farm in Sheapcote Lane in Wheathampstead. I stripped the car to its chassis got the local blacksmith, yes we did have a blacksmith in the village in the seventies, to weld two box sections to it, rebuilt the engine and the gearbox and sprayed it with the original maroon colour. I managed to get the parts from a company in the Midlands who had bought the entire stock of spare parts from The Roots Group who were responsible for the Sunbeam-Talbot marque which produced the Alpine model when Chrysler disbanded the marque in 1967. Sadly I had to sell that car because we were going to America for a year and I had no way to storing it.

In September 1980 we arrived in Philadelphia, the founding city of the Nation, on a World Health Organisation Fellowship. We were allowed to stay in the faculty apartment at the Wistar Institute, University of Pennsylvania, for two weeks while we hunted for a house to rent. After many viewings we managed to lease a colonial style house in Springfield, west of Philadelphia. The three bedroom house with a basement in Shellburn Road was very comfortable and the garage had been converted into a games room with a full size table tennis table. Joan worked her magic and made the house into a home fit for her family. We took Lisa and Chris to the Middle School, walking distance from the house, and they spent a very enjoyable and productive year at the school where they made many friends and even swore allegiance to the flag. We experienced our first heavy snow in the USA when we woke one morning to find that three ft of it had fallen overnight and our car was hidden under it. Kevin Mooney our neighbour's son was clearing the footpath in front of our house.

The state of Pennsylvania decrees that every household has to clear the footpath in front of its house. The Mooneys lived on one side of us and a widow on the other and they were very friendly neighbours. The first house in Springfield Road was occupied by Stan Milkowski a retired Army Colonel who became a good friend and later visited us in England many times. We integrated with the local community by joining the country club and other organisations. Chris, Lisa and I joined the Scout groups and went on many adventures/camps with them. All three of us learned to snow ski on one of these camps in the Pocono Mountains. Chris went to the Adirondacks during the summer holidays and I went with the girl scouts to help them and also be with Lisa. The senior scouts in the troop initiated me into the Pennsylvania section of the Order of the Arrow at the end of our stay. It was a gesture to thank me for helping out with the troop. The family went white water rafting on the Leigh High Gorge. *(See page P-14, Pic. 36: White water rafting on the Leigh High George).*

Just before Christmas we drove to Oswego on Lake Toronto to visit Michael O'Kane, Joan's nephew, who had settled there after marrying a local girl he had met in Europe. On the way back we were caught in a snow storm that was so severe that the windscreen wipers of the car could not cope and we had to stop for two hours until the storm abated.

In February 1981 we hired a motor home and drove down to Disney World on Interstate 95 visiting and staying overnight in the main city of each state. In Virginia we visited Colonial Williamsburg and Jamestown Plantation. *(See page P-13, Pic. 34: Chris at the North Carolina Border).*

In North Carolina we stayed overnight in Raleigh, and took a guided tour of the town. In South Carolina we stayed in Charleston and took a guided tour to see the highlights of the city. Savannah was our overnight stop in Georgia and it was of interest because the architect who designed the Arcade in Bristol was responsible for the architecture here. In Florida we visited the Kennedy Space Centre and spent three days in Disney World, which was a real treat, especially as we were able to park right in front of the gate in the disabled spaces as Chris was on crutches due to a sprained ankle sustained in a basketball game at school. *(See page P-14, Pic. 37: Joan, Lisa and Chris in Disney World).*

We then travelled to New Orleans to spend time with Kamal, Adarsh and Priti and also to see the Mardi Gras. *(See page P-14 and P-15, Pic. 38: Chris watching the Mardi Gras Parade; Pic. 39: Me, Joan, Lisa with Kamal and Priti in New Orleans).*

We were in New Orleans for 4 days and thoroughly enjoyed our stay and the MardiGras. Chris and Lisa had great fun trying to collect doubloons from the people on the parade floats. We cruised part of the Mississippi on the paddle steamer Natchez and had gambo and beans for lunch while calliope (a steam powered organ) was playing.

We visited New York City many times and saw the Statue of Liberty, Empire State Building, Central Park, Grand Central Station and skaters in Washington Square. We had many meals in China Town and Chelsea.

I used to commute from Springfield via trolley bus to the 69th Street station and then via subway to 36th and Spruce where Wistar Institute is situated in the middle of the University of Pennsylvania campus. Wistar Institute was founded in 1809 by General Isaac Wistar and contains the anatomical collection of his great uncle Casper Wistar. I shared an office and a lab with John Di during my year-long stay. We spent many a happy hour on Friday afternoon enjoying beer and pretzels in Tom Tawhasky's laboratory. My work at the Wistar resulted in a publication in the journal Cancer Research in 1983. At the end of my stay I was made an Alumnus of this institute.

In 1984 I was invited to Sweden to work at Uppsala University, birthplace of modern genetics Where Gregor Mendel, carried out his original research in genetics with the green pea plants. There is a museum about his work at the university. I was invited by the director of the Zoo physiology Institute, Professor Lindhal-Kessling to collaborate in research using a certain cell line that I had brought from Philadelphia. One day Professor Lindhal-Kessling asked me to go to the Agricultural University at Ultuna, near Uppsals, to listen to a seminar instead of her.

She said that she has telephoned people at Ultuna University to inform them that I will be attending the seminar instead of her. Before he started delivering the seminar the speaker said, I have changed my seminar from Swedish to English because of the presence of a scientist from England. He apologised to the fact that he did not have enough time to change his slides from Swedish to English. At the end of a very interesting lecture I thanked the speaker for his kindness in changing the language of his talk. I worked at the institute for 4 weeks and also got an opportunity to visit Stockholm (Sweden). We travelled by train from Uppsala and alighted at the magnificent Central Station when we reached Stockholm. I managed to visit the national museum and the Royal Palace. I

POZNAŃSKIE TOWARZYSTWO PRZYJACIÓŁ NAUK

WYDZIAŁ _____

KOMISJA *CHEMII KLINICZNEJ* _____

zaprasza na wykład:

dr *TARLOCHAN S. BHATT*

z *St. Bartholomew's Hospital* w *LONDYNIE*
pt.:
BIOGENIC SILICA FIBERS

w dniu *7 września '92* o godz. *13⁰⁰*
w *FILII im ADAMANSA (w Grunwaldzka 6)* Ip.
BIBLIOTEKI GŁÓWNEJ A.M w *POZNANIU*

Pic: D - 11

also managed to travel around Sweden. The work on the effect of 11-me-17-ketone on DNA resulted in a publication in 1984 in the journal "Carcinogenesis." In 1990 I was invited by the Polish Academy of Sciences to deliver a seminar at the University in Poznan.

I asked the organisers if they would pay for Joan's hotel accommodation and I would pay our travelling expenses. We drove to Poland through Germany and stayed in Berlin for three days at a friend's house in Spandau in the British Sector. It was exciting as the wall was coming down and we were able to go to the eastern sector, Brandenburg gate and the Chancellery.

Special Seminar:

Departments of Microbiology, Pathology, Molecular Pharmacology and Toxicology, the Institute of Toxicology and the Kenneth Norris Jr. Comprehensive Cancer Center

"Biogenic Silica Fibers and Mesotheliomas".

Tarlochan S. Bhatt, Ph.D.
Staff Scientist
St. Bartholomew's Hospital
Department of Reproductive Physiology
University of London
London, United Kingdom

Norris Cancer Hospital and Research Institute
5th Floor Conference Room
11:00 A.M.
Friday, May 29, 1992

Host: Joseph R. Landolph, Ph.D.
224-6526

Pic: D - 12

I was given a small piece of the wall by my host. In May 1992 I was invited by Prof. Joe Landolph of the Norris Cancer Hospital and Research Institute, University of Southern California to deliver a seminar on Biogenic Silica Fibres. I flew to Los Angeles from Texas as I was working at the MD Anderson Cancer Center. Adarsh drove me to my talk venue and was asked to stay and listen to my seminar by Joe Landolph.

In the summer of 1997 my brother Gurmit was going back to Toronto after a short break in London. I told him that I was asked to deliver a seminar in the Biochemistry Department, Toronto University by Prof. Sarma. We travelled together in Air Canada 3000 as Gurmit worked for them at that time, from West Midlands airport. I stayed with him for three days in

Toronto and he took me to the university. Prof. Sarma asked Gurmit to stay and listen to his brothers Seminar while enjoying his coffee.

In March 1991 we celebrated *Bibiji's* 70th birthday with a party at my squash club in Potters Bar. Majority of the Bhatt clan plus extended members of the family were there to celebrate the 70th birthday of the great lady. *(See page P-16, Pic. 41: Bibiji's 70th Birthday; Pic. 42: Picture of all those who attended Bibiji's 70th Birthday Party at my club)*

Bibiji wanted to perform wanted to perform *'Dadak Shak'* ceremony for her grandson and grand daughter-in-law. She asked me to arrange a party at the club for the Bhatt clan where she performed this ceremony in front of all the family and friends. *(See page P-17, Pic. 44: Param helping Bibiji with the jewellery for Gillian while Chris watches; Pic. 45: Now its Christopher's turn).*

Bibiji was a woman of immense strength and character. She learned to read and write Punjabi; spoke fluent Swahili. She gave birth and brought up 10 children, all of whom are very successful in life. She loved and cared for all her children. She was very religious, forthright in her comments. Her death in 2003 came as a shock. It was Sunday the 3rd February and I was just finishing my lunch when the phone rang. I answered and heard Jasbir saying *"Bibiji"* been rushed to Whipps Cross Hospital (WXH) could you please come." I said "I am leaving now" and immediately telephoned my brother Sawarn and when he answered, I told him that "If you want to see your mother alive then get in your car and drive to WXH." Dundee (Sawarn) in his usual way started making all sort of excuses, I repeated my request three times about coming to the hospital to see *Bibiji*. When there was no response except accusations and innuendos; I placed the receiver on the cradle and left for WXH. I was in a hurry and when I got to the Chingford Reservoirs there was a row of cars moving very slowly. I overtook them and then went through the traffic lights as they were turning red. As soon as I reached the gates of Chingford Rugby Club I heard the siren and flashing lights of an unmarked Police Vehicle. This white van was the one that was travelling at the appropriate speed between the reservoirs slowing the flow of traffic. I gave my driving licence to the officer that approached my car and told him "I know I am breaking the law. If you have to give me a citation, then please hurry as I have to get to WXH because my mom is in a critical state and she is not going to survive. I want to get to her before she departs this earth." He went to his vehicle to talk to his companion and then came back a few minutes later. He handed me my driving licence and said "follow us" I followed the Police Vehicle, lights flashing and siren going all the way to the gate of WXH. The officer got out of his vehicle and made sure I was turning into the gate of the hospital and said "let this be a warning, don't do it again and good luck with your mother" I thanked him, drove in to the hospital car park and got to my mom's bed side in time. I was holding her arm when she took her last breath at 3.15 PM. I was overcome with emotions and broke down when I read her eulogy on the day she was cremated.

Our friends Pam and Roger Hartley who lived at 32 Kimpton Road introduced us to their immediate neighbour John and Joan Biles who lived at 28 Kimpton Road. One New Year we were invited for a drink by the Biles. I noticed a shield from Zanzibar Police hanging on his wall. John said he was in the Colonial Police Force and Commissioner of Police in Zanzibar was his last post. I told him that I was in the Kenya Police and was stationed at the CID headquarters opposite the Anglican Cathedral on Ngong Hill. He told me that my boss was Chief Superintendent Cartwright, a Battle of Britain Pilot, and he named some other people that we both knew. It was amazing to think that two people living at Blackmore End were at one time in East Africa in the Police force at different times and knew the same people. A very small world, indeed.

One morning at breakfast Joan said to me, "Can you move toes of your left foot?" I said "yes but why do you ask?" She could not move her toes and I said, "I think you have had a TIA." So we went to see a cardiologist at BUPA Hospital in Harpenden. He examined Joan and said, "You don't need me but you need to see a neurologist." We did, and he said Joan was suffering from Parkinson's disease. This was confirmed by two other neurologists at The National Hospital for Neurological Diseases, Queen's Square, in London. After many tests they came to the conclusion that Joan was suffering from a nasty form of the disease called Multiple Systems Atrophy. After a lot of research on MSA, I found out that the average life span was 5 years but the top parameter was 11 years and of course Joan lasted 11 years with this dreadful condition. The year of diagnosis was 1996 and Joan carried on looking after the club and the house for a number of years before she started to slow down. Her deterioration was gradual and it was heartbreaking to see her body systems die slowly. I used to take her onto the squash court and make her hit the ball, trying to keep her muscles and limbs moving. She had played squash at a very good standard for many years. I also used to take her for long walks in St. Albans Park making her walk round the lake up-to the Cathedral always using the excuse that I had to use the toilets there. The distance from the car park to the top of the hill was about a mile. One day as we were coming back from the Cathedral and had just gone a little way by the lake Joan stopped and said "I can't go any further" I tried very hard to make her walk but in the end I had to carry her to the car. At this stage of her illness, Joan only weighed 94 pounds. After her death I had a bench placed near the site where she stopped walking. The brass plaque on the bench read's, 'In Loving memory of great wife and mother. Joan Louise Bhatt nee Read. 1932-2007.' *(See page P-16, Pic. 43: Bench in St. Albans park in memory of Joan Bhatt).*

In the early stage of her illness one morning while we were having breakfast, Joan looked at me with those beautiful green eyes full of tears and said. "You are going to put me in a home?" I immediately responded by saying never, and I looked after her for seven years except the last two months of her life when she went into a BUPA home in Elstree. Within four years of the illness being diagnosed, Joan had deteriorated so much that I decided to close my laboratory at St. Bart's Hospital at the end of December 1999, so I could look after my squash club and Joan. At this stage Joan had a Piper Alarm round her neck which was so sensitive that the control could hear her whispers. One evening the control telephoned and told me to get home because Joan was in trouble. I rushed home and found her head stuck between the bed and the bedside table; obviously, she had tried to get out of bed and fell. After seeing to Joan I had to go back to the club to lock up because I had left the club open with members minding the facilities. I found it very hard to do both the jobs and, after 18 months, I made a decision to sell the club and devote my entire time looking after Joan because I did not want her to go into a care home. I received a telephone call from Chris at 2 PM on Sunday the 19 April 2007; he said he had received a call from the care home saying his Mom was rushed to Barnet General Hospital. When I reached the hospital I saw the Consultant in the casualty department who told me Joan had Pneumonia. She said we could prolong Joan's life by two weeks with antibiotics, and then asked what we wanted them to do? I said I had to consult with my children before I make the decision and I immediately telephoned Lisa and then Chris. They both said that I should let Mom go because she had suffered enough. The Hospital put her in a room and fed her intravenously and we all visited with her every day and made sure that at no time she was left on her own. Joan took her last breath at 5.30 PM on the 24th April 2007 in Barnet General Hospital with Lisa, Chris, Gillian and me each holding on to a part of her body.

On a glorious day in July 1997 our son Christopher married Gillian at St. Andrews church in the village of Little Berkhampstead. St Andrews is a pretty little church dating back to Saxon times. The village is famous for the fact that William the Conqueror accepted the surrender of the City of London here after the Battle of Hastings. I remember the day really well for two reasons, one because of our son's wedding and two, the cannon showed a great deal of interest in the tie I was wearing. I told her that it was the Royal Society of Chemistry tie and that I was a fellow. She said that she was chemist and a member of the society before she took holy orders. A year earlier Joan had been diagnosed with MSA and, therefore, not feeling hundred percent. She looked stunning in her beige outfit and a beautiful hat and she was elated at her son's wedding. There were a large number of people from both sides of the families, from Chris and Gillian's work and also from our squash club. *(See page P-22, Pic. 57: Chris and Gillian on their wedding day).*

While I was taking care of Joan at home I had to be with her 24 hours a day, as she was unsteady on her feet and not able to attempt many tasks. Therefore, I was not able to go to the club for squash and exercise so I started to run around the block as soon as Joan use to go to sleep. I would come out of the house, turn left into Kimpton Road and start running. About half a mile at the brow of the hill, I would turn left into Porters End Lane, run past a dozen properties in Porters End to the cross roads and then turn left into the Slype.

About a mile and half at the cross road, I would turn left into Kimpton Road and complete the 3.2 mile circuit when I reached home. The Social Services used to supply me with a sitter for Joan for three hours on Thursdays to go shopping and 4hours on Fridays to go to the club. The Friday sitter used to let me down 50% of the time. One day about a year before Joan departed this earth, Tony Bowen, a friend and neighbour, came to the house and asked me to go for a walk with him. He was feeling very upset because a few months earlier he had lost his wife Brenda to breast cancer. We waited until Joan went to sleep and then walked the route I used for my daily run. When we reached the last house on the right hand side at Porters End Tony stopped to talk to a young woman working on the borders outside the house while I stood back. After a while he said, "Oh, by the way this is Tochi. He is a friend and lives at Blackmore End" I said hello and thought, "What a gorgeous woman," and we were on our way. Many times afterwards during my run I would look around whenever I went passed the house but never saw anybody. One day, I think it was on a Tuesday, a year after Joan died, I saw that woman outside the house and stopped and talked to her for a short while, and then went on my way. I had sold my house at Blackmore End and bought a smaller house in Broxbourne to be near Amelia. I was also on my way to Texas to work for 4 years at the MD Anderson Cancer Centre where John Digiovanni was now the Scientific Director. Just about a week later, on Thursday the 12th February, I was doing my usual run and turned into Porters End Lane. When I had covered 200 yards, I saw a blue car slowing down. I thought to myself that somebody had lost their way and wanted direction from me, but as it happened, it was the young woman from the last house at Porters End with who I had spoken the previous Tuesday. She talked to me, gave me a lovely smile, and told me where she was going but her companion; following in another car behind was impatient and started blowing the car horn. After I had run another half a mile, I said to myself, "Stupid, stop! The woman gave you a lovely smile and talked to you for a while. Don't you think she is worth pursuing?" This was two days before Valentine's Day and I decided to send her a card. So I rushed home, showered and went to W.H. Smiths in Harpenden to buy a Valentine's Day card. When I started to write the card I realised I did not even know her name, so I telephoned Tony Bowen and asked him if he knew her name. He immediately said, "Why do you want to know?" "I just want to know" was my answer, and I started looking in the local telephone directory as I knew the name of the house. Tarbox was the name that corresponded to the name of the house in the directory so I addressed the card with that name, wrote in it that I was sorry that I did not know her first name and at the bottom I wrote, "An admirer" and posted it. In the back of my mind I thought it would be thrown in the trash can because I had no idea if the lady was married or not. I do not know what I was expecting but after the weekend I realised that the person I sent the card to would have no idea who was it from. Monday morning with tongue in my cheek I telephoned and said I am the gentleman who goes running past your house and I am having a farewell party for my neighbours on Saturday, "Would you like to come?" When she answered "Yes," I nearly fell out of my chair, as I was not expecting that answer. At the party I saw her but did not get a lot of time to talk to her as I was talking to my other guests. She talked to Chris, Lisa, Gillian and Amelia for most of the night. At the end when everybody had left I went over to Lisa and Mrs. Tarbox (don't forget I still did not know her first name) because they were the only guests left, and the first thing she said to me was, "Where is your squash club?" I said, "It is in the playing fields of Mount Grace School in Potters Bar." She started to laugh and said I went to that school and we used to live in Potters Bar. When she said I love your grand daughter and your family I just had warm feelings for her and, as she was going out of the front door, I said, "By the way, did you get my Valentines card?" She said, it was you! Why did you not follow it because I waited for a knock at the door?" Andre was also going out to his car at the same time and he turned around and looked at me in complete surprise. I asked her for a date and she said, "On one condition, if you come with me to a talk on diabetes at Luton and Dunstable Hospital one of our local hospitals. Pauline and I went to the talk and, while walking to the lecture theatre, we met one of my colleagues from the past, Nargash Despande, whose first words were, "What are you doing on my patch?" In fact, he was the lecturer. Pauline could not believe that I knew somebody at L&D. After the lecture we went for a meal at our local Indian restaurant in Wheathampstead. The waiter there recognised me because he was the relative of the owner of Pubali in Potters Bar. At this point Pauline remarked, "Does everybody know you?" It was a very good first date. I took her out for her birthday to a restaurant in Harpenden; Graeme and Sinead, Pauline's son and daughter-in-law, sent a bottle of champagne as a surprise. I gave her a gold necklace with a heart pendant and told her it is a Manglasutra. A *manglasutra* (from Sanskrit mangal, meaning holy and sutra meaning thread) is a sacred necklace that a Hindu ties around the bride's neck. Hell!! I am not even a Hindu, but it does not matter because the thought was pure when I gave her the necklace. *(See page P -19, Pic. 48: Pauline and Me)*

It was interesting to find that Pauline's family had also come from Islington. Her father had a butchers shop in Kings Cross road and her uncle, Donald William Bromfield lived in Middleton Square and was the Mayor of Islington in 1969. Joan's family lived in Holford Square and her parents were married in St Marks Church in Middleton Square. Both the families had Dr. Bhattacharya as their general practitioner who had his surgery in Kings Cross road and he was affectionately known as Dr. Batachacha. To crown it all Pauline is the split image of Joan's younger sister Lillian, my God-son, Andre's late mother.

When Joan passed away John DiGiovanni a long-time friend and currently Scientific Director of Research at The MD Anderson Cancer Research Centre in Smithville Texas, telephoned from Texas and said, "Now you have nobody to worry about and you have been on holidays for too long, so come and work in the lab and see how you feel." But first In May 2007, I took a short trip to India to trace my Dad's side of the family and also to find some details about my mother's two brothers who were in the Indian Army during the Second World War. I had seen their picture in uniform clutching their .303 Lee Enfield Rifles.

One of the two brothers Pritam Singh Rekhrao is still alive and I stayed with him for three days. He was not very forthcoming with information on the first day, but on the second day at noon, he loosened up and told me that he and his brother had enlisted in the army in 1939 in Jalandhar. He said after training he was posted to the signals branch and posted to Kala Pani (Andaman Islands) and his army number was 4089, he reached the rank of corporal. His commanding officer was a Punjabi speaking General McCarthy (see note below) was who had some boats, hidden in the reeds round the islands and as soon the Japanese invaded the islands (the only part of India the Japanese occupied) he took his men in the boats to Calcutta. Pritam told me that his elder brother corporal Lal Singh Rekhrao, army number 3838 was in the Military Police. His unit was transported to Sumatra to guard these East Asian islands but they fell back with the Japanese advance and were captured at the fall of Singapore. As POW Corporal Lal Singh witnessed Japanese atrocities. He returned home bald, emaciated in 1946 and narrated his observations

of the horrible conditions the prisoners were subjected to. His unit's medical officer, Captain Diwan Singh, was tortured, mutilated and finally shot in front of his men. Diwan Singh was accused of helping the English. On my father's side I was able to trace up to nine generations to the first of his ancestors and mine who settled in Noganwan. I also visited other relatives who I had heard of but never seen. Overall a very satisfying visit to the birth place of my father.

Pic: Cpl. Lal Singh and Cpl. Pritam Singh Rekhrao

Then in August of the same year I went to Texas and worked in John's department and enjoyed being in the Laboratory working on the bench. I have always been hands-on scientist. *(See page P-15, Pic. 40: Members of the DiGiovanni laboratory at the MD Anderson Cancer Center).*

Note: *When I researched the name General McCarthy in the India Office Library I found that he was a Major and was in command of a detachment of 300 soldiers of the Sikh Regiment. The Sikhs were augmented by a Gurkha detachment of 4/12 Frontier Force Regiment of the 16th Indian Infantry brigade in Fort Blair in the Andaman Islands.*

At the end of my three month visit, John managed to arrange a 5-year contract for me to start in 2008. I moved to Texas in May 2008 and rented 506 Olive Street, Smithville, a quaint little Texas railroad town. It's famous because the movie "Hope Floats" was filmed there and, in fact, the house in which the characters lived is at the top of Olive Street. I joined the local Methodist Church, which was the next block from the house I lived in, and made many friends like John and Jill Lube, Earl and Maryann Walborg, to mention a few. I would walk to the church every Sunday for the service and also helped with the youth activities. Through some jiggery-pokery (on the waiting list for membership) by Terry Krugger I managed to join the casserole club and through it met many more people living in Smithville. I bought a light brown coloured 2004 Toyata 4 Runner which I sold to John for his son Jason at the end of my 4 years stay in Smithville. At lunch time John, Karen (another professor at the MD Anderson Cancer Centre) and I use to go for bike ride around Buescher State Park for exercise. One day we went towards the state road 71. The road bends and slopes down considerably and we were moving fast. John stopped at the junction and I realised that I was going too fast, I panicked and pressed the wrong sequence of brakes. I immediately realised that I was going to go over the handle bars, so I turned the bike towards the grass thinking I would fall on the grass instead of the tarmac. But luck would have it that the handle bar got stuck in my shorts and, therefore, the bike came on top of me. Karen, who came behind me, shouted at John to stop. When I opened my eyes, the first thing I saw was Karen's beautiful face; she told me I had been out for a minute. I was taken to Smithville General Hospital where I was checked thoroughly and was told that, apart from the shoulder and knee injury on my left side, I was OK. Karen, a true friend, stayed with me all afternoon in the hospital while I was going through all the tests. After the tests when they brought me into the recovery room the elderly nurse was ready to give me a Tetanus Jab and told me to take my pants off. I was nervous and trying to joke, and said to the nurse, "I am shy," she said, "I am not, so bend over" and slammed the needle into my right Gluteus. The result of this accident is a slight limp in my left leg. This is due to the fact that I destroyed some nerve endings in my left quads. I have worked hard in the gym to get the quads back to original strength and still maintain the strict regime.

Pauline came to visit me in Smithville a few times and I also went home a few times during those four years. Pauline and I drove to Dallas to spend very enjoyable weekend with Rachpal and Inderpal about a dozen times. Inderpal still calls her "half *Mamiji;* he says that's because we are not married. *(See page P-19, Pic. 49: Pauline cooking on the famous Inderpal Tavi).*

In 2009, I was one of the scientists from the United States invited to the first USA/China Symposium on the future of cancer research held in Changsha, a city three hours flying time north of Beijing. John DiGiovanni and I flew from Dallas to Beijing via Tokyo, a gruelling 18 hour flight time. We stayed overnight in Beijing before taking an internal flight to our destination.

For recreation we were taken to an outdoor theatre, a traditional Chinese story beautifully narrated by hundreds of actors on this vast outdoor stage illuminated by thousands of light bulbs. Three days after a very successful meeting we flew back to Beijing for rest and sight- seeing. We saw and walked through the Forbidden City and Tiananmen Square; we also saw and walked about a mile on part of the Great Wall (The Mutianyu Great Wall near Beijing). The wall is indeed a wonder of the world.

Pic: The Three Musketeers

There was a second China/USA symposium on the future of cancer research held in Guangzhou (Canton) in 2010. This time I gave a talk on Biogenic Silica Fibers and also chaired a session. We were taken for traditional Chinese foot massage. Guangzhou is the birthplace of this kind of foot massage. We were flown to a town near the Tibetan border to see and experience the local cuisine and observe their traditions; in fact John played his guitar here. The 6hr drive to the old city of Lijiang (The city is famous for its Silver mines and Silver ware) following the course of the Yangtze river through the mountains was breathtaking. *(See page P-20, Pic. 50: First USA/CHINA Symposium on the frontiers of Cancer Research, Changsha, 2009; Pic. 50: Second USA/CHINA Symposium on the frontiers of Cancer Research, Guangzhou, 2010).*

SCIENTIFIC PROGRAM

DASAN Conference on
"Integrative Strategy and Global Network for New Direction of Translational Cancer Research"

Aug. 12 (Thu)

SESSION 1

Chair: Nicola McCarthy

8:40-9:00	Daehee Kang (Seoul National University, Korea) Cohort Study for Gene-Environment Interaction
9:00- 9:25	John DiGiovanni (The University of Texas, USA) Growth Factor Receptor Signaling Pathways as Targets for Cancer Prevention
9:25- 9:45	Jae-Yong Han (Seoul National University, Korea) Beyond the Mouse : the Application of Transgenic Chickens for Animal Models
9:45- 10:05	Jaydeb Kumar (Seoul National University, Korea) Role of eFIA2 in Skin Carcinogenesis
10: 05- 10:30	Yong-Yeon Cho (The Hormel Institute, University of Minnesota, USA) A Novel Chemopreventive Target of RSK2 in Human Skin Cancer
10:30- 10:50	Coffee Break

SESSION 2

Chair: Tarlochan Bhatt

10:50- 11:15	Zigang Dong (The Hormel Institute, University of Minnesota, USA) The Role of Membrane Receptors in Skin Cancer
11:15- 11:40	Okkyung Rho (The University of Texas, USA) Targeting mTORC1 Effectively Inhibits Tumor Promotion
11:40- 12:00	Young-Sam Keum (Dongkuk University, Korea) Role of Histone phosphorylation in the UVB induction of AP-1 expression
12:00- 12:20	Junho Chung (Seoul National University, Korea) Development of Anti-hepatocyte Growth Factor Antibody as an Anti-glioblastoma Agent
12:20-12:40	Jeong-Mook Lim (Seoul National University, Korea) New Approach for the Application of Stem Cells
12 :40- 2:00	Lunch & Poster Presentation

Pic: D - 13

In August 2010 John Di and I were invited by Saul University to Dasan Conference on "Integrative Strategy and Global Network for New Direction of Translational Cancer research." The meeting was held in Jayju Island and we flew there from Dallas via Tokyo. I chaired a session on the second day. On our free day we were able to visit the magnificent botanical gardens and walk round the base of Mount Halla. We wanted to trek to the peak at 3060 ft to see the volcanic crater but the peak was encased in dense fog.

Registrar

Dr T S Bhatt MPhil CChem FRSC
Dept.Reproductive Physiology
St.Barts Hospital Med.College
West Smithfield
London
EC1A 7BE

Thomas Graham House,
Science Park, Milton Road,
Cambridge CB4 4WF,
☎ 0223 420066
Fax: 0223 423623

Our Ref:233397

16 July 1992

Dear Dr Bhatt

I am pleased to inform you that you have been admitted by the Council to Fellowship of the Royal Society of Chemistry with effect from the date on the enclosed certificate. As a Fellow of the Society, you are entitled to use the designatory letters CChem FRSC.

The Society does not inform referees of the outcome of applications in which they have been named since it is believed that applicants would normally prefer to do this themselves.

I am sure you would like to be aware that the names of newly admitted Fellows of the Society are published in the Times, usually within a month of the meeting at which they have been admitted.

Yours sincerely

B A Henman CChem FRSC

☎ International+44 223 420066 Fax:+44 223 423623 Telex: 818293
Founded 1841   Incorporated by Royal Charter 1848

Pic: D - 14

I was also invited to the International Cancer Research symposium 2010: Defining and Translating Science for Disease Prevention and Treatment held in Thiruvana-thapuram, Kerala in December 2010.The meeting was sponsored jointly by Jawaharlal Nehru University, Delhi and Rajiv Gandhi Centre for biotechnology, Thiruvanantha-puram. At this meeting I chaired a session and also delivered a seminar. *(D 14).*

I had never fished in my life until I joined John in Texas. He introduced me to this inexpensive hobby that does not require many skills, is a stress buster and a good excuse for drinking with friends. Fishing provides you with anexcellent way of unwinding while connecting with your colleagues and friends. It teaches you the art of staying still. Waiting for a nibble from a fish requires patience, especially if you are aiming to catch a particularly large fish. Once you get a bite, however, then it's time for some action. The challenge presented by pulling in a big one can be one way of relieving all that accumulated tension. We have been fishing at Port O'Connor south of Matagorda Bay on the Gulf of Mexico, for a number of years since my first introduction in 2008. In 2010 I caught a 31 inch Red Drum and took it to the taxidermist in La Grange to be processed. I told him this fish was going to England as a trophy. He processed it and mounted it on a special piece of driftwood. It is now at West Lodge, on the wall of the downstairs clock room with the two photos of me. *(See page P-20 and P-21, Pic. 52: At Port O'Connor; Pics. 53, 31: inch Black Drum I caught in 2013; Pic. 54: Two Black drums; Pic. 55: Ugly Fish; Pic. 56: Another large Black Drum I caught in 2014; Pic. 56a: Small Shark).*

I have been to Port O'Connor with our fishing group many times and the last time I caught a 24 inch Red Drum and a couple of keeper Black Drum. Fishing as a hobby continues to this day. On every trip my casting has improved thanks to John and another friend Kent Pruit. I can also maintain my own fishing equipment. Our last trip to Port O'Connor was very successful in that three of us netted our quota of Red Drums, three spotted mackerels, one flounder and many Black drums. I caught the biggest, 28 inch, Red Drum.

Mountain climbing has been one of my passions. It started when I was 17 year old. Climbing is a challenge that involves risks, danger and hardship. The sheer joy of reaching the summit of a mountain is unbelievable. Lying on a ledge watching the eagles and large birds soar above you and the panoramic views is breathtaking. I am sad to say that because of the bicycle accident in 2007 my climbing days are over. My last attempt at a serious climb was in 2010 when we went up Mount Lemon in Arizona. John DiGiovanni and I have known Tim Bowden for many years. He is a professor at the University of Arizona and is afflicted with Parkinson's Disease. His wife telephoned John and asked if he and Tochi would accompany him to the top of Mount Lemon.

At 9159 ft (2079 m) Mount Lemon in the Coronado National Park, north of Tusca is is the highest peak in the Santa Catalina Mountains. *(See page P-23, Pic. 58: At the start of our climb on Mount Lemon, Arizona)*

Tim, his wife Diane, John and me started our climb at 6.30 AM and worked our way up without any hitches. At about noon my left leg started to bother me, this was the leg that was injured in the bicycle accident back in 2008. We decided to stop for lunch break at about 8000 ft. When we resumed our climb I was dragging my left leg. At this point John decided that we were going back down the mountain. As we started our descent my leg got heavier and heavier. I dragged it until we were a mile short of the base; I said to John "I cannot move any further." John telephoned the Sheriff who alerted the mountain rescue team who arrived within a short period. They had a trolley with one central wheel upon which was mounted a stretcher. I was placed on this stretcher and brought back to the base a mile and half down the mountain. *(See page P-23, Pic. 59 and Pic. 60: Rescue team on Mount Lemon)*

I was checked by the Physicians at Smithville General Hospital when we got back to Texas. After a thorough medical examination, MRI scan, and many tests they told me, that I was fit and there was nothing wrong with my leg. In their opinion I had suffered a severe muscular fatigue. Anyway that was the end of my climbing. I feel very sad at the situation because to me climbing was everything.

Pauline and I have been together now for, very happy, 6 years. We have settled into a comfortable life at West Lodge and enjoy gardening plus DIY and travelling. We enjoy each-others company and have travelled quite a lot. Apart from our regular visits to the Condo on the Cost del Sol in Spain we have been on interesting trips to various countries. We went to India for six weeks and were met at New Delhi by the agent who arranged our trip. They garlanded us with marigold garlands; it was especially interesting for Pauline. We booked into a hotel in Karol Bagh in Delhi and used it as a base. Our first trip from here was a drive to Chandigarh where we stayed in the Taj Hotel at Chandigarh, a city designed by Le Corbusier, is a very interesting place to visit. It has many tourist attractions like the Rock Garden and International doll Museum. We went to Shimla for three days. Shimla was the summer capital of the Raj. The city's buildings are styled in Tudor, Elizabethan and Gothic architecture dating from the colonial era. It is strung along a 2 Km ridge but the town centre is Scandal point. The pedestrian only Mall runs west to East and Christ Church Cathedral stands at one end of it. We saw the Viceregal Lodge, the building looks like a cross between Harry Potter's Hogwarts School and the Tower of London. It is now the Indian Institute of Advanced Study. We took a 30 minute, walk up to the Jakhoo temple(Hanuman Temple), in fact Pauline got altitude sickness and we had to descend fast. We travelled on the famous narrow gauge railway that runs between Kalka and Shimla that was built in 1903, now a World Heritage Site. Our Journey was from Shimla to Taradevi station where we were greeted by the station master and had a picture taken with him in his office. Before the picture he insisted that he goes and put his jacket on. *(See page P-24, Pic. 61: Standing behind the Station Master of Taradevi Station on Kalka-Shimla narrow guage rail track built in 1903, now a World Heritage Site).*

We took a two day trip to Amritsar to see the Golden Temple and also the crazy ceremony at the Wagha Border. From our hotel we walked to the Jallianwala Bagh where we

saw a group of school children being told the story relating to this place.

A gentle walk to the central religious place of the Sikhs, a symbol of human brotherhood and equality is a fantastic sight. The sheer grandeur of

the Golden Temple and the hues create an enigmatic sight. It's a place of cleanliness, peace and tranquillity. The serene environment in and around is wonderful.

The visit to Wagah Border was well worth the effort to witness the flag lowering ceremony. A bizarre spectacle carried out each evening involving the border guards from India and Pakistan and both countries treat it as a bit of good natured rivalry. From the "Ministry of Silly Walks" marching up and down, formal lowering of the flags, what is going on is so obviously tongue and cheek that it is difficult to take it seriously. *(See page P-24, Pic. 62: At Wagah Border)*

On our way back from Amritsar we went to Noganwan via Fatehgarh Sahib. I wanted Pauline to see the family home and she graciously agreed to spend the night in the village. We slept upstairs in the bed *Papaji* use to sleep. Pauline got on well with Chapo's wife, Gurpreet and Jaspreet and saw Baba Sheed's shrine. Pauline said to me that she liked Fatehgarh Sahib more than the Golden Temple. After our visit to Punjab we came back to our base in Delhi for a night and travelled to Rajasthan via Agra and Fatehpur Sikri. The Taj Mahal in Agra is indeed a magnificent monument.

Pic: At Taj Mahal, Agra

The three week tour of Rajasthan was very informative and memorable. Rajasthan is the land of Rajputs where stately palaces and hilltop forts look over desert sands, cultivated plains and densely wooded hills. It is a land of colour, clamour and sheer intensity. We travelled extensively: from Jaipur to Udaipur via Ajmer and Pushkar. Jaipur is known as the pink city and its main attractions are the palace of winds, Jantar Mantar (a royal observatory notable for its massive sundial); and imposing city palace. We took an elephant ride to the hill on which the majestic Amber Fort is situated. The Amber fort is set in picturesque and rugged hills are a fascinating blend of Mughal architecture and were constructed by Raja Mann Singh, the fort is constructed with red sandstone and marble.

The city palace located in the heart of the old city, is a blend of Mughal and Rajasthani architecture and the royal family still lives in this palace.

Udaipur, our next stop, is one of the loveliest cities in Rajasthan, with its imposing creamy-white palaces with domed cupolas that overlook the shimmering waters of Lake Pichola. We saw Kumbhalgarh fort set in gorgeous hilly countryside. The fort is crowned by the so called cloud palace; encircled by 1.5 Kms of walk-able walls. We bumped across the singed country North from Aravalli hills. The Acacia-dotted plains were interspersed with farmland and white washed shrines atop rocky outcrops. We visited the Jain Temples at Ranakpur on our way to the blue city of Jodhpur. Its stellar attraction is the massive Meharangarh fort which stands theatrically on a great lump of rock high above the blue city. The living fort of Jaisalmer a massive sandcastle rising from the sandy plains of Thar Desert is like a mirage. Inside the fort are shops swaddled in bright embroideries, a royal palace and many businesses. Beneath the ramparts the narrow streets of the old city conceals magnificent Havelis, all carved from the same golden-honey sandstone as the fort, hence Jaisalmer's designation as the Golden City. Our camel safari in the sand dunes was an unforgettable experience especially for Pauline.
(See page P-26, Pic. 67: Pauline enjoying Camel ride!!!)

The next stage in our journey was Bikaner a vibrant, dust-swirling desert town with Junagarh fort which evokes an energising outpost feel. Its atmospheric old walled city with its magnificent Haveli's and Rajasthani wall paintings of this region are worth seeing. This region was once part of the silk route. I had seen a documentary about a Rat temple in Rajasthan on the BBC a few years ago. When I asked around and was told it was very close to Bikaner we took a detour of

30 Km to visit this temple. It is called the Karni Mata Rat Temple and literally hundreds of Rats live in it and people travel great distances to pay their respect. Pauline stayed in the car with the windows shut because she is terrified of the Rodents. I stood near the gate to observe these rats and was amazed to see that they approached the gate but did not go across the threshold. Thinking about it they had no need to go out as they had enough food, milk and water in the temple donated by the worshippers. *(See page P-28, Pic. 71: Karni Mata Rat Temple near Bikaner in Rajasthan - India).*

We returned to Delhi via JhunJhunu and and Nawal Garh. The three week tour of Rajasthan was fascinating, exhilarating and the 2500 miles covered produced its own problems.

Our four star accommodation was in Heritage Hotels which are mostly old castles and Maharaja's hunting Lodge's. Another item of my wish list satisfied.

Another night's stay at our base in Karol Bagh in Delhi we then flew to Kochi (Cochin) Kerala. Fort Cochin is the name of the old town and it was the centre of spice trade for centuries. Old Cochin is a charming series of lively streets. We visited some very old churches and the oldest Synagogue in the Commonwealth. The silhouettes of Kochi's giant Chinese fishing nets, as menacing as monsters from Hollywood horrors, sink into the horizon behind us then we were on our way to the misty mountains of Munnar in the Western Ghats. When you enter Munnar, a popular hill station, you are greeted by miles upon miles of lush tea plantations. As far as your eyes can see the hills are a mass of greenery consisting of bulbous tea plants, occasionally there are some colourful bushes by the side of the tea plants. We saw women in ruby, turquoise and emerald saris plucking tea leaves and flicking them into net bags that hung from a broad band tied around there head. We visited the Kolukumalai Tea Estate very early in the morning. This was in order to view the sunrise, the tea factory also the tea museum to look at the fascinating history of tea production in these hills. In the tea factory we were taken on a guided tour, from a noisy airless room where tea leaves tumble on conveyor belts until they wither and Oxidise, to a light filled room full of large drums where leaves are baked to stop the Oxidation process according to the type and strength required. At the end we were given different types of teas to taste. Most of the tea manufactured was black, but with awareness of health benefits of green tea is now also produced. *(See page P-25, Greenery consisting of bulbous tea plants on way to Munnar and Thekkady (Kerala - India).*

The drive to Thekkady through the cardamom spice hills is spicy to say the least. The walk through the spice plantation near the town of Kumily was very aromatic and informative. We took a two hour boat ride on a man-made lake, which encircles the Periyar Wildlife sanctuary. Next morning after breakfast we drove to Kumarakom. The three hour drive through the mountains of the Western Ghats was breath taking. At the key side of our hotel we boarded a Ketuvallom. Kerala is criss-crossed by 5 major lakes, numerous canals, estuaries and deltas of many rivers to make the backwaters where these house boats ply. We cruised for two days in our 5 star house-boat exploring the back waters of Alappuzha. After a week spent exploring the mountains we returned to the serene beaches of Kovalam on the Arabian Sea to relax and chill out for a few days. Strolling around the complex at Uday Samudra Hotel I came across a gift shop. In the window of this shop was a water colour of the Golden Temple in Amritsar from a very unusual angle. I decided that I was going to have this painting. It took me two days of haggling with the shop keeper, fortunately for me he was the owner of the shop. Can you imagine a scene where an Indian is haggling with another Indian? In the end I won the day and got the painting at a considerably reduced price. I had it framed in Hitchin to match the frame of another Indian painting we have at home. Both the paintings are hanging in the lounge at West Lodge. Kerala's regal if dusty heritage, soothing waters, bright and prosperous dwellings, friendly natives and fantastic cuisine is worth every penny. After spending six weeks exploring just a small part of the sub-continent of India we came to the conclusion that it was well worth the effort. One would think that after a six week touring we would take a breather, no that was not the case here, we were on another adventure.

The Alaska cruise in 2012 with the Holland-America shipping line was most interesting. We combined it with a visit to our friends, Gary and Jackie, in Seattle. We stayed with them in their house at Coyle on the Hood Canal for a few days. Sitting on the deck at 100 meters above the Hood Canal with a glass of gin and tonic watching the boats cruise past was a real treat. After three days we travelled to Vancouver via Amtrack. We boarded the train at Edmonds Station close to Gary and Jackie's house in Seattle. The track meanders along the coast line and we enjoyed the endless views along the coast that passed in an almost cinematic way along our journey. Right across the Pacific Central station in Vancouver we took the Sky-train line to Pan Pacific Hotel for an overnight stay. Next morning we had to join the line to board the Zuiderdam moored by the side of the hotel for our Alaska cruise. We sneaked our way through the line to board the ship after 12 PM in time to enjoy the lunch and settle into our cabin. Our luggage was already in the cabin. It was a lovely sunny day and was glorious setting sail from the jetty and gliding under the Lions Gate Bridge with Stanley Park on one side. *(See page P - 29, Pic. 73: Pauline and I, Alaska Cruise, 2012)*

We sailed through the inside passage with its dramatic scenery, abundant wild-life and calm protected waters to Katchikan, our first port of call. The city is backed by forested slopes and distinctly shaped deer-mountain. We walked through the downtown area which is the main commercial district. The Saxman Native Village Totem Park has a large collection of Totem Poles from various villages around the inside passage. A stroll through this park was impressive because you learned the history of the tribes and their immense woodcarving skill. *(See page P-30, Pic. 74: Saxman Native Village).*

Pic: Saxman Native Village, Ketchikan, Alaska

We also saw other historical sites like Dolly's house museum. Next we docked at Skagway which is known as the gateway to Klondike. It was made famous by the gold rush in the Yukon. Juneau, the capital city of Alaska, is very much an outdoor place has wonderful system of trails within a short walk of downtown (at least that's what we were told by the guide). Next we sailed into Glacier Bay and stayed there for a few hours. We were very close to Margery Glacier which is famous for multiple calving activities. The phenomenon of "Calving" is breaking and dropping of ice into the sea. I just happen to be filming the glacier when some calving took place, what a scene. I was just lucky to be filming at the right place. After 7 days cruising we came back to Vancouver and stayed another two nights at the Pan Pacific hotel and explored the city. We visited one of the city's most iconic sites Capilano Suspension Bridge Park. The cliff walk hangs for 700 ft and is 300 ft. high. This stunning walkway, made partly of glass, hugs the granite Cliffside as it offers a panoramic view of the rainforest below. We walked around Stanley Park and also went to Deadman Island where we had lunch in one of the many restaurants. We found the highly recommended Indian restaurant "Salam Bombay" at the corner of Robson Street and Burrard Street. The food and ambiance was excellent, in fact we went there two days running. On Monday morning we took a cab to the Rocky Mountaineer Station for our journey to Kamloop. There were refreshments available while we waited for the train to depart. The train departed on time and we were off to the Rockies. We travelled Gold Leaf with all meals included, the meals were very good. Kamloop is situated at the junction of North and South Thompson Rivers in which Salmon are found in abundance. The hotel was very good considering it is only the equivalent of a four star hotel. In the evening we were told that due to track problems ahead we will not be able to travel in the Rocky Mountaineer and that our journey to Banff will be in a coach. The convoy of ten coaches departed from the convention centre at 9 AM for Banff. The coach trip through the Columbian mountains and the Rockies was scenic. This is a good way, just sit back, relax and look at fantastic Canadian country side and the mountains. We toured around downtown Banff and took the Gondola ride to the 7460 ft. mountain top.

(See page P-30, Pic. 75: Pauline and I on the Gondola ride).

The views from this vantage point are magnificent. Next morning we were picked up by the "Webster Inc." transport company coach from our hotel. The coach picked other passengers from other hotels and departed for Calgary Airport for our three hour flight to Toronto. Gurmit met us at the airport and we stayed with him for three days. He showed us around Toronto and also took us to Niagara Falls.

In Feb. 2015 I was invited to an International Symposium on Current Advances in radiobiology, Stem cells and Cancer Research held at Jawaharlal Nehru University in Delhi. At the end of the 4 day meeting I was presented with a "Plaque of Honor." *(Pic. 72a)* On our free day we were taken for a tour of the magnificent Taj Mahal. *(See page P-28, Pic. 72: At Taj Mahal 2015)*

I am great believer in natural justice. I had to borrow money from a commercial bank when I bought Potters Bar Squash club. Because of the dodgy accounts the high street banks were not willing to consider the proposition. It took me three years to persuade one of the big four banks to re-mortgage the club. My solicitor, Mrs. Shaeen, telephoned me on a Monday morning to say she had received the redemption figure from the commercial bank and this figure was inclusive of one week's interest added on. When she mentioned the figure I was taken aback but did not say anything except "redeem the loan as soon as possible but at least by Friday. When I looked at the figure which I had written down it appeared lower than what I had calculated. Had the commercial bank made a mistake in calculating the figure, was the question on my mind. When I telephoned my solicitor late Friday she said to me "Dr. Bhatt we were not able to redeem because our bank did not have the paper work ready on time, so I have asked the commercial bank for another redemption figure which they have promised on the following Monday." My heart sank but there was nothing I could do. My solicitor telephoned on Monday afternoon and gave me the revised redemption figure which was the same as the one previous week plus another week's interest. I instructed my solicitor that it is imperative that we must redeem the loan by the end of the week. I was very relieved when I received a call from the solicitor on Wednesday that week to say we have redeemed the loan and that she had received confirmation to that fact by E-mail. The miss-calculation on the part of the commercial bank accountant/s amounted to £ 15,000.00. I waited with baited breath to see what was going to materialise, but weekend passed and nothing. However Monday morning I received a telephone from Mrs. Shaeen who said "the commercial bank solicitor has been on the phone and said that they made a mistake in calculating the interest" and they wanted to give us new figures. I asked her what was our legal position and she said that it was solid because they had given us two redemption figures two weeks running. I told her to reply, in legal terms, whatever she thought was a suitable reply. A day later she telephoned me again and said "I have heard from a Dr. Sennit (one of the director of the commercial bank) who says he is a friend of yours." I told her I don't know the bastard, to this she replied "that's all I wanted to hear from you." The commercial bank accountants had indeed made mistake, a massive mistake, but they could do nothing because we were in the right. To me this was poetic justice because I was given the money they had charged us at a exorbitant interest (24.9%) in the past three years.

I have had a good life so far and have no regrets, my children are both successful and I am extremely proud of them. I have a brilliant granddaughter who is the sunshine of my life. I have been blessed with two English roses in my life, the first one I knew for 50 years and the second I have known for only 6 years, but what a women.

I am very lucky because I have another English Rose who is beautiful, loving, kind, and caring. I am fortunate enough to be able to commute to Texas to work and fish. Sadly I have had to call an end to climbing, not because of age but because of a bicycle accident I had in 2007. Pauline and I continue to go on adventure vacations and each time I am able to cross another item of my "to do list before I die."

Pic: Me and Pauline

Pic: Me and Jaon

Bhatt's of Noganwan (Panjab, India)

My brother Jagdish Singh Bhatt and I, Dr. Tarlochan Singh Bhatt, are the sons of the late Sardar Naranjan Singh Bhatt of Noganwan, Panjab, India. For many years we have been ruminating about the name Bhatt and have been interested in trying to trace the background of said name in the hope that we will also unlock the history of our family. In investigating this we also had in mind the future generations of the late Sardar Naranjan Singh Bhatt. Here we present our findings.

The name Bhatt, meaning 'priest,' is a last name that is common in many ethnicities in India. It originates from Kashmir and over the centuries it has branched into many variations like Bhat, Bhatti, Bhatnagar, Bhattacharya, Batt, Butt, Brambhatt, and so on. Bhatt's were Brahmans of priest and warrior class who lived in Kashmir and were descendants of the Aryans a people of Indo-European origin.

The Sanskrit speaking Aryans were nomadic herdsmen of white race who arrived into the Ganges valley from the shores of the Caspian sea in the eighteenth century B.C. and advanced as far as the present day Delhi. The Aryans, who used the chariot, were militarily superior to the original inhabitants (the Dravidians). They imposed a religious tradition contained in the Vedas, a collection of sacred writings covering two thousand years preceding the Christian era and forming the substance of the Hindu religion. No literature, anywhere at any time, has been so widely propagated.

The division of Hindu society into four main castes occurred at this time. In the myth Brahma created the world, from his mouth emerged the Brahman, in whom sacerdotal authority was vested; from his arms came the Ksatya (Kshatryas), the nobleman and warrior; from his loins came the Vairya, the tradesman or craftsman; and from his feet, the Shudra, the servant or peasant.

In the sixth century B.C. two factions protested against this caste system and opposed the authority of the Brahmans. They were Cakyamauni Prince Gautam (Buddha, 'The Enlightened one') and Mahariva, who founded Buddhism and Jainism respectively. Their doctrines were based on nonviolence; they championed respect for life and equality of all human beings before God. To counter these two new trends of thought, Brahmanism embraced other cultures and became Hinduism, the cult of Shiva and Vishnu. This is now the most wide spread religion in India, with five hundred million believers.

As the Aryans migrated towards Panjab and Delhi a large number must have colonised and settled in the tracts of land in and around Delhi. Some of these Brahmans became the Rajputs and Jats of which there are many branches throughout India. One branch of the western Rajputs became the Bhat's. Bhatti is the Rajputana word for Bhati. This is the same as Bhat, which is the title of the great modem representative of the ancient Jadubansi's royal Rajput family descendants of Krishna and therefore of Lunar race. Their traditions tell us that they were in very early times driven across the Indus; but that returning, they dispossessed the locals and others of the country south of the Lower Satluj some seven centuries ago, and founded Jaisalmer.

In the 17th century the then Mogul rulers of India tried to convert all of India to Islam by whatever means necessary. The fifth ruler in this dynasty, the fanatic Aurengzeb (1618-1707), third son of Shah Jehan, was determined to crush Hinduism and Sikhism. He issued an edict to this fact and told all his Provincial governors to put those who did not convert to Islam to the sword. Iftikar Khan the Governor of Kashmir followed the edict with a great deal of zeal.

The Sikhs, at this time, were small in number but were determined not to be crushed under the yolk of Islam. At the time when Aurengzeb was ruler, the 9th Sikh guru, Tegh Bahadur, was in Anandpur at Gurudawara Thore Sahib, a place from where he use to preach to his followers. In 1650 Kashmiri Pundits came to Anandpur to see Guru Tegh Bahadur and seek his help in ending the persecution of Kashmiri Hindus at the hands of Iftikar Khan.

Guru Tegh Bahadur told Aurengzeb "if you can convert me to Islam then all the Kashmiri Pundits will convert to Islam." Aurengzeb tried but failed and in the end he murdered Guru Teg Bahadur on the 24th November 1675 (based on the Nanakshahi Era calendar) Chandni Chowk, in Delhi.

It appears that many Brahmans from Kashmir had already settled in the vast plains of India, especially Panjab and Rajasthan, many centuries before the new wave of Kashmiri Pundits. The latter came to the low lands of Panjab in the 17th century to escape the persecution by Moguls and strike root wherever employment and trade was possible. It is irrelevant when the Bhatt's came to Panjab, whether with the initial wave about 8 centuries ago or with the new migrants in the 17th Century, but it is clear that the Bhatt's (Bhat or Bhatti) came from the Brahman stock of Kashmir and therefore, are the direct descendants of the Aryans.

It appears that some of our ancestor settled in the village of Noganwan and became woodblock printers and later tailors *(Darzi).* (The Panjabi word *Darzi* denotes a trade and it is not a caste).

We feel that after reading this some misanthropists will say "Bhatts cannot be of Rajput or Jat origin." All through our research we have found that the caste system is mutable. There are many examples of metamorphosis of castes and tribes to trades acquired which then becomes the new hereditary caste. Thus, caste in Panjab is based primarily upon occupation but also upon political position.

We say the caste system is mutable and there are many incidences-of this throughout Indian history. It is worth mentioning here that the Sikhs did much to weaken the caste system in Panjab. In our notes below we have tried to assure our reader by citing a few examples, in reality a whole book can be written on the subject.

Notes: -

1) As in all countries society is arranged in strata which are based upon differences of social or political importance, or of occupation. In India the classification, under Hinduism, is hereditary rather than individual to the person involved under it. An artificial standard is added which is peculiar to caste and which must be conformed to on pain of loss of position. The rules which forbid social intercourse between castes of different rank render it infinitely difficult to rise in the scale. Also it is next to impossible for the individual himself to rise. It is the tribe that alone can improve its position; and this it can do only after a lapse of several generations, during which time it must abandon a lower for a higher occupation and thus separate itself from the caste to which it belongs.

2) Nothing can be more variable and more difficult to define than caste. The fact that a generation is descended from ancestors of any given caste creates a presumption, that that generation is also of the same caste, a presumption liable to be defeated by an infinite variety of circumstances.

3) Bhat are described as a great Kashmiri tribe and Bhatti are said to hail from Kashmir in earlier time. We have shown, above, that both Bhat and Bhatti came from the same stock so it is in the realm of possibility that the two words are identical under Hindu society and that Bhatt is a variation of the two names.

4) The whole of India was priest-ridden under the Brahmans, who could at first claim no separate descent by which they should be singled out from the Aryan community. The Brahmans sought to exalt their office and to appease their political rulers, who were the only rivals they had to fear, by degrading all other occupations and conditions of life. The principle of hereditary occupation was of utmost importance to them. As they increased in number, these numbers necessarily exceeded the possible requirements of the laity. Thus they ceased to be wholly priests and a large number of them took up other occupations like agriculture. It was at the time in Hindu history when Brahminism was substituted for Hinduism. The Religion became turmoil of impure and degraded doctrine and sectarian teaching from which the theory of the hereditary nature of occupation seems to have taken its present form. The word caste is not Indian but comes from the Portuguese word casta (breed or race). The Sanskrit word for caste or a group of people is varna, which signifies an endogamic group, its members linked by heredity, marriage, custom and profession. Professions became diversified with the evolution of society and whole groups of people took on new identities associated with the economic activity of their group. Therefore, it appears that the caste distinction was based upon occupation.

5) Those Brahmans who took up other trades over time acquired that caste. For example Chauhans of Delhi are no longer recognised as Rajputs because they have acquired other professions. There are whole traditions of the Panjab tribes of the Jats and Gujar, which state that the' are descended from the Rajputs. The Sahnsars of Hushyarpur were Rajj until the beginning of the 20th Century, when they became market gardeners. Some of the Tarkhans (carpenters) and Lohars (blacksmith) are known to have been Jats and Rajputs who within quite recent times have taken to these occupations and thus through their trade have acquired hereditary castes.

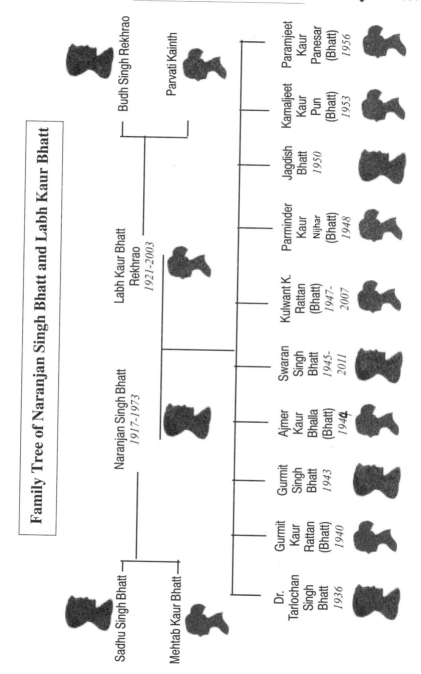

Family Tree of Naranjan Singh Bhatt and Labh Kaur Bhatt

Sadhu Singh Bhatt

Mehtab Kaur Bhatt

Budh Singh Rekhrao

Parvati Kainth

Naranjan Singh Bhatt
1917-1973

Labh Kaur Bhatt
Rekhrao
1921-2003

Dr. Tarlochan Singh Bhatt
1936

Gurmit Kaur Rattan (Bhatt)
1940

Gurmit Singh Bhatt
1943

Ajmer Kaur Bhalla (Bhatt)
1944

Swaran Singh Bhatt
1945-2011

Kulwant K. Rattan (Bhatt)
1947-2007

Parminder Kaur Nijhar (Bhatt)
1948

Jagdish Bhatt
1950

Kamaljeet Kaur Pun (Bhatt)
1953

Paramjeet Kaur Panesar (Bhatt)
1956

Return to India after 30 Years

I reached Delhi at 7.20 AM on Wednesday the 5th May 1993. Gurmeet and Dev met me outside Indira Gandhi Airport, where I had been waiting for about 20 minutes constantly being accosted by *Rickshawallahs*. It Was very hot (we discovered later the temperature that day was 46° C). My first taste of Indian busses (bone-shaker's) was when we took a small bus to the main bus terminal in Central Delhi. The main delights of Delhi were yet to come!!!

Delhi bus terminal is a stinking dump- bodies all over the place I have only been here 3 hours and I want to go home. Gurmeet eventually manages to get two tickets on a 'Delux' bus to Chandigarh. The only thing delux about the bus was the fact that there were only 5 passengers in it. The bus was not air conditioned and the seats were torn. We left on time and headed towards Punjab at great speed. The bus went through some really squalid parts of Delhi and there are so many people thousands.

Heat and dust was the order of the day. After a 2 hours dusty ride we stopped at a motorway cafe (shack, petrol pump and a tap for drinking and washing). We eat our stuffed *parathas,* cooked by Dev's wife, and drank some mango juice called Frooti. After a 10 minutes stop we left. Oh! We did wash our hands at that tap. I was very tired and hot, therefore, decided to occupy the rear seat and went to sleep. Gurmeet woke me when we got to Chandigarh. Just as we got of the bus another bus close-by was ready to leave for Fatehgarh and the conductor said he would stop at Nogawan for us. Not only Punjab, I am sure, the whole of India is criss-crossed by these so called buses. They are old, rickety, wooden seats and the stink plus diesel fumes are thrown-in with the cheap fare. The 54 seater carries about 100 passengers crammed inside and on top of the roof and I am sure if they could they would carry them on the wheels too. The delights of many rides in these' 'bone-shakers' was to come. By the way they are driven on Diesel and I don't think they would pass an emission control test let alone a MOT. Driving in India is an experience because it makes driving in Rome look very tame in comparison.

We reached Nogawan at 4.30 PM and were greeted by the family and the two aunties from Kalka – doesn't the younger one talks a lot. Balbir and his wife had left that afternoon after waiting for us for 24 hours. Chapu (uncle's son) was dispatched to Samrala to bring them back the next morning. Throughout the day and evening many visitors came to talk and pay homage to Papa's ashes. Thanks to electricity at least we could leave the fan on all night but Mosquitoes did not leave us, even for a second. In the morning we were covered with bites allover.

Thursday the 6th May, 1993 was Puran Mashi and we were up at 4 AM and got ready to leave for Kiratpur with Dads ashes.

Balbir his wife and Chapu arrived at about 6.30 AM and we left for Morinda at 7.15 AM. At Morinda we changed buses for Kurali where we had to change yet again. The temperature was beginning to rise thus indicating another scorching day ahead of us.

The bone-shaker dropped us in front of the temple at Kiratpur at 11.45 AM. We went straight to the Sarover (Ghats) on river 'Sutlej' behind the temple where a sant was praying. Gurmeet, *Chacha,* Balbir and myself got undressed. Gurmeet said to me "Paji don't take all your clothes off…" I wasn't going to. In fact I had put my swimming trunks on before we left Nogawan. *Chacha* told me to hold the red bag containing Dad's ashes and all four of us went in to the water up to our waists and I poured Dads ashes on to the water of the 'Sutlej' the others touched the bag and we threw flowers and said our last goodbye to Papa. We all had a dip in the 'Suljej' including *Massi* and *Mammi.* We gave Papa's shirt, the yellow cloth and some money to that sant and he said *Ardas* for Papa. After this we went and registered. Gurmeet and I signed the register. We paid for the *Parsad* and went into the temple and had them say Ardas with Papa's full name and we gave them a *'Rumalla.'* After this we had some food. On our way out we distributed money and no begger was refused.

We followed *Chacha* who was keen on showing us other temples and sites of historical interest. We bought a small pot from one of the shops and had Papa's name and date engraved on it. We then sat and drank a local drink called *'Skangvee'* (it is made of small limes, and has an odour like that of Sulphur dioxide) which made me feel sick. This drink was to make my stomach turn later on in the week- see below.

We walked to Baba Gurdita's shrine, reached after climbing 100 high steps in temperature of 44° C. We needed to rest twice before we reached the shrine where we had Ardas said for Papa and gave them a *'Rumalla'* and paid for the Parsad. We then went all the way down across the canal and up again to Baba Guden Shah's shrine. Here we rested for twenty minutes and drank some water and had *Ardas* said for Papa and gave them a *'Rumalla.'* All this time we distributed money to the poor beggars. We walked about two miles back to the bus stop and start our journey back to Nogawan at 3.30 PM. Balbir and his wife got off at Roper for Samrala and we continued via Kurali and Morinda. At Morinda I made my second mistake and drank some sugar-cane juice which tasted of oil and smelled of sulphur dioxide. We reached Nogawan feeling happy that our mission had been successfully completed.

After a lovely meal cooked by Shinde (Chapu's wife) we went to bed and to resume our battle with mosquitoes at about 9 PM.

My impression of India so far "Heat dust, bone-shakers, flies, mosquitoes and miserable beggers"

On Friday morning Gurmeet left for Nawanshahr (Shaheed Bhagat Singh Nagar district) to visit a friend and agreed to meet us in Samrala that evening. Massi Peto and I were to leave for Samrala at about 4.30 PM. At 10.30 AM Chapu and I decided to go to Fategarh Sahib where we donated a *'Rumalla'* and had Ardas said for Papa. After lunch I went to sleep for two hours. Massi and I caught a bus for Samrala via Morinda at 4.15 PM. When we reached Samrala Gurmeet was already there having failed, to meet his friend (though agreeing to meet the next day). We had a very pleasant evening with a smashing family in there cool house and lots of good food.

On Saturday morning after a heavy, I mean heavy, breakfast Gurmeet left for Nawanshahr while Massi Peto and I left for Nogawan. During the journey back my stomach felt a bit queezy. When we got off the bus at Nogawan I bought some Mangoes as they looked delicious. After lunch we had some Mango slices. There were many visitors in the house and we were sitting talking when at about 3.30 PM there was a violent 'thunderstorm' in my stomach and I had to make a mad dash to the 'loo' where I was violently sick at both ends.

In fact I was so long in the 'loo' that Massi came to look for me. I had a bath and went to bed and stayed there until Sunday morning. On Sunday at noon time we had to perform a ceremony at Baba Shaheed's shrine. I went although I felt sick, had diarrhoea, felt dehydrated and thirsty (classic sign as of Cholera). There was no way I could get hold of some antibiotics until we reached Delhi.

We left for Chandigarh at about 4.30 PM and after two 'bone-shaker' rides we reached Chandigarh where we were met by *Fauji* Teja Singh who entertained us. While in Chandigarh we had the pleasure of visiting two hospitals (a General Hospital and a Post-Graduate Institute of Medical Science). I

Pic: D - 15

was very disappointed at the state of both the Hospitals. If they were in this country they would be closed as they would be considered a health hazard. The state of these two hospitals makes Whippps Cross hospital look like a palace. For a city designed by Corbusier and a capital city at that, I must say, it looks like a dump. We stayed the night and left for Delhi at 4.30 AM. The delux bus stopped at another motor-way cafe in Haryana which was clean and well stocked with shops and restaurants. It was like a motor-way stop in this country. We reached Delhi at about 10.30 AM and caught a Scooter Rickshaw and headed towards Gurmeet's in-laws house. The ride through dirty, polluted, smelly and often narrow streets was hot and tiring. As I said before there are no rules about traffic, so you just sit with your eyes closed and pray. It's like being in a field with a couple of hundred lawn mowers spewing two-stroke mixture fumes at you. In the next two and a half days we were to experience many of these rickshaw rides through the streets of Delhi and all the time wishing we were not here.

In Delhi we went to the two main Gurudwaras, Sis gunj and Bangla sahib, and had *Ardas* said for Papa and donated a *'Rumalla'* to each. We walked round the old bazzars, Pahar ganj, Chandni chowk and saw the underground shopping centre where we did our shopping. Gurmeet is extremely generous and super to be with especially when shopping. It was interesting to see many foreigners walking around, eating, shopping and thoroughly enjoying themselves in these dirty, narrow streets.

I left Delhi on Wednesday the 12th May 1993 at 22.50 determined never to return again, but I am having second thoughts.

NOTE:- To be fair my comments are my personal and own view. These not directed towards the whole of India but only to those parts that I had the chance to visit.

Though good air conditioned buses, cabs and fast trains with clean air conditioned (AC Class) accommodation and limited stops (for cities and big towns) are available but these are on specific time schedule with advance online reservation. So one has to be careful in planning and choosing these options for comfortable journey in India instead of going for 'bone-shakers.'

Bibliography

1. Coombs and Bhatt, Cambridge University Press, 1987.
2. Khushwant Singh, A history of the Sikhs, 1999.
3. John Keay, A History of India, 2000.
4. The Census Report on the Races, Castes and Tribes of the Panjab by Sir Denzil Ibbotson. 1881.
5. Panjab Castes by Denzil Ibbotson. 1916.
6. History of India by John Keay. 2000.
7. The Arts of the Sikh Kingdoms. Edited by Susan Strong. 1999.

◁ Pic 1
The Church
built by Italian
prisoners of
war by
the side of
Nairobi to
Nakuru road
(Text p. 14)

Pic 2 ▷
Amelia - Winner
100 Meter Final
(Text p. 19)

◄ Pic 3
Amelia
the Hockey
Wizard
(Text p. 19)

▽ Pic 4
Socialising with
Rachpal, Inderpal
and Chris
in Old Dallas
(Text p. 41)

◀Pic 26 -
With Lisa
beside Lake
Nakuru
(Text p. 67)

⚡Pic 27
Lisa and Chris beside
Lake Nakuru
(Text p. 67)

⚡ Pic 28 -
At the start
of the Rift
Valley
(Text P. 68)

◀Pic 29
Lisa and
Chris at the
Equator,
Kenya
(Text p. 68)

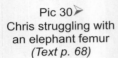
Pic 30▷
Chris struggling with
an elephant femur
(Text p. 68)

◁ Pic 31
Joan at Bambury
chalet on the
Indian Ocean,
Mombasa
(Text p. 68)

Pic 32▷
Adjusting the
Pelota basket
(Text p. 72)

△ Pic 44
Param helping Bibiji with the jewellery
for Gillian while Chris watches
(Text p. 80)

△ Pic 45
Now its Christopher's turn
(Text p. 80)

▲Pic 46
Bhatt Family*(Text p. 17)*

▲Pic 47
Me and Jaon - *(Text p. 17)*

⋏Pic 48
Pauline and Me *(Text p. 86)*

⋏Pic 49
Pauline cooking on the famous Inderpal Tavi *(Text p. 89)*

⌃Pics 50 - First USA/CHINA Symposium on the frontiers
of Cancer Research, Changsha (China), 2009 *(Text p. 89-90)*

⌃Pics 51 - Second USA/CHINA Symposium on the frontiers of
Cancer Research, Guangzhou (China), 2010 *(Text p. 89-90)*

Pic 52⌃
Fishing at Port
O'Connor on the
Gulf of Mexico
(Text p. 92)

ENGINEERING SYSTEM SAFETY

Engineering System Safety

by

G.J. Terry   CEng   FIMechE

Mechanical Engineering Publications Limited
LONDON

First published 1991

ISBN 0 85298 781 1

A CIP catalogue record for this book is available from the British Library.

Typeset by Saxon Printing Ltd, Derby
Printed in Great Britain at the Alden Press, Oxford

Contents

Introduction

The field of safety is one that encompasses much of everyday life. For engineers, scientists, and managers many aspects of safety are covered by regulations and codes of practice. For example the Health and Safety at Work Act controls a wide area of activity. However there are frequent occasions where there is either no clear guidance or where additional requirements are appropriate. The book is not intended to act as a guide to regulations or Health and Safety Executive (HSE) activities generally but is intended to cover the area not encompassed by predetermined controls.

It is a fact that life is temporary; nonetheless, the general attitude is that it must be preserved. It should be noted that the statement does not include the words 'at all cost' as is so often added. As will be shown in this book, the question of cost and convenience often produces compromises in safety. It is, however, very rare for any person or organization to actually declare they have decided that to spend more to avoid death or injury is just not worth the money. To some extent studying safety brings to the student a certain amount of cynicism, and a view that people are somewhat irrational and unscrupulous when it comes to safety decisions.

Engineers and others have to make sense of the conflicting demands and ensure that products are safe to use. The scale of their responsibilities can range from the simple domestic item, such as a tin opener, to nuclear power stations and spacecraft, the latter two having the potential for worldwide effects.

The book is intended for those who need to have some knowledge of the many aspects of safety, but who do not wish to become specialists. The scope is such that an appreciation of the thinking and procedures is given enabling the reader to understand the activities of specialists and also the factors that influence safety decisions.

The degree of safety afforded or demanded of an engineering system is dependent upon many factors, some of which are easily expressed as clear requirements whilst others are much less tangible. The need to appreciate the pressures raised by bias and lack of logic is essential if a manager is to ensure his 'product' is successful.

There is no magic formula or process that will ensure a product is safe and, as it is usually the simple thing that goes wrong in the first instance, the need to be meticulous at all stages of design, development, and production is essential. Considering some major accidents, the loss of the *Titanic* was primarily caused by the lack of a good lookout arrangement, the Clapham rail crash by bad wiring, the Kings Cross fire by piles of rubbish (as was the Bradford Football Stadium fire), and the *Challenger* disaster by a leaking 'O' ring, the possibility of which was being examined for possible modification. Cultivating the ability to think not only in depth but also laterally is a prerequisite to a successful design. A healthy degree of scepticism is necessary, as frequently the information supplied is based more on hope than fact, even though it is offered in good faith.

The increasing role of organizations specializing in safety evaluation technology results in a variety of activities that influence design, operating procedures, and disposal of material. These influences affect complexity, cost, and timescales to such an extent that managers must understand the broad basis of the activities in order to better control projects at all stages. To some extent safety studies can be self sustaining and, in the end, an 'executive' decision has to be made to bring them to a conclusion.

Many large organizations have considerable in house expertise, with entire departments dedicated to safety. Therefore, staff in other departments, or joining the organization, will wish to have an understanding of the technologies and thought processes involved. This requirement is particularly important for graduates, who may well find the concept of safety evaluation is not covered by the normal education syllabus. A notable exception to this lack of acknowledgment of safety is the Institution of Chemical Engineers which require the subject to be studied before granting membership.

The techniques developed for reliability are the basis of much of the thinking on safety, and it is only the end objectives that differ when comparing the two fields of work. Much of the material in this book could be equally well applied to design, and this illustrates the point that safety is design carried that little bit further. The engineer or user concerned with performance stops at the point where the equipment performs to specification. This target is usually measured in clear quantitative terms such as speed, power, output of material, and the like. Safety goes past this point and asks what happens when something fails, what are the consequences and effects on people and the surroundings. The performance limit is more aimed at making sure the product is reliable and the activity virtually ends at that point.

The reader may consider too many examples are drawn from transport when there are many other types of engineering around. The reason for this bias is that it is possible to comment on something with which most people are familiar; for the reader, of whatever persuasion, the points made can be understood, whereas drawing upon some of the more specialist fields, such as chemical plant, might take the reader into unfamiliar territory. Besides which, transport supplies such splendid examples of the attitude to safety.

1

Prologue to Safety

Whilst the scope and complexity of science and technology have grown at an ever increasing rate in the last one hundred years, the full implications of these advances did not, in many instances, begin to be understood by the public until the 1980s. Indeed, it is frequently obvious that even the 'experts' closely involved in such developments fail to understand the potential consequences of their actions. Advances in transport, power generation, and chemicals in particular have often been 'sold' on their direct and obvious benefits, rather than on a full disclosure of their consequences. The designers of engineering systems have, frequently, been able to place their main priority on performance, with the consideration of safety a secondary objective.

Arguably the first awakening of the public interest in the long term implications of new technology was (in the UK at least) brought about by the book *Silent Spring*. The disastrous impact of DDT became recognised across the Western World and its ban was fortuitously aided by further developments in that field of chemistry. In the USA Ralph Nader's book *Unsafe At Any Speed* was the real starting point of 'consumer associations' and the realization by much of the public that they actually did have a positive role to play in decisions regarding both old and new technologies.

The nuclear reactor incident at Three Mile Island (TMI), USA, prompted a very critical look at the overall safety of that source of power. Paradoxically, the TMI event demonstrated to scientists and engineers that the overall safety of the plant was in many ways satisfactory, in that a major catastrophy was prevented despite the events which occurred. Not unreasonably this optimistic interpretation was not shared by the public.

From these beginnings there have sprung strong lobbies that try to examine every feature of modern life from a safety point of view. Thus, the everyday activities of engineers and scientists are being probed by groups of people whose knowledge, ability, and attitude are not always appropriate or positive.

Many potentially dangerous or hazardous systems are controlled by regulations of varying authority and substance, for example, domestic electrical appliances, passenger aircraft, shipping, buildings, and so on. There are, however, times when systems are outside regulatory control. From the requirement to treat safety as a subject in its own right, coupled with the developing interest and concern of the public, has sprung a whole new field of technology. This branch of engineering and science is engaged on analysing systems for the determination and evaluation of hazards and their consequences, together with estimating the probability of occurrence of accidents.

It is probably fair to say that the driving force in this new 'industry' has been nuclear power, which in some people's eyes is closely related to nuclear weapons; thus, there is a considerable emotional and political impact, as well as genuine technical concern. The aircraft and chemical industries are also leaders in this new field. Whilst the first of this trio has been, in no small way, driven by the concern of the public for it's own safety the aircraft industry, and to some extent the chemical industry also, appear to be driven by different pressures. The airlines have required their machines to be safe enough to keep the passengers assured but still operate as cheaply as possible. These organizations, therefore, wish to avoid crashes which will cause a loss in revenue. This somewhat cynical view is supported by the fact that there has never been a public enquiry about the design of a new aircraft before it enters service, whereas enquiries at the proposal stage of projects are often initiated for many other industries.

The majority of engineers may never become directly involved in formal safety evaluations. However, the procedures, consequences, and attitudes arising from the activities in the major fields of concern will inevitably keep expanding into lower levels. It is likely, therefore, that engineers remote from the 'front line' will eventually feel the impact of these new attitudes, and the implications of safety in its broadest sense need to be thoroughly understood throughout the engineering industry. (Fig. 1.)

Safety is not in itself a precise state or situation and it cannot be described in absolute terms. The difficulty, therefore, with safety is that very few people can agree, in any one situation, as to what it really means. A simplistic view of safety is the definition that 'Safety' is the 'Prevention of an unwanted event leading to damage, injury, or death'. The Oxford English Dictionary defines 'Safety' as 'The quality of being unlikely to

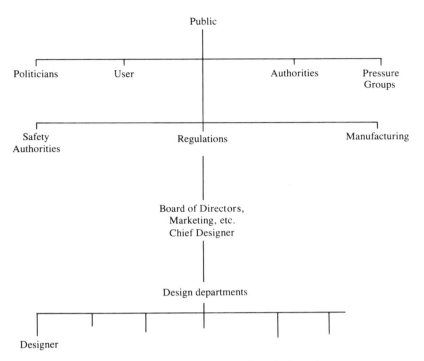

Fig 1   Safety comes down to the designer in the end

cause or occasion hurt or injury; freedom from dangerousness'. Within that definition the key word is 'unlikely' and this is the major problem. The debate always centres on what is acceptable in quantative terms as 'unlikely'. Typical of the difficulty in defining what is to be regarded as safe is the necessity to take unquantifiable decisions. For example, consider the dilemma of choosing between two designs. One has the extremely remote possibility of causing an accident, although if it occurs it will cause many deaths. The other has a significantly greater (although still very remote) chance of an accident, but one which will result in far fewer fatalities. (Fig. 2.)

There have been numerous attempts to place a value on life. Generally these values have been obtained by an analysis of what has proved to be acceptable in existing systems. The figures have not been a conditioned

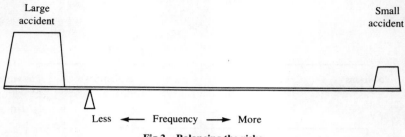

Fig 2   **Balancing the risks**

response to the question of how much should be spent in a particular instance. Past practice has been largely on the lines of determining the costs of safety features that have been accepted as necessary. These costs have then been attributed to the number of lives they have saved and a 'cost per life' established. It would for example be most unusual for the specification of a plant or vehicle to contain the statement 'it is only worth spending [so much] for each life saved'. Yet this is what happens in practice. More lives could be saved if aircraft had wider spacing between the seats and wider gangways, but this is not done because revenue would fall or fares have to be increased. For most applications the acceptable level of safety is one were people believe an accident will not happen, particularly to them. There is a strong objection to regarding something as being safe when it is predicted there will only be a 'small' accident. The public find it difficult to grasp the concept of probability, except in the broadest of terms, and judge acceptability against the chance that it will not happen to them in their lifetime. In rough figures, the fatality rate on the roads is $130:10^{-6}$ and that of the home and work $120:10^{-6}$ and $30:10^{-6}$, respectively; these figures hardly reflect the public's understanding of risk, when home is regarded as the safest place.

Of some interest is the report that in Bangladesh in 1990 tigers killed 200 people, this being an increase of 50 over the 1989 figure. The proposal to create a reservation for the tigers was costed at £30 million, a sum which the Government could not afford. If the killing continues at the current rate, then in 5 years there will be 1000 victims, so the value placed on life in Bangladesh is less than £30000. If an industrial plant caused half as many deaths it would be closed overnight.

Engineering is essentially the art of making things, whether they are small single components or complex systems, such as the space shuttle or a chemical plant. Therefore, the engineer must participate in the definition of safety as he has the responsibility of providing the means of achieving a safe design and, hence, product. The likelihood of a design or project engineer being pitchforked into taking the responsibility for the safety of a major system at an early stage in his career is remote. It is, however, quite probable that he will be playing a support role, albeit, at times, almost unwittingly. Decisions taken at the detail level of a design have a profound effect on the safety of complete systems. It may at times appear that senior staff are unnecessarily concerned about detail when a system is being evaluated. To appreciate their interest in the minutiae the junior engineer must understand the philosophy of safety, which unfortunately varies from occasion to occasion and system to system. The pressures on those charged with endorsing or recommending a system as safe are not confined to technical matters; as a minimum there is a need to balance cost, efficiency, reliability, and time (or programme) constraints. (Fig. 3.)

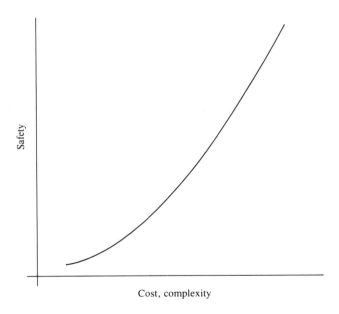

Cost, complexity

Fig 3   As safety increases, so cost and complexity escalate

Designers, managers, and project engineers need a balanced perspective of the various factors influencing activities and decisions. The normal education of these management staff includes the properties of materials, the way in which stress is encountered, the mathematics and science of the system, and the management techniques, including accountancy, marketing, and so forth. Frequently safety is not identified as a separate topic, yet in many systems it is a major cause of cost, delay, and complexity. It is not necessary, or indeed desirable, for all involved to become expert in Fault Tree Analysis, Failure Modes and Effects, and the like; there are adequate numbers of specialists to deal with such problems in detail. Management of an engineering organization should be acquainted with the needs and principles of safety. The accountant, administrator, contracts manager, and so on, will, in one way or another, be involved in safety activities. Unless they recognise the increasing importance in the need for resources to support safety they will not be able to separate the various activities in a project and make the balanced judgements necessary for effective management. What is essential for the 'management' is to have a grasp of the possible complications and requirements in the same manner as they have one of the availability of manufacturing processes, the market and the cost. Increasing safety is like building a stronger wall: you either have to add more bricks or improve their strength. With safety you have to increase the effort or the quality (by using specialist help?). (Fig. 4.)

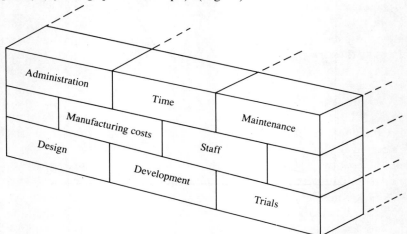

Fig 4   To increase safety, all areas have to be increased

The introduction of safety features can be regarded as an overhead; an extra that adds nothing to the performance or simplicity of the system. There may be far reaching ramifications involving the setting up of training courses, the writing of manuals of instruction, or the creation of monitoring teams. The provision of aircraft simulators at very high cost is, in part, the result of safety requirements; aircrew can practice manoeuvres that would be risky in flight trials. Even when a system reaches the end of its working life there may be safety costs. The decommissioning of nuclear plant is a prime example of very high expenditure being involved in disposal.

As with many management problems, the difficulty often lies not in finding the answer but in finding the question. Accidents and failures generally occur due to a series of minor unforeseen events rather than a catastrophic single happening. In other words, it is the unexpected that causes the problem. The mechanism for finding the potential accident or failure path may be aided by logical and mathematical analysis, but in the end the means of seeking the required information depends upon experience and imagination.

Ideally, one would be able to express safety as clear, numerical, levels in the same manner in which performance is commonly specified (velocity, power, reliability, and so on.). The problem is that, even if one could set numerical levels, they are likely to be so small that in many instances they could not be demonstrated. To show that a piece of equipment might fail once in 10^6 operations is almost impossible without an unrealistic amount of testing and user experience. The best that can be done is to produce a logical assessment of the likely failure of the component parts and add to that assessed data on the other aspects (such as user errors) to finish up with a figure that seems acceptable.

In very many instances safety is considered to be satisfactory if certain criteria of design, manufacture, and use are met. There are specifications and Codes of Practices, many with legal backing, that limit the engineering activities. On other occasions it is necessary to argue and agree the criteria. This is particularly so where new systems or environments are encountered, or when an unexpected change of circumstance occurs. The Kings Cross Underground station fire in London resulted in a complete re-evaluation of the system which, when viewed in the long term, had an apparently quite acceptable safety record. This particular accident was the result of a few simple things going wrong, all of which were clearly predictable and, indeed, resulted from observable conditions.

Most safety regulations concentrate on the physical features, for example, stress factors, materials, insulation, and the like. There are very few examples of regulations addressing the human factor area, yet it is human error that causes a great many accidents. The UK domestic driving test arrangements are directed to establishing that a certain level of skill has been achieved and then assuming that this will not deteriorate over a lifetime. This is equivalent, in engineering terms, to testing a boiler when it is made and then neglecting effects of corrosion over the ensuing years.

In English law the charged person is presumed innocent until proved guilty. When dealing with safety the designer has to prove his innocence against not only the initial charges but also those that are developed by his peers as his case develops. Safety evaluation relies a great deal on the use of imagination to determine the likely sequence of events leading to accidents. Whilst the authorities examining a design may have clear requirements to start with, it is not unusual for these to be expanded and developed as the time passes. It is important that this philosophy is such that there is a need to prove the system is safe rather than proving it is unsafe.

Unfortunately people's ideas on safety, or risk, are frequently more influenced by circumstance than by pure logic or even common sense. Who, in an industrial situation, would agree to untrained people standing next to fast moving machinery without adequate safety measures? However, passengers are allowed to stand on the edge of a crowded underground railway platform without any barrier either between them and the train or, indeed, between them and the throng of other passengers trying to move along the platform.

Having accepted from the outset that the term 'safe' is by no means definitive, it is logical to assume that it can only be used to indicate an agreement that, under certain circumstances, those persons affected are, or will be, satisfied that the equipment or operation is acceptable to them. At best, and with a considerable amount of data, analysis, and imagination, safety can be numerically defined by the two terms 'probability' and 'consequence'. Naturally the credibility that can be given to such values is entirely dependent on the available data and the precision of estimates and assumptions.

It follows that a logical and essential first step in the process of determining safety is to obtain an agreement as to what it means. It may not be possible, for a number of reasons, to agree firm values of probability and the full scope of the consequences of an accident in the initial stages of a design or project. This does not detract from the requirement to start with some target values and criteria. The preliminary work must include the perceived importance of safety as well as the actual risk. Frequently the originators of a project will not wish to determine the actual importance of safety and accept a target for cost. It is often thought that the safety standard will somehow emerge without specification and at zero cost. Accountants will enthusiastically undertake cost benefit studies for systems but will be unwilling to put a price on the amount to be allocated to safety features and the demonstration of their effectiveness.

The cost of safety should be identified in exactly the same way as the costs of marketing, manufacture, development, and so on. By showing the costs allowed for safety it is possible to highlight the importance of this aspect when reviewing work programmes. When breaking new fields of technology or practice it is not always possible to establish from the outset what the ramifications of each design decision will be. Those responsible for approving a design may require time to consider and evaluate fundamental points before being able to set the criteria. The designer will need to be in a position to judge the likely attitudes of the assessors when, at a later date, they examine the product. For this to be done designers must understand not only any regulatory requirements but also the likely attitudes and prejudices of those in authority that will evaluate the system. Meeting regulations does not necessarily mean that people will accept something is safe; they often demand more. Typical of the complexities of making decisions in the safety field is the fact that people will on occasions demand less safety than regulations dictate. The use of protective clothing is a prime example of this, as are safe practices in the use of scaffolding and the like. The usual reason given is that the use of precautions delays work or makes things inconvenient.

There are a variety of techniques for assessing risk in numerical terms, but the derived values do not necessarily reflect the views of the participants in an activity. The expert evaluation of probability and consequence may be of little help in satisfying nonspecialists that a situation or system is safe. Not surprisingly the majority of the population is largely illiterate on matters of engineering, science, and statistics. This deficiency includes many professional people in positions of influence. In setting safety standards it is important to appreciate the need to present the facts and arguments in a meaningful way, and not to rely on a totally technical evaluation requiring expert understanding.

The concept of risk being a product of probability and consequence is not readily grasped by the general public or, indeed, many professionals. The public, generally, is principally interested in consequence and fails to appreciate the fact that, in many instances, it is quite impossible to accurately state that an accident will not happen under any conceivable set of circumstances. The Royal Society has defined 'risk' as 'the probability that a particular adverse event occurs during a stated period of time, or results from a particular challenge'; this does not really provide a useful definition for the layman.

The advent of nuclear power and, as has already been mentioned, its close association in the public mind with nuclear weapons, made a tremendous contribution to bringing safety into the area of open debate. For many years the topic of safety was a matter of agreement between knowledgeable people. public enquiries now proliferate, either before or after the event. Engineers and scientists must adjust their thinking to allow for this exchange of views between the 'expert' and 'lay' audience. Whilst the public has little chance of fully understanding the safety concepts, this will, quite rightly, not stop them demanding involvement.

The technology of 'reliability' studies was primarily developed to improve or establish quality. They do, however, also provide an evaluation of safety. This brings with it the concept of using the reliability engineer to determine the likely safety standard. The reliability specialist will then have the role of asking how the system will fail rather than the designers main thought of how will it work. If such a method becomes commonplace the reliability analyst will have to obtain a much broader education. In analysing the performance of a system the goals are stated in the specification; does the system measure up to the set standards? In analysing safety, the task, in many instances, is to find the feature of operation that has not been thought of.

It is, of course, convenient to adopt a methodical, analytical approach to the safety of a system. The weak link is obtaining reliable data. Too often the methodical approach instils an unjustifiable level of confidence, as it appears that the topic has been thoroughly examined. Accidents do not normally occur due to the single, obvious event taking place; they are far more likely to arise from the unexpected, or from an unusual combination of the expected. Safety is often achieved by someone using their imagination, rather than by just asking the obvious questions. Systematic analysis is, quite rightly, highly valued, but it can lead to false confidence when staff believe they have completed the exercise, but have failed to look for the unusual.

Many people derive a high degree of assurance when told a risk is a one-in-a-million chance; they fail to realise that this still means the unwanted event may occur the next day. A once-in-a-hundred years storm can easily be encountered twice within a short period. It may well be that, to even things out, the third occourance is two hundred years later, but that is of little practical comfort or use.

There is no doubt that in most engineering systems absolute safety can never be assured. What must be achieved is an acceptable level of safety. In determining acceptability the criteria often become less certain, as the arguments for standards vary with both time and situation. One of the greatest influencing factors is the 'perception' rather than the 'understanding' of a situation, either by the public or the authorities. Attitudes, be they positive or negative, towards a proposal, will not necessarily be logical. Personal safety standards are variable and, at times, illogical. At work there is a demand for risks to be reduced to a negligible level, yet, at the same time, many workers will accept a 'risky' task if given compensation. They will engage in high risk sports, such as skiing and parachuting, yet refuse to undertake quite ordinary tasks in a factory without elaborate precautions. The loss of an aircraft with 100 fatalities or the drowning of 20 people in a pleasure boat causes headline news coupled with calls for legislation and the expenditure of vast sums of money. Yet the yearly deaths of several thousand people on the roads is accepted as a part of life. People will generally accept high self-imposed risks, but will reject lesser ones forced on them.

The attitude toward injury or death varies greatly not only from country to country but also within societies and from group to group. Within the groups there are further subsets. The average person's attitude to a faulty pushchair injuring a child would be to ensure the manufacturer changed the design. If the same sort of injury was regularly caused by a do-it-yourself tool, then it is quite probable, given that the number of incidents were fairly modest, that the matter would be ignored, the attitude being that the innocent must be protected, but the majority should be left to their own devices.

In road safety there are many excellent examples of the change of attitude with time, and also of lack of logical and consistent thought. In the early days of the motor car in the UK it was necessary for them to be preceded by a man with a red flag – despite the probably better control achievable by the car when compared with the horsedrawn carriage. Seat belts are a requirement in the front of cars, but not in the back. The front seat passengers are saved from impacting the windscreen or facia, but can be hit by the people behind. Lap seat belts are fitted to aircraft, but not coaches. To compound the lack of logic, the use of lap belts ensures the user pivots about the hips, thus hitting his or her head, whereas in the car the whole body is restrained.

Transport in general seems to attract illogical and inconsistent attitudes. Some of these are due to economics and others due to opinion. Aircraft are fitted with forward-facing seats, despite the obvious advantages of rear-facing ones. It is argued that passengers would not wish to travel 'backwards'. Yet half of the seats on most trains face that way, and many luxury coaches have some seats facing backwards. Five abreast seating and narrow gangways in aircraft show that cost considerations outweigh those of safety. Evacuation exercises or tests are carried out without the drawbacks of hand luggage, the old and infirm, or the aircraft being on anything but an even keel.

The existence of the anomalies must not, however, cloud the real value of practical experience in assessing risk. As mentioned earlier, the practice of passengers standing next to fast trains has proved to be acceptable. The filling of cars with a volatile fuel of low flash point has, in practice, been shown to be low risk. However, if, from the beginning of the use of cars, the process had been examined using today's criteria, then it would almost certainly have been rejected. There would have to have been a sealed transfer hose operated by trained staff, and most likely there would have been a requirement to earth the car to avoid static electric sparks.

In many instances the passage of time changes perception and requirements. If the car had been proposed under modern circumstances would the design of a vehicle capable of 100 mile/h which required the use of all four limbs, at the same time, making coordinated but different movements, in the dark, on a wet road have been considered practical?

Death and injury/incapacity through natural causes has, particularly in the Western world, markedly decreased in the last century. This reduction means that 'technological' accidents (notably the motor car) have contributed an increasingly large proportion to the whole mortality equation. It is, therefore, not surprising that the public's attention is turning from many traditional, natural hazards (plague, famine, weather, and the like) and concentrating on the artificial ones. This change in attitude is despite the technologies, particularly in land, sea, and air transport, having become significantly safer.

Different attitudes to safety are sometimes dictated by circumstance. Most safety systems are designed to prevent a hazard arising from the system not working correctly. With military ordnance the situation can be considered to be somewhat different. Military equipment is designed to remove from the enemy the will to fight. This is generally achieved by depositing large amounts of energy in his vicinity in the most uncomfortable manner that can be devised. Thus, it is possible to argue that military ordnance devices are potentially fast-moving accidents being restrained from happening. This restraint is usually achieved by the design of the control, fusing, and firing systems, so that they have to progress to their proper function through a series of 'gates' which restrain them. It is, therefore, the function of the system to become more unsafe as it approaches its designed task. It is necessary, in many instances, to approach the safety of military equipment in a different manner from the safety of civil systems.

The differences in approach within the civil area are also illustrated by the attitudes of the aircraft and chemical and nuclear industries. The first is little concerned in the consequences of an accident as these are often fatal to all concerned. They are not interested in trying to decide if a 'little crash' will happen. Their philosophy is to avoid crashes irrespective of size. The aircraft industry does not differentiate between full and the near empty aircraft and assess the number of passengers that might be killed. The other two industries tend to examine quite closely the consequences of an accident. Will it be a small leak or a large one? Will there be many people in the affected area?

Safety costs time, money, and performance. The engineer is, therefore, faced with evaluating a number of factors to reach a compromise. Indeed, he has not only to deal with the immediate situation but also anticipate the future, when changes of circumstance may well render his current decisions useless. Building safety into a system affects the following.

Timescales

The effort required for evaluating safety of a project can be significant and produce complications in other areas of activity. There may be a need

Engineering System Safety

to delay decisions affecting the design of a system to await the outcome of safety analysis, trials, and assessments. The time taken to use a piece of equipment may be lengthened by safety procedures, the use of protective equipment, and so on.

Performance

Any system embodying safety features is likely to lose performance. There may be weight penalties, reliability may be decreased by an increase in the number of working parts, safety factors for structures may be increased leading to additional material, lower working speeds or pressures, and so on.

Cost

Any of the above factors will have cost implications. There will be more costs arising due to the need to demonstrate safety – for example, laboratory car crashes to show passenger protection is satisfactory.

System safety separates into a number of levels depending on the size of the work. Irrespective of the size and complexity there are common areas of questions to be addressed.

– What is the cause of a breach of safety ?
– What is the consequence of an accident ?
– What is the probability of it happening ?

There is no standard correct and formal way to analyse the system and arrive at a totally acceptable answer. There is always the need for human judgement and decision making.

There are a number of basic techniques which must be used to approach the analysis. Evaluation and judgement must always be logical, understood by all concerned, and written down. Before analysing a system there are essential ground rules to be established.

– What, in the particular set of circumstances, is to be considered as 'safe' ?
– What type of information is likely to be needed to demonstrate safety has been achieved ?
– What importance is attached to 'safety'; is it to be safe at all costs or are there commercial or operational limitations that allow for a higher than minimal level of risk?

– What are the standards likely to remain valid throughout the life of the system ?
– What needs to be done when the system is eventually scrapped ?

As has been stated earlier, safety is very much in the eye of the beholder. Having accepted that absolute safety is impossible, there are a number of options to choose from. Should the standard be:

'as low as reasonably achievable' (ALARA);
'as low as reasonably possible' (ALARP);
'to the minimum level of risk';
'the tolerable level of risk';
'to the generally acceptable level for existing equipment'.

Foremost in the minds of designers is the need to make the system work; after all, that is the purpose of the exercise which is absorbing resources. By their nature safety features are additions to the system as a whole and do not contribute to the efficiency or economy of the system. Indeed, by stopping things happening, safety features frequently introduce a degree of unreliability. The more parts there are, the more there is to go wrong. Nobody has set out to justify the creation of a design for a system whose main function is to be safe and incidently perform some useful task.

In the pursuit of safety there are two broad approaches. One is the attempt to introduce zero- or minimum-cost features that will add to the safety standard. The other is the introduction of special safety features. Obviously it is preferable to utilize as many zero-cost options as possible. These might be simple things, such as properly grouped controls and instruments, or painting in suitable warning colours; the standard practice of making electrical plugs and sockets non-interchangeable is an example of minimum-cost safety.

At the time a design is initiated the current safety standards are frequently governed or guided by legislation, codes of practice, and other controls. That may not be the full story as coexisting with the appropriate requirements at any one time is the continuing potential for change due to a wide range of remotely-connected circumstances and developments. A designer of a vehicle for carrying highly toxic substances will have a whole range of requirements to guide him as to the standards he must meet. If during the design phase there should happen to be a particularly nasty accident with a similar cargo then, possibly for political reasons or due to public outcry, the specifications might change in a very short time. A similar second-order effect might arise due to no fault of the designer but, say, to the chance discovery that the potential cargo has adverse long term medical effects which were previously unknown. The realization that blue asbestos was a major health risk completely changed the acceptability of insulating material almost overnight.

An area that is causing increasing difficulty with regard to producing a convincing safety assessment is the use of computer control of processes and systems. With electrical and mechanical systems there are many opportunities to apply test loads and generally exercise the system to demonstrate the margin of safety. A computer program is not so easily checked to show that there are no possibilities of error. As programs are complex structures not easily observed there is always a fear that a rogue command is hidden in the depths in a similar manner to a virus. Demonstrating the problem does not exist is very difficult indeed.

The route to achieving and maintaining a safe system is often long, expensive, and fraught with difficulty. Whilst the scope of analytical techniques is improving and the data base expanding the use of experience and imagination remain paramount.

2

Physical Causes

For an accident to occur there obviously has to be a cause. Causes generally fall into one or more of four broad areas:

– inadequate understanding of a situation;
– human error;
– equipment failure;
– poor design.

The sources of accidents or failures can often be attributed to some physical phenomena. In dealing with the phenomena likely to be encountered there is a good case for arguing that the considerations are more appropriate to a treatise on design than one on safety. Whilst this is to a large extent true the fact remains that analysing phenomena and their effect on performance designers often fail to identify the perhaps unusual, but entirely predictable, cause of a failure. The tendency is for designers to concentrate on the normal situation rather than the abnormal.

Nearly all accidents are caused by some event or physical phenomenon that was entirely predictable at the design concept stage. The reasons as to why such obvious potential hazards are not identified or catered for are numerous. However, all too often the reason is 'we didn't think of it'. The design process is usually a random approach, with any methodical analysis being left to the end, to 'optimize' it. Ideas are put on paper in a disorderly fashion and the design gradually evolves one step at a time. As problems are encountered they are solved piecemeal, until the completed design is often quite different from that first envisaged. Whilst this undisciplined attack on problems in many instances works quite well in practice, on some occasions the results are literally disastrous.

The difference between the criteria and considerations used for design and safety are not generally very large; it is normally only a question of degree. Safety often requires just that bit extra imagination of what might be encountered, and just that bit extra performance margin. Safety requirements are not necessarily different to performance requirements, but are an extension of them.

Thus, when reviewing a design for safety it is important to methodically and thoroughly detail and understand all of the physical phenomena (for example, corrosion, pressure, temperature, and so on) that might become the cause of a failure. It is natural that the design specification should adequately describe the environment under normal conditions, but it should also consider the abnormal ones.

Design and performance specifications are generally optimistic regarding the extremes of the various criteria. This is understandable, as the more complex the specification and the more extreme the phenomena, so the more expensive and complicated the design often becomes.

Diligent examination for the scenario that might cause failure must encompass all conceivable phenomena that might degrade the system. The physical phenomena that might be considered could well be divided into the following areas.

(1) Chemical reactions:
  – combination;
  – reaction etc;
  – change of state.

(2) Mechanical energy:
  – kinetic;
  – potential.

(3) Thermal effects:
  – heat;
  – friction;
  – temperature:
    – actual;
    – gradients;
    – rate of change.

(4) Electrical:
  – voltage;
  – current;
  – insulation;
  – capacitance;
  – frequency.

(5) Pressure:
  - absolute;
  - rate of change;
  - difference.

It is essential when analysing a design to identify within it the sources of energy, the chemical make up, the areas where transients and changes occur in such properties as temperature, velocity, material, and so on. It is also necessary to visualize the same features in reverse, as inputs into the system, that is, the external environment.

Chemical reactions are frequent reasons for equipment failure. These reactions may range from simple corrosion having a strength-reducing effect to explosive reactions causing complete devastation. When assessing the potential of an accident occurring a methodical survey of the likely causes should be undertaken. This should be part of the design process aimed at an effective design, and safety implications, over and above those of performance, make such examinations vital.

The method of analysis will be dependent on the design as, at times, the possible source is reasonably obvious and, at others, is only determined by considerable thought. A design and its environment might well be considered under the headings given above. This must be done with regard to the design itself and in addition the surroundings must be carefully examined to see if they may have an input. There is, in effect, a two-way process: there is the direct potential for chemical effects within the design package (for example, the use of cooling water for an engine) while on the other hand there is the possibility of external attack, such as is caused by the use of salt on the roads to prevent icing. It is useful to consider the system as a box with internal and external activities which interact.

Different materials or chemicals represent a potential source of degradation of a design. At all places where there is a change of substance there is a potential weakness. One of the most widely recognised of these problems is the use of dissimilar metals that may, in the presence of moisture, cause electrolytic corrosion. Similarly there might be a migration of one constituent of a material into the other, causing one or both to become weaker. This can occur even with materials in their solid state, although the reaction is less vigorous than when liquids or gases are involved.

In some instances long term failure can occur after relatively short exposure during the manufacturing process. Maraging steel is at times susceptible to inter-granular corrosion when exposed to chlorines. In a particular instance, as part of the NDT process during manufacture, pressure vessel units were immersed in a chlorine-based fluid. Despite rigorous controls some of the units were insufficiently well sealed and a minute amount of fluid seeped into the vessels. Although this was later removed by a cleaning process the material structure was damaged enough to cause failure at a later date. The problem was two fold: first, a primary error in allowing the leak path to occur, and, secondly, not recognising the potential risk from the process.

The analysis for chemical effects must encompass not only the final build of an assembly but the exposure to potential troublesome materials throughout the manufacturing process. Chemical attack is often particularly difficult to identify in its early stages, especially in the cases where chemicals are absorbed without staining or surface-finish changes.

Mechanical failures often result from the release of stored energy, and failure analysis should be directed at identifying where energy is stored in the system. The existence of fuels and pressurized gases is fairly evident. What is less apparent is the existence of other phenomena such as strain energy – and this may not only exist as direct deformation, such as of a spring.

It has been accepted for many years that pressure tests of systems are best done with a relatively inert fluid such as water or oil. However, this guideline was established in the era when most systems were constructed with metals whose Young's modulus is high. With the advent of non-metallic materials pressure vessels can be made using wound filaments. The fundamental difference is that whilst, for example, steel has a relatively low expansion under pressure (within the elastic limit) non-metallic composites can show significant dimensional changes – strain – whilst still remaining within their working stress. The result of this difference is that a non-metallic pressure vessel can store a considerable volume of fluid under pressure due to the expansion of the walls. This may be suddenly released if a failure occurs. If the failure takes the form of a small crack any oil released under pressure may form a fine mist that could present a fire or even explosion risk. The jet alone could result in physical injury. The message is 'beware of deflections' as they often represent stored energy. (Fig. 5.)

Kinetic energy is obviously one of the major causes of accidents, and in most instances this is easily identified. What must be examined are the

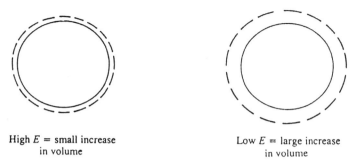

High E = small increase
in volume

Low E = large increase
in volume

Fig 5   New materials require a new appreciation of the consequences

potential paths that the energy can take in the event of an accident. Modern car design typifies the manner in which energy being transferred in a crash is diverted to less hazardous paths and areas. Car bodies are designed to deform and absorb energy as well as deflecting various masses to avoid critical areas. Rotating systems are commonly dealt with as items that may fragment and cause damage from the impact of the particles acting as missiles. There is a less commonly recognised phenomena associated with rotating systems that are encased in shields. What is often not visualized is the fact that fragments literally fly off at a tangent from a disintegrating body. In providing shields it is all too easy to imagine that the fragments hit it in such a manner as to penetrate the shield. This is only true if the shield is some distance from the fragment source. If, for example, a tube were spinning and suddenly disintegrated then if the shield were close to the outside of the tube the fragments would hit the shield where the tangent intersected it. In all probability this means the

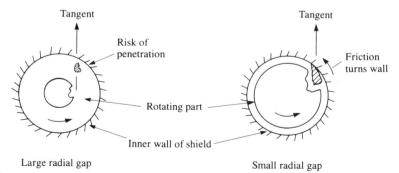

Large radial gap   Small radial gap

Fig 6   Failures do not always have obvious results

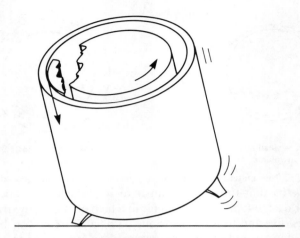

Fig 7   Out-of-balance forces can topple equipment

fragments would slide round the inside of the shield and in so doing exert a centrifugal force on the shield. Friction between the sliding fragments and the shield would give the latter a turning force. (Fig. 6.) If the system were a free standing device there could well be sufficient turning force as to cause the whole assembly to become unstable. Allowing a sizable gap between the rotating parts and the shield allows the fragments to impact at a steep angle, reducing the turning force but increasing the penetration effect. (Fig. 7.)

The rotating reaction may be of minimal relevance in most shielded systems, but where the complete system is not restrained, such as a fairly portable centrifuge, the resulting forces may topple the equipment.

Kinetic energy is often underestimated where very large masses moving slowly are concerned. A load of several tonnes has considerable kinetic energy when it has swung just a short distance before hitting another object. Pendulum effects can be quite destructive, as the potential energy is transformed to kinetic.

Potential energy is fairly readily identified as its availability usually takes the form of an object being above a level to which it can descend. This release of energy does not always show itself as a falling object. Piles of loose material are essentially unstable and given the right sort of event will redistribute themselves. This may not matter in an open space but in a confined area can be the cause of considerable sideways pressure. Thus, a container of particles is, in many respects, similar to a pressure vessel. However, the similarity does not extend to uniform pressure. There will obviously be a difference in pressure, or force, depending on the 'depth' of the material. Dependent on the particle size and other characteristics there may not be a uniform pressure at any particular depth. If, for example, a fairly large-sized particulate material is in a container with sharp corners there may be a wedging action in the vicinity of the corners, relieving the pressure in that area. This, in some instances, may be an advantage, but in others this lack of uniformity can cause unwanted distortion.

The unexpected behaviour of particulate material, including slurries, has been the cause of many accidents. Whilst the material may act like a very viscous fluid, the introduction of some other material or energy can cause a complete change in the characteristics. As a simple example damp sand is a moderately rigid substance capable of holding its shape. The introduction of a modest amount of extra fluid can suddenly change the apparent viscosity from high to very low. This change is often observed in spoil dumps from mining activities. Spoil that has remained stable for long periods, say years, can slump in a catastrophic manner after prolonged rain; the ensuing slurry is extremely mobile and exerts strong forces on obstacles in its path. In calculating the potential forces produced by such a slurry one has to take account of the specific gravity of the mixture rather than that of the fluid. Thus, a mixture containing particles which have a specific gravity greater than water – for example, mixture of glass particles and water – may well have a combined specific gravity of two or even three times that of the water alone. This means that a container of dry material will exert much greater pressures if it is then filled with liquid, perhaps by a leak from a pipe

Thermal effects are normally centred around temperature. Heat is a store of energy and, as such, only represents a hazard when its quantity changes, achieved either through a change of temperature or state. In visualizing effects of temperature people are much better at appreciating the scale of temperatures above the normal ambient than below it. It is relatively easy to recognise that 60°C is a bit hot to touch and 100°C can cause burns. After those levels most engineers understand that the melting point of such metals as solder scorches rather than burns material, and that red hot is getting into a significantly damaging level for many materials. Reversing the scale is by no means as clear. The freezing point is fairly well understood, but how does this compare with, say, the temperature of solid CO_2? Frequently, because they are not encountered in everyday life, the physical aspects of low temperatures are not readily visualized. The temperature of liquid air is such that, if a material is exposed to the atmosphere at that temperature, liquid oxygen may form on the surface. This could well form a hazard if oil were present on the surface as well.

Temperature change can be as much of a problem as actual temperature. The stresses induced by temperature gradients across a material can be significant and, if cyclic, may well lead to fatigue effects. Normal performance trials can be misleading when determining temperature gradients. Unless the environmental conditions are exactly representative, the rates of cooling and temperatures reached can be quite different to those encountered in service. The inevitable movement that occurs as surfaces heat and cool can cause them to rub together, and this can result in damage to protective coatings.

Safety can, of course, be affected if there are hot surfaces where they might be touched. A very hot item might be dropped or a sudden reaction might cause an accident.

Care must be taken when changing materials that have proved satisfactory without fully considering the consequences. For example, the military authorities issued nylon and similar clothing to personnel and introduced an injury problem under accident conditions: cotton and other natural materials merely burned in the presence of a fire, but the synthetics exacerbated the injury problem by melting.

Spontaneous combustion is usually associated with organic materials in their natural environment. In the past, before grain and fodder were artificially dried before stacking, there were regular haystack fires across the country. Fires in ships' holds were also frequent when the cargo became damp. Within industry, spontaneous combustion can occur when simple materials, such as oily rags, are stored in a confined space. Therefore, the confinement of any organic material must be suspect in this respect. The confinement may be no more than a small heap of material and does not have to involve any special circumstances other than the availability of a small supply of oxygen and sufficient insulation as to prevent the heat escaping at at least the same rate as it is generated.

The potential risks from electrical sources are a study in themselves. Apart from the obvious dangers of high voltage supplies, the presence of static electricity is of major concern where flammable materials are present. The generation of tens of thousands of volts is readily encountered where large sheets of material are involved. The discharge of the voltage is by no means easy as a simple earth point on a sheet may not discharge the whole surface. Whilst it is unlikely that damage to personnel will occur from static charges, there is a risk of people encountering the charge being hurt enough to make them drop something or make sudden movements, perhaps in dangerous surroundings. Large capacitors can gain a substantial voltage by means of static, and in this case there may be sufficient charge to become a real hazard. For this reason very large capacitors should always have a shorting device applied to bleed off any potential charge. Conveyor belting can also build up a substantial electrical charge, as can dust clouds. The risk is not confined to dry materials as water sprays, such as are used in cleaning ships oil tanks, can produce sufficient voltage to ignite fumes that may be present. The apparently contradictory feature – that water can carry a static charge – is easily reconciled by considering the voltage carried by thunder clouds. It all depends on leak paths; unless the charge can leak away at least as fast as it is formed then obviously it will build up.

Pressure of either a gas or liquid is a prime source of stored energy and the explosions of the Industrial Revolution era provide many examples of the failure of boilers through over pressurization. Many years ago bakers' ovens were heated by inserting sealed steel tubes containing water through the wall that formed the back of the oven and the side of the furnace. There was, therefore, on one side the fire and on the other the oven. (Fig. 8.) The function of the tube was to convey heat from the furnace to the oven by boiling water on the furnace side and allowing the steam to condense on the oven side; the tubes sloped downwards to the furnace so the condensate ran back to that end. The advantage of the system was that the bread was baked in a clean environment. Failures occurred when the tubes were not filled with enough water to prevent total evaporation. Once all the water had boiled the steam became superheated, with a very considerable and sudden rise in temperature. As no venting or safety valves were fitted the tubes failed in an explosive manner. The lesson to be learnt is that a change of state can cause a significant rise in pressure. As most liquids expand on freezing the effect on containment can be to subject it to high pressures; hence the risk of burst water pipes on freezing. If pressure rises suddenly in a vessel containing a fuel or oil vapour, the accompanying rise in temperature can cause ignition (dieseling) resulting in an explosion. This phenomena can

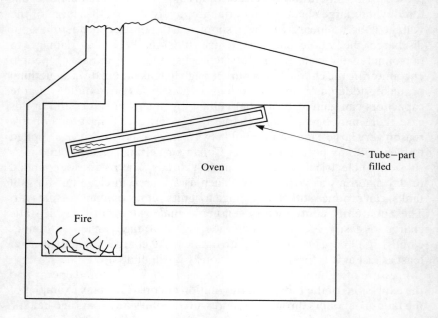

Fig 8   A sudden change of state can generate large forces

be encountered in unexpected situations. Tight fitting dowels, if driven into a hole containing oil, can cause this reaction.

Cyclic pressure has long been the cause of fatigue failure in metals, one of the most famous examples being the Comet aircraft. Much damage is caused by pressure differences, and lack of balanced vent paths can give rise to large differential pressures. It is important to select the correct size of vent, particularly for gases. If the pressure ratio for air exceeds about two to one, then, in some instances, sonic flow is established across the orifice, and no matter how much greater the pressure difference the flow rate will not increase. The flow through an orifice will, for any reasonable pressure difference, cause a drop in temperature which can be enough to cause ice to form; this may restrict the flow, or the melting ice may wet parts of the system.

Any person concerned with safety would be well advised not only to understand the range of phenomena normally encountered in the environment for his sphere of activity in design, but also to attempt to identify and explore all of the unusual chains of events that sometimes result in an accident.

3

Safety Criteria

As stated earlier, the first and most important criteria to establish is whether the requirement is to prove a system is safe or to prove it is not safe. This is akin to the principle of having to prove someone is guilty of a crime as opposed to them having to prove they are innocent. The safest course to follow is the need to establish something is safe and there is an opinion that the US *Challenger* disaster occurred because under the pressure to launch the policy was changed from the former to the latter.

To establish the requirements for a system, or to determine the safety standard of an existing system, it is necessary to decide on the criteria that will be adopted. The instinctive reaction, particularly among nontechnical people, is to demand that there shall be no safety risk. For virtually all practical purposes this is an ideal that cannot be reached. It is possible to divide the approach to the task of achieving a safe design into two main regimes. Firstly, that there will be sufficient safety built into the system so that a fault is so contained as to prevent any external hazard being created. Alternatively, there is an acceptance that safety will be breached at some time, and the problem is countered by other means.

Criteria are often set by precedent. Instead of deciding the requirements from a logical analysis of the situation, it is found to be more convenient simply to apply the criteria already in existence for current or past systems. It is, of course, prudent to look back at past experience, but there is always the risk of carrying forward requirements that are not entirely appropriate for a more advanced technology or for a change in application.

In determining safety criteria one cannot ignore trying to define what is meant by 'safe' in terms of the total existence of a system. After an accident has occurred to, say, a road fuel tanker, does 'safe' mean that immediately following the accident there was no loss of fuel, or does one have to take into account the subsequent recovery process, as this might be quite hazardous. In a similar manner it might be quite possible to commission a chemical or nuclear plant and operate it for many years, but find the subsequent scrapping of the plant to be a major problem.

As an example of different criteria in similar fields of activity (transport) it is accepted that accidents at sea will occur, but lifebelts and lifeboats are offered as a means of reducing the risk of an event that is unacceptable. The aircraft industry takes a different view and tries to reduce the risk of a major accident to the level where parachutes are not needed or indeed practical. The provision of aircraft life jackets and life rafts may not contribute to overall safety as the increased weight and complexity puts an additional demand on the aircraft structure and fuel requirements. It is doubtful whether the use of these aids has saved enough lives as to warrant the cost; the money expended would probably have been more useful in added fire precautions, especially in eliminating the production of toxic gases from the fabrics and decorative panels of the cabin. For rail travellers the organizations show even less regard for protection of the passengers if an accident should occur. There are no seat belts to restrain the occupants against even a low speed crash. Additionally, in some regions of the UK, there is a deliberate policy of not providing enough seats, so that a sudden stop at even very low speeds is likely to cause injuries. Not only will the standing passengers be liable to injury if there is an unexpected stop, but they may in turn injure the seated ones by falling on them.

Whilst it is easy to suggest criteria, such as 'intrinsically safe', 'safe by design', 'fail safe', 'safe by procedure', and so on, in practice the exact definitions and meanings of these are not always clearly definable. Given enough imagination and determination most critics can devise scenarios that will show almost anything is a potential hazard. Even a simple lump of clay can be considered hazardous if one assumes it can be dropped on the floor creating a situation where someone might slip on it. As is mentioned elsewhere the continual problem is that it all depends on what you mean by 'safe'.

As a prime example of the tortuous route whereby something as inert and apparently safe as river water can cause an explosion, one has to consider the case reported of the kerosene tank in Lincolnshire. In the 1930s there was an explosion in a kerosene tank which had a layer of river water in it. The enquiry concluded that the water produced methane gas by bacterial action. This gas then ignited and set off the kerosene fumes. Even more intriguing is the theory as to how the spark necessary to ignite the methane was generated; namely that further bacterial action was the cause. It was believed that pyrophoric iron sulphide was formed by sulphate-reducing bacteria in the water. Any person suggesting this as a scenario prior to the event would have probably been derided.

There is one approach to safety which lacks a certain amount of logic. This is to reduce the risk of an accident or failure to a relatively low probability and then to pay workers some compensation for the risk they are taking. It has been argued that coal mining was a hazardous occupation and that the wages should reflect this fact. However, far more people are killed and injured in the agricultural industry of the UK than in mining.

The highest level of safety is that of 'intrinsically safe'. That is to say, the system is such that even with a failure no significant incident will occur. The battery powered razor is an intrinsically safe electrical device. The mains rechargeable battery razor is conceivably liable to give the user an electric shock if used with the mains lead connected; although the chance of this happening is so remote as to be discounted. The latter system is, then, 'safe by design'. It is extremely difficult to make systems intrinsically safe as to operate they usually have to undergo changes that will have the potential for causing accidents. Generally speaking electrical systems are more amenable to being made intrinsically safe than are mechanical ones. Electrical systems can operate with low voltages, current limiters, and the like. Mechanical systems have mass, velocity, and pressure, all of which, in one way or another, are connected with energy. Once there is significant energy present in a mechanical system it has eventually to be removed to avoid hazard. It has been said, of course by an electrical engineer, that there are no electrical failures, only mechanical ones.

'Safe by design' is the most common and practical criteria, and provided the standard of safety can be agreed, is the one most easily and convincingly met. The perennial problem arises of first defining the level of safety to be deemed acceptable and then demonstrating this has been met. In devising the means of ensuring safety it is often convenient to consider a tiered strategy. Assuming an untoward event is generated (for example, an acid leak), then perhaps the first line of defence might be some containment. Should this be breached then there might be a countermeasure, such as a neutralizing agent; and if this fails a means of evacuating those at risk. A simple example is the kitchen of a public facility. The cooking range would be under an extractor hood taking out the fumes and flames from a fat fire; if the fire spreads there might be a sprinkler system or at least fire extinguishers. If these steps failed the fire

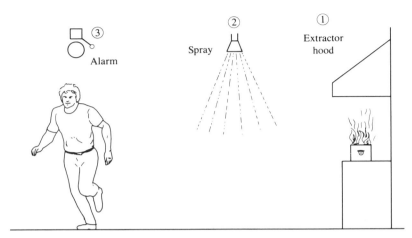

Fig 9   Several levels of response

alarms would, hopefully, ensure staff and customers were evacuated. (Fig. 9.)

Defence in depth is more effective than a substantial single barrier; however, in providing the depth there is likely to be added complexity. At times, of course, depth cannot be avoided, and thus it becomes important to determine the true nature of the risk and to ensure the 'barrier' is capable of meeting the demands placed on it. The designer of a submarine is likely to be allowed only one pressure hull and thus he has no real series of barriers. The safety can be increased by several simple additions, such as surrounding the hull with fuel and ballast tanks, thus reducing the externally applied forces on the vital pressure (hull) barrier. In addition, weak points in the hull, such as valve and pipe penetrations, are, wherever possible, sited below the centreline. If a leak occurs it might be possible to increase the boat's internal air pressure to reduce the flow of water from a hole below the centreline; a hole above the centreline will more easily allow air to leak out as the water comes in. This latter problem applies even if the pressure is not increased. The makers of antisubmarine torpedoes are very aware of the characteristic and try to produce weapons that attack from above. For surface ships the reverse is true and the favoured point of attack is from below. (Fig. 10.)

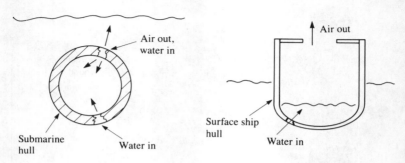

Fig 10   Some areas have a higher risk than others

To follow the 'safe by design' route means that it is necessary to declare the risk and consequences that might arise in the event of an accident or failure. The designer is, therefore, faced with the necessity of stating he has an unsafe system to start with, but that he has countered it in an acceptable manner. This invariably leads to over-design of not only the basic system but also the safety features.

A system that is designed to be safe must demonstrate this not only in its inherent design features but also in appearance and general acceptability. For example, a handrail may be adequately strong but flimsy in appearance. It is likely that the general user will not appreciate the true strength but will judge the acceptability of the rail on its appearance. The reverse can also be true. If the handrail is substantial, but poorly fixed, the user is likely to trust the appearance rather than the design. A noisy machine, or one that creates a lot of movement, will be judged to be unsafe as there is no other measure or standard on which the user or bystander can judge the situation.

When safety is ensured by a design feature the weak link frequently occurs with the introduction of modifications or change of application or usage. Adequate arrangements must be made to identify safety-related features in both the design department and in the field. This requirement is particularly important where subtle, unusual, or innovative design features are used. The disciplines of most design offices are regrettably slack when it comes to recording the features in question; they are rarely identified in a clear manner on drawings and in specifications. The usual method is to rely on memory, which either requires a continual employment of the same staff or a good hand-over system.

On large and potentially dangerous systems, such as in the aircraft, nuclear, and defence industries, the significant facts are likely to be formally recorded. In many other areas, as there is no requirement to create good recording systems, then the information is likely to be lost. Aircraft, nuclear, and defence systems often have very long working lives which extend beyond the careers of the designers. Record keeping under these circumstances is particularly difficult. It is not easy to persuade the management, particularly if not of the engineering discipline, to set up and maintain the expensive system of data banks and archives to ensure adequate records are kept. Indeed the accounting pressures may be such that space is not made available for storage of this documentation, let alone its upkeep. It is equally difficult to ensure the engineers record their reasons for certain design features that are often only described by drawings. These are in most cases, only, or primarily, intended to supply manufacturing information and not that for design.

Whilst it is frequent practice to define designs by drawing and specification it is also regrettably common for modifications to be introduced as manufacture proceeds. Good housekeeping demands that accurate records are kept of the changes introduced, but the weak link comes in ensuring safety is considered in each instance. For example, the introduction of a stronger strut may well be quite acceptable, and hardly merit comment, when examining the design for the effects on performance. However, the new strut may well transfer a load to some other part of the system, making it vulnerable to failure from a safety angle not previously considered.

The modern design of cars, with crumple zones to protect the occupants in a crash, is a prime example of the careful distribution of strength to ensure safety. In the chemical industry storage tanks are commonly made with weaker welds at the top than the sides and bottom. This ensures the 'lid ' lifts to release unexpected excess pressure, rather than a leak forming lower down.

One way of reducing the failures of safety systems is to ensure they have no 'common mode' of failure. For example, if excess pressure is prevented by a blow-off valve, fitting a second one may not be effective if, say, that too is vulnerable to ice or snow jamming the mechanism. To avoid this problem a second device might well be a burster disc, whose failure mode is likely to be quite different to that of a valve. In isolating pipework, not only should the valves be locked shut but blanking plates

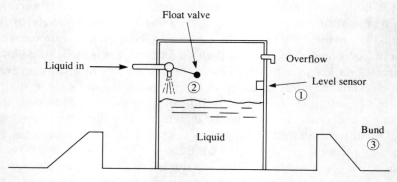

Fig 11   Defence may be in depth

should be inserted if there is any possibility of the valve being moved from its safe position.

It is not always possible to have two separate and different systems, and some alternative means should be provided. With modern technology it is much easier to introduce a 'voting' system into controls and alarms. If two out of three readings are the same then the output from those is taken as the accurate one. If safe functioning relies on an electrical safety key, then the key should be fitted with a pennant and it should not be possible to remove the key when the system is functioning.

Design can provide defence in depth, as with the typical case of storage tanks – the level monitor, the cut-off valve, and the containment (bund). (Fig. 11.) Alternatively the system can rely on one safeguard backed by a series of checks that it is in good order. Assume that there is a high voltage area, entry to which is restricted by a key that isolates the voltage and also unlocks the door. The key is the safety feature, unless it is in the control panel the voltage cannot be applied and even if it is removed entry is barred until the door is unlocked by the same key. The design of both the control panel and door locks must be such that the key is captive when inserted and turned to the active position

Another concept of attaining safety by design can be that of the use of 'weak' and 'strong' links. The principle is that, under fault or accident conditions, some features are damaged so they can no longer perform their normal function whilst others are extremely robust and survive. The principle may be used in the military field, for example, in a system containing, say, a battery, fuse, and explosives or propellant. In the event of a fire the design is such that the battery will be destroyed, thus removing the energy source, whilst the switch system is robust and remains as an isolating device. The weak/strong principle can often be used to obtain safety by careful design of the system without the need for additional devices. A domestic equivalent is the valves fitted to oil-fired central heating boilers; these have a fusible handle or wheel and in the event of a fire the handle melts allowing the valve to close under spring action. (Fig. 12.)

Not only does 'safe by design' cover the construction and use phases of the life of equipment, but it must also apply to the eventual disposal. With the ever-increasing concern for the environment the disposal of many materials is becoming both difficult and costly. The problem has existed for many years; in one instance there was a site which was used for the dismantling and scrapping of crashed aircraft. It was the practice of the site users to throw broken instruments onto a scrap heap that was eventually buried under a thin covering of earth. Many years later when the site was required for a different use the pile of earth was examined and found to be radio-active. The luminous paint of the instruments had not been recognised as a hazard and had just been buried in a casual manner.

It is, of course, not possible for the designer to cater for hazards that have not been identified at the time the design is undertaken, although by

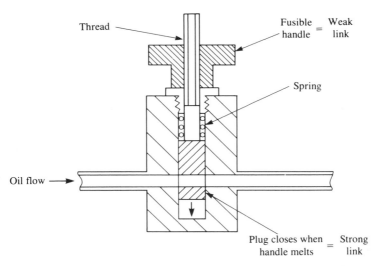

Fig 12 **'Fail safe' under fire conditions using 'strong' and 'weak' links**

keeping an ear to the ground some judgement might be made of any restrictions which are approaching over the horizon. An interesting and debatable point is whether the designer and supplier have a responsibility for adding the cost of disposal to equipment or whether the user has to pay at the time it is scrapped. Often manufacturers are the only organizations with the means of achieving safe disposal. An example is the use of CFCs in refrigerators; when it comes to scrapping them the manufacturer is best placed to reclaim the filling. Similarly, modern batteries such as mercury cells are better dealt with by the makers. The time may well come in the not too distant future when systems will be sold not only on their performance but also on their 'friendliness' for scrap. This will, in many instances, generate cost penalties, and restrict performance; the former will probably be reclaimed at the point of sale rather than by manufacturing economies. Currently the trend is to make the polluter pay for the remedial action.

'Safe by design' must, therefore, be achieved not only in the conception and development process but must also be maintained throughout the product's life and, in some instances, the disposal process.

'Fail safe' designs are a variation of 'safe by design' criteria. The principle is that, should an accident occur, the system hazard is disposed of by a predesignated route. The hazard must be progressively diminished and not maintained at the same level as it encounters each palliative barrier.

One such device, in the simplest form, is the train vacuum brake where if the pipe fails then the loss of the vacuum applies the brakes. It is, however, possible to advance a scenario where this does not happen, although it is an exceedingly remote possibility. If a train were ascending a long slope and the coupling at the engine broke, the brake pipe would be broken by the carriages pulling away. The scenario could be postulated where the trailing pipe falls onto the track and sucks in a mixture of wet snow and gravel which seals the pipe and maintains the vacuum. The carriages would then run back down the slope as the residual vacuum would be holding the brakes off. If this 'snow plugging' example is considered unlikely, then one could postulate the broken pipe falling across the rail and a wheel running over it and pinching it flat. No doubt this problem has been fully examined in the analysis of train brakes, and it has been decided these are not credible events.

Structural safety in aircraft can be enhanced if sheet materials are correctly sized and positioned so that any crack stops at a joint rather than progressing across a large sheet causing unacceptable weakness. The safety of pressure vessels can be enhanced, or the effects of failure mitigated, by selecting a material (for example, steel) that is ductile and therefore tears rather than fragments.

'Fail safe' invariably takes one into the need to establish weak links. In a very simple instance a specialized vehicle company made most of the nuts in its designs weaker than the bolts. The idea was that if there was a failure then there was a chance of the bolt remaining and perhaps reducing the hazard. Similarly they fitted all vertical bolts on the chassis with the head uppermost so that the bolt could not drop out. Fail safe features have to be clearly identified. It is of little use putting fusible plugs in a pressure vessel to prevent over pressurization in the event of a fire if the fire brigade play cooling water onto them yet fail to keep the vessel adequately cooled.

The invention of the automatic brake for lifts lead directly to the building of skyscrapers. Until this 'fail safe' mechanism was provided the concern over cable failures was the holding factor over very tall buildings.

One of the most critical 'fail safe' mechanisms has arisen with the advent of antiskid braking for vehicles. These brakes function by effectively disconnecting the breaking forces on the skidding wheel. If this mechanism fails the wrong way it would mean the driver would have no means of applying the brakes.

Designing a 'fail safe' system demands a high degree of understanding of the events involved and the tolerances of the failure mechanism or feature. Taking the most simple device, the shear pin in a mechanical system is designed to protect part of the mechanism from excessive loads. The pin strength has to be a carefully chosen value that gives sufficient margin over the normal operating loads and yet is weak enough to fail before the mechanism it is protecting is damaged. The simple electrical fuse or trip has to be a compromise between the current that can be allowed, the rise time of the change in current and the time for the device to function. A too-sensitive fuse will blow under the imposition of harmless transients unless it has characteristics that are devised to delay it's failure until a harmful current is reached.

In all cases 'fail safe' devices need extra care in design. The example of the shear pin illustrates this point. If the pin design is such that shearing frequently occurs, someone might be tempted to substitute a pin of different material. In this case it would be wise to select a nonstandard pin size so as to avoid the use of such things as bolts. By choosing a slightly odd diameter, say 4.5mm, then a 5.0mm bolt or rod cannot be used; even better is the introduction of some unique physical shape. There is a recorded instance of an error with a trial installation of a missile carried on the launch rail of an aircraft. A shear pin was used to hold back the missile until the thrust had built up. The shear pin was of two different diameters the 'function' one being the smaller. As was inevitable, the pin was one day inserted the wrong way round, and whilst the aircraft survived, the experience was most uncomfortable for the crew, who found themselves flying with twice the thrust on one side of the aircraft as on the other.

The use of 'multiple paths' is a frequent solution to both reliability and safety problems. For mechanical systems 'multiple paths' can at times present problems. For instance, a chain is used to lift an object and, for safety, a second chain, which happens to be slightly longer, is used alongside the first. Should the first chain break the load applied to the second chain is not that existing in the first but is much greater, because suddenly applied loads exert far more force than steadily applied ones. It is necessary to consider not only the normally applied loads but also the effects of their sudden transfer. Four-legged slings are not necessarily capable of lifting a third more than three-legged ones as it is not easy to ensure all legs carry the same load when attached to a rigid body. The use of a four-legged sling can actually decrease the safety. With three legs, lifting more or less over the centre of gravity, all share the load, but a fourth leg means that only two opposite legs take the greatest load if the sling lengths are not identical. (Fig. 13.)

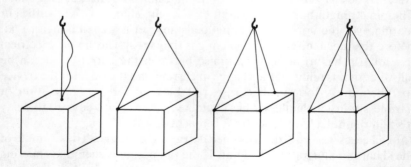

Fig 13   An increase in structure does not always give an increase in safety

'Multiple paths' or systems to increase safety do not always lead to the straightforward gains that might be expected. Taking aircraft as an example, and assuming engine failures are evenly distributed among similar engines, one can produce an interesting exercise in evaluation on the use of multiple units. On the assumption that all engines have the same failure rate the premise must be that more engines mean more failures. A single-engine aircraft is totally reliant on the one engine and failure means there is a problem of some magnitude. If twin engines are used then if one fails it should be possible to maintain normal flight on the remaining engine. However, if the engine fails on take-off, particularly under bad weather conditions, the additional safety might not be so assured. As two engines have twice the failure rate of one it could be argued that two is less safe than one. With three engines there will be three times as many failures, but it is probable that the power available will be more symmetrical, which lessens the risk on take off. Four engines have four times the failure rate, but there are three engines to take the load if one fails. However, as landing an aircraft is probably the most dangerous part there will be the need to evaluate the increased chance of more unscheduled landings due to engine failure. This illustrates the point that simply multiplying the paths may well increase the overall probability of failure.

In many instances it is necessary to rely on procedures to ensure safety. The 'rules of the road' that require drivers to obey certain conventions are an obvious example, although it is also a clear demonstration of how hazardous it can be to rely on procedures. To have any chance of success procedures must be simple and clearly defined. What is more they should be common within an area of activity wherever this is feasible. A military aircraft landing at London Heathrow crashed into the ground because the procedure for civil pilots was to set the barometric reading for the altimeter to local conditions but that for the military was to make an additional adjustment for the effects of the airfield height above sea level.

The need for clear and logically laid out procedures is well illustrated by the US comedian Bob Newheart's sketch on defusing a bomb. It goes along the following lines. "Cut the green wire" [over the page] "but it is first most important to remove the red knob". If procedures involve the use of controls or instruments care must be taken to ensure consistent layouts are adopted. It might look nice for a control room to have mirror image panels at each end of a display of racks, but it is unlikely to add to safety. Care must be taken to avoid the designer of equipment being more concerned with the overall appearance than with allowing vital items such as switches and valve controls to 'stand out' by colour and shape. If a procedure, for safety reasons, requires one of a number of switches to be operated in a hurry, then that item must be clearly identified both visually and by touch.

The method of writing, issuing, and controlling procedures has to be appropriate to the degree of safety required. All too often the procedures for a system are primarily written as operating manuals that happen to contain vital safety information. The use of coloured printing to identify safety instructions and warnings is undesirable, for should these documents be photocopied, then the whole of the text will appear in uniform colour. It is preferable to highlight safety instructions and the like in the text by 'boxing' or 'sidelining'; underlining often leads to a crowded and unclear text.

The use of procedures and the introduction of modifications to either the equipment or the documentation requires a study on how the changes are to be implemented and controlled. If the equipment is changed and there is both modified and unmodified material existing at the same time it is necessary to take considerable care in ensuring the user can easily identify the appropriate documents. If it is the document that is modified then there must be a positive means of ensuring the user is aware of the changes and is clear on their application.

In summary, if the use of procedures is the only practical method of achieving safety, it must be recognized that the chances of error are high and the need for clarity is paramount. Allied to procedures is the use of training, and this is an area that is even more difficult than the procedure route. Any equipment used in training courses should be fully representative of that likely to be encountered in real use. If manual controls are involved they should have the same 'feel' characteristics. The same requirement exists with instrumentation. If, in the real system, a gauge is subject to fluctuations due to feedback, then the training gauge should behave in the same manner.

At times it will be necessary to provide protection against the consequences of an accident or failure. There are two broad types of protection: that built into the equipment and that provided extraneously. The latter may be divided into two further classes, one being personal protection such as safety gloves, glasses, and the like, and the other taking the form of screens, water sprays, extractors, and so on. The safety protection built into equipment presents fewer problems than the unattached type. Having identified the probable risk, the designer then adds the appropriate protection. Care needs to be taken to make the added protection compatible with the working of the system. This particularly applies to the man/machine interface. There is nothing more guaranteed to encourage the modification of a safety protection system than its interference with everyday working. The machine tool industry suffered greatly from the practice of operators removing guards from equipment. On a different level, operators of, for example, halls and theatres, have long been plagued with illegal entries through the safety exit doors, and it is not unknown for these to be chained up.

As a general rule a safety feature will add to complexity, interfere with operation, reduce reliability, and increase maintenance problems. With this in mind it is necessary for the designer to take as much care over the features of safety items as over the performance-related systems. Safety features should not be treated as 'add-ons' of little consequence, but as an integral part of the equipment. Indeed, at times, the viability and efficiency of the safety items may be a major selling asset.

The design of a safety feature should make not only its identity self-evident, but also the fact that it has functioned correctly. For example bolts and locks must have visual indicators that they have functioned correctly. The need for care in design is illustrated by the example of a large piece of special lifting equipment. The lift was by means of a large eyebolt that screwed into a block of metal that was itself fitted to a crane hook. To secure the eyebolt a pin was fitted across the thread to stop any tendency for it to unscrew. Maintenance schedules required the equipment to be stripped and examined for corrosion. Following a maintenance strip the eyebolt was not screwed fully home and consequently the pin passed across the top of the threaded portion rather than through it. Eventually, after a period of use, the eyebolt started to unscrew, and fewer and fewer threads were engaged, until finally the weight stripped these and the load fell to the ground.

Protection by external means has its own difficulties. The field of protective clothing and the like is well covered by specialized industry suppliers and presents little problem to the designer. However, for the following reasons it is better to build protection into the equipment than rely on personnel protection. Even though great strides have been made in making safety apparel more comfortable, it still lacks both the style and comfort offered by general clothing. An exception to this might be safety shoes which at times are much valued at home – for gardening, for example. Likewise, being able to obtain a pair of prescription safety glasses has its attractions. Visitors to equipment frequently have to be kitted out with protective glasses, hats, and so on, and here the problem lies in providing a sensible range of sizes and styles. To allow visitors access and not to demand they use the same protection as the 'workers' tends to devalue the requirement in the eyes of the latter.

Portable protection equipment, such as screens, barriers, and warning notices, are all liable to go missing or not to be used correctly. Warning notices rapidly loose their effect through prolonged use or being left in position when no longer required. Temporary speed limit signs on motorways are soon ignored when, after obeying ten miles of temporary 50 mile/h signs no obstacle is seen. Portable protection equipment is a last resort as, being susceptible to damage and 'walking', there is difficulty in ensuring it is used. There must be clear guidelines on the use of such equipment to avoid damage, and a record must be kept to ensure it is maintained properly.

When it is necessary to restrict access to certain areas of equipment or a facility, then the selection of a suitable guard screen is highly dependent on the choice of locks. The padlock system, although secure, is open to abuse, for if someone loses a key there is the very real risk they will fit their own padlock, thus destroying any key control arrangements. Similarly, it should not be possible to remove a key from the lock unless the equipment is safe and secure. For any protective system of this type to be effective there must be a very efficient key control system. Keys must be available in the event of an emergency, they must only be issued and retained by authorised users, and they should be regularly audited. If an electronic coded lock is used the combination should not only be closely safeguarded but must be changed at regular intervals; this also means the coding should not be obvious.

The laying down of standards in whatever form is of no consequence unless they are, firstly, clear, secondly, appropriate, and, thirdly, followed. Despite many people's and organizations' ambitions, safety is all too often compromised by failing to meet one of these three requirements.

Setting Standards

As well as asking 'How much?' and 'When?' management, customers, and indeed the public are likely to ask 'How safe?'. It is possible to respond to the question and establish the safety of the system using analytical techniques and giving a 'probabilistic risk assessment'. Alternatively there may be a standard, code of practice, or similar instrument that will set the level of safety. In adopting the latter course it is most unusual for any figures to be quoted; the knowledge that the requirements will be met is usually enough. There is some comfort when numbers are offered, particularly if they are impressive, such as a one-in-a-million chance of an accident. It is unfortunate that numbers are not always what they seem, yet we have little else to offer apart from reassuring words. All too often physical evidence is difficult to obtain or, if obtained by tests, leads to endless and meaningless discussion.

It is often reassuring when the design of systems has been made to conform to specified standards or codes of practice. Sometimes these will be mandatory and may limit originality in design as they are usually based on proven technology. Alternatively it might be appropriate to adopt advisory requirements which, although not mandatory and, therefore, apparently allowing flexibility, are ignored at some risk. Codes of Practice in particular have the advantage of avoiding the long and difficult course of generating and enforcing statutory requirements, and whilst having no legal status may almost assume that standing by default.

Frequently it is assumed that following the necessary regulations will ensure that safety is obtained. One problem with all types of specification, regulation, or whatever is that there is a tendency for people to think in no greater depth than is necessary to meet the requirement. This leads to a false sense of security. An example of the fact that regulations do not cover even fairly ordinary events is illustrated by the crash of an aircraft chartered to fly a number of US Marines back to base. The civil airliner was loaded in the normal manner with its full compliment of passengers and luggage. At take off from an intermediate stop the plane crashed. It was found that the regulations for loading this type of plane were, as for all civil aircraft, based on a normal spectrum of passengers. The 'model' load assumed a range of men, women, and children, of average weight, carrying typical luggage. The marines were much above average build and were all male. Their luggage was heavy, although not excessive for military personnel. All this meant that the plane was overloaded and this, coupled with other problems, caused the crash.

The Health and Safety at Work Act dominates UK thinking on safety, and for that and other legislative standards the designer is well served by publications and specialist advisers. When designing a system it is advisable to seek this specialist help regarding legal requirements to ensure the information is correct and, most importantly, up to date. There are frequent court cases that affect the interpretation of various Acts of Parliament, and it is only those who are deeply involved on a day-to-day basis that have the facility to keep in touch with developments and to interpret the impact of judgements across the board.

In some instances there is a reluctance to specify how a standard of safety shall be achieved as this restricts the flexibility of designs. The cynic might suggest that, should an accident occur, then the producers of a regulation must share the blame, and the reason for not being specific is to avoid this happening. The UK Building Regulations, although not entirely devoted to safety, are an excellent example of how the requirements can be written to maintain standards and yet give guidance. The requirements are written to cover certain aspects of buildings such as the foundations. These are followed by design information that is 'deemed to satisfy provisions'. If he wishes, the designer has the principles of good building design to follow; alternatively he can innovate, but he will bear the responsibility of demonstrating that the mandatory requirements have been met.

In setting standards or targets for designs it is necessary to first determine some form of measure or scale that can be used to quantify or qualify the design. Numerical values are attractive in that they give a scale that can be compared, albeit at times with difficulty, with other situations and systems. They are, however, difficult to demonstrate. An alternative is to show that a new design is equal or no worse than existing ones. This brings in two problems, firstly to find out what an existing design standard is, and secondly to show the two designs have comparable characteristics.

Taking the case of establishing numerical values the initial problem is in determining not only what a particular value should be but also how it is possible to demonstrate it. For some reason or other the public, and indeed many technical people, consider one in a million to be an acceptable value. There are, of course, much more logical ways of determining appropriate risk levels than just deciding on what appears to be a comfortable number.

One example of controls or standards being set almost by default is illustrated by the insurance companies. Whilst these organizations do not, as a rule, issue standards, by virtue of their accounting system they do, in fact, impose them. Using the simple instance of the domestic car, every owner knows that his insurance premium depends upon a number of things. Primarily, the car owner incurs a penalty if he gains a bad record for accidents, and therefore pays an increased premium. The owner wishing to keep his premiums low minimizes his claims. He therefore takes care to secure the car, takes care to avoid damaging it, and takes care to whom he lends it. We have an instance here of the operator reducing the risk, not because he is legally enforced to, but because he has a financial incentive.

As a parallel in industry management, designers, for example, are concerned with making equipment and plant operating conditions safe, as otherwise they might find the premiums for insurance become sufficiently high to affect the company's profits.

In some areas insurance companies impose fairly specific conditions, and perhaps the oldest of these is the shipping industry. Boiler insurance companies are also adamant that certain standards are followed. To some extent the standards of this type of control are, in many instances, retrospective in that the imposition of higher premiums are additional conditions following a series of accidents when losses have become significant.

One cannot really consider standards for safety without at the same time considering their enforcement. In any civilized (and some uncivilized) societies there are three tiers of control over the activities of individuals, groups, and organizations. Hardly any group of people can coexist without drawing up rules of behaviour to ensure that existence is to some extent harmonious. The organization structure, be it a country or the local cricket club, usually encompasses their activities. Firstly there is the definition of the requirement (law, code of practice, rule, or similar) which may be written or unwritten. The second activity is the monitoring or policing of the actions of different parties to ensure that the regulations are being followed. The third activity is the taking of action against those in breach of the rules by the application of punishment, correction of the misdeed or, if appropriate, ensuring compensation is paid in money or in kind.

It is clear from this experience of organized human activities that those who have to set standards must also ensure there is a system set up to make sure that they are taken seriously. It is not enough to just write the rules, as the probability of their being followed is uncertain, especially if they cause inconvenience or loss of resources (time, money, materials, and the like).

The Health and Safety at Work Act is an example of the type of 'regulation' that places the emphasis on setting out what has to be achieved but not defining the route that shall be taken. The prime requirement is that the employer shall provide a safe installation, safe means of work, and adequate management, the latter embracing not only discipline but also training and instruction. The employer is left by the act to decide what is 'safe'. The Factory Inspector is at liberty to disagree with the employer and may enforce his views by serving an Improvement or Prohibition notice. It must be noted that the requirements of the Act are governed by the 'as far as reasonably practical' principle, and not by absolute standards.

Whilst the Health and Safety at Work Act is not intended to lay down the way in which safety is achieved, there are, associated with it, codes of Practice that the person concerned is supposed to follow, unless he can demonstrate that he has devised a better alternative. The Act is enforced by the the Health and Safety Executive, which embraces various organizations, including the Factory Inspectorate, the Agricultural Inspectorate, and the Nuclear Installations Inspectorate, to name but three.

The fact that the Act does not define what shall be done is, in many ways, advantageous, as the employer can adapt his working equipment and methods to suit changes in technology whilst still meeting the requirements. This would not be the case if the Act defined the way of working or the construction of equipment. The Authority's Inspector has only to establish that a method of working or a plant is unsafe, taking into account what is reasonably practical, or does not meet generally accepted practices. In other words, the Inspector does not have to show that a regulation has been broken – only that the equipment or working practices are unsafe.

In many cases safety relies in part or in whole on documents such as assembly instructions, maintenance manuals, and operating instructions.

As they form a fundamental element in the safety system they must be treated in a manner appropriate to their importance. Too often manuals and instructions are either read upon issue and forgotten or they are ignored from the beginning.

The problem lies with the policing role, and unless the appropriate management steps are taken the wilful disregard of instructions is almost certain to occur. In the extreme the most appropriate way to ensure instructions are followed is to have one person read out the check list or instruction whilst the other(s) carry out the tasks. This is standard practice for aircrew when preparing for a flight, and there is no reason why it should not be applied in other fields.

Where these manuals and instructions form part of the plant or equipment design intent there must be a proper hierarchical control system that not only ensures that the documents in the field are up to date but also that there is adequate control over modification. There should be a family tree of all such documents, some of the more important features of which are the authorizations and cross-links with other parts of the system. All-important is the establishment of a formal and easy route for proposals for changes to be fed back up the system. Failure to provide feedback at best means frustration and at worse leads to unofficial modifications.

As with many things the method or system that appears to have advantages almost always has disadvantages. To produce a standard for design or operation implies that anything that meets the standard is safe, and will always be so. The problem is that standards are much like check lists in that they inhibit thought. It becomes too easy to narrow one's considerations to the scope of the standard and either miss some important point that might lead to a failure or, alternatively, to miss some other aspect that could lead to cost or material savings. It could be argued that the final passage in any standard should read 'and what else should you have thought of ?'.

It is common practice for organizations to produce their own codes of practice, standards, and instructions, either for internal use or perhaps for their subcontractors or customers. To ensure these documents are effective it is important that they are written in such a manner that they retain credibility throughout their working life. Some essential features of these documents are as follows.

(1) The title should clearly describe what the document is about. All too often, especially if the document is one of a series, the title is either jargon, abbreviations, or just plain misleading. It should also be constructed so that in an index it falls into the area that people are likely to search. 'Brass pressure vessel safety factors' might be better as 'Pressure vessel safety factors – brass '; then if there are others on copper or steel, they will appear in sequence.

(2) There should be a coherent and clear numbering system. When numbering it is a good plan to always have the same number of digits. If documents start at 1 and run to, say, 170 it is relatively easy for errors to occur if a digit gets missed. For example, '3' could be '33', but if '1' is shown as '1001' and '2' as '1002', then it is always going to be clear as to how many digits there should be. With issue numbers it is convenient to follow the plan that draft documents are alphabetical and authorised issues numerical.

(3) The issuing authority should be clearly identified.

(4) The scope, in either task, equipment, or geographical terms, needs to be clearly defined. Similarly, if there are times when the standard should be modified or when it is not applicable, it is important that these are identified. For example, equipment may have to be operated in a certain manner except when under test. Electrical installations may have cut-out switches to isolate areas, but under maintenance or test these cut-outs may have to be by-passed, in an authorised manner.

(5) The contents should, of course, be laid out in a clear and unambiguous manner. In particular, information should not be mixed up. If there is a description of equipment then the safety instructions should not be inserted into it without some clear identity. It is important that paragraphs are numbered.

(6) Finally, the document should look right, and if it forms part of a suite, then there should certainly be some attempt at uniformity. If single sheet instructions are used, then they should all be the same size. Mixing A4 and A5 is a recipe for losing documents, and the economy in paper just not worthwhile. If the document is important it should look respectable and arrangements should be made to ensure distributed copies are maintained in a decent condition. There is nothing more calculated to ensure something is ignored than to have

a tatty piece of paper bearing the name and signature of some long
gone Managing Director

Whilst there is every intention that people should follow requirements,
there are, in practice, many occasions when this not practical. The
regulations regarding ferries operating from the UK have been modified
in the light of the Zeebrugge disaster. The ferry companies clearly cannot
rebuild their ships overnight, so the requirements have been 'waived' to
allow time for the changes to be implemented. In establishing a waiver
system it is important to ensure that the user party does not also find itself
in the position of also being the concessionary party. This unsatisfactory
situation has arisen on many occasions, and Government Departments in
particular are very practiced at the art of granting themselves concessions
against requirements they have established. The UK Government's use
of Crown Immunity is probably the greatest waiver of safety standards in
the Western World.

5

Risk Assessment

This chapter is an introduction to the concept of risk and the basic considerations for evaluating it. Whilst the assessment of risk is obviously very complicated for major systems, the basic techniques used for simple cases are similar; the variations are largely ones of scale. One of the greatest difficulties is the estimation of probability, and advanced and complex statistical methods have to be employed, especially as, in many instances, the database is small or unreliable.

In a subject that is governed by prejudice, judgement, and decisions formed in the face of inadequate data, it seems that the use of mathematical solutions to problems is an unlikely and unrewarding approach. This is not the case, and modern methods of examining designs, operating procedures, and the like can do much to bring order to even the most complex safety scenarios. By using modern techniques it is possible to examine the most complex of systems and estimate the likelihood of occurrence of even very rare events.

A dilemma that exists is the need, wherever possible, to set minuscule levels of risk and at the same time present designers with usable specifications, which should give numerate levels for the standards of safety to be attained. Assuming the favoured, but often illogical, one in a million probability of a failure leading to an unacceptable event, then this is clearly impossible to demonstrate by trial or test. The designers' solution may well lie in breaking the system into units, each of which contribute to the safety. If there can be three such items in parallel and each has a probability of failure of one in a hundred then the chance of all three failing is the much-coveted one-in-a-million. It is then often practical, if not easy, to show that a subsystem failure rate of better than one in a hundred can be achieved. To attain safety by the 'parallel' approach care must be taken to avoid any common features in the design of the units to avoid one incident or phenomenon causing two units to fail at the same time. Of course the parallel system applies to items that have to remain functional, such as a relief valve, a burster disc, or a fusible plug, all three of which might be aimed at preventing excess pressure in a

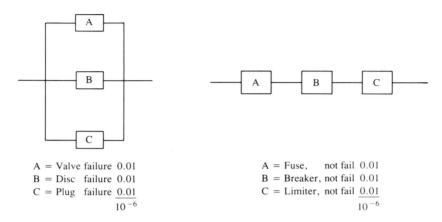

A = Valve failure 0.01
B = Disc   failure 0.01
C = Plug   failure 0.01
                   10^{-6}

A = Fuse,   not fail 0.01
B = Breaker, not fail 0.01
C = Limiter, not fail 0.01
                      10^{-6}

Fig 14   One-in-a-million ($1/10^{-6}$) obtained by sub-systems

tank that was subjected to a fire. If, however, the items are to 'fail', then they will need to be in series – for example, a fuse, a circuit breaker, and a current limiter. (Fig. 14.)

The role of management in risk assessment activities is crucial to the success. In recognising the task is one which demands attention to detail and is time consuming management must allocate adequate resources. Unless the organization is well versed in risk assessment and it is a regular feature of the organization's activities, there is much to be said for placing the work with a specialist contractor. However, this will still require a considerable amount of in-house work to provide information of various types.

Before considering the available methods of assessing the safety, or otherwise, of a system it is important that those involved understand and agree the language being used. The concepts of 'risk' and 'consequence' are key features and really determine the acceptability of a system; these and some other keywords and their definitions are as follows.

Risk	the chance or possibility of danger,loss, injury, or other adverse consequences.
Consequence	the result or effect of an action.
Hazard	a physical situation,that can cause an unwanted dangerous effect.
Probability	the chance that something will occur.

Event   something that happens, either as part of the functioning of the system or as an outcome.

Fault   failure.

These definitions are central to the analytical methods used in establishing the safety or otherwise of systems.

Whilst most people recognise the term 'risk' from everyday experience, the concept of *quantifying* it is less well known. Probabilistic Risk Analysis (PRA) is a method of establishing the magnitude of risk in such a form that comparison can be made between different applications and circumstances. It can be used to compare the risks of a diverse range of activities, either against each other or against a common standard.

Risk, then, can be considered to be a function of frequency of the event and the consequence of its occurrence, thus

$$\text{Risk} = \text{f(Frequency)} \times \text{(Consequence)}$$

It can be seen that there are two simple choices in reducing risk: either change the frequency at which faults might occur or change the consequence. Alternatively one can reduce both, or change the balance between them, so as to obtain a smaller risk figure. One might, therefore, choose to accept a smaller consequence but expect an increase in the probability of its occurrence.

It is convenient to approach risk assessment in four steps by determining the following.

(1) What is likely to go wrong?
(2) When or how often is it likely to happen?
(3) What are the likely results – consequences?
(4) Is the result acceptable or unacceptable?

The following techniques are derived from the above.

HAZOP   The identification of hazards in their qualitative form – that is, HAZard, OPerability study.

FMEA   Failure Modes and Effects Analysis can be used to identify the weak points in a system and therefore show where failures can occur.

FTA   To determine the faults that may occur in a system the design has to be analysed in a step by step manner using a network with accepted conventional 'gates'. Fault Tree Analysis represents in a diagrammatical way the build and function of a system

PRA/HAZAN   Method of determining in quantitative terms the chance that something will happen is called Probabilistic Risk Analysis (PRA) or HAZard ANalysis (HAZAN), the choice of title being fairly arbitrary.
Note that it is relatively easy for HAZOP and HAZAN to be confused and for this reason there is merit in using the term PRA instead of HAZAN.

Before embarking on PRA the management question to be asked is 'Will the effort be worth the result?' as it must be recognised that it is labour intensive. In some situations there is, however, a firm requirement to apply this technique. The real problem lies in the fact that so often where the method is employed the probability of an accident is exceedingly small. The lower the risk the more difficult it is to determine a realistic probability. Having established the risk is remote the debate usually centres on whether it is acceptable and whether the calculations are correct. In addition, a very low risk is almost impossible to demonstrate by trials.

The bottom line is 'What can you do with the result?'. In most instances the best approach is to compare the risk and consequences with existing situations. Here we run into the 'perception of risk' problem. If you tell a member of the public the risk is greater than flying he will probably reject it; if, on the other hand, you say it is less than driving a car, it will most likely be accepted. Yet flying is the safer of the two. In the perception of risk it is often the consequence that people concentrate on; even if the probability is very remote they still direct their attention to the former. The consequence of an aircraft crash is usually perceived as fairly terminal for those involved whereas the consequences of a car crash are usually considered to be injury, and only at worst, death.

To understand risk it is necessary to be clear what we mean by 'consequence' and 'probability'. Consequence is what happens: I fall over and the consequence is broken teeth. The probability is low, perhaps once during adult working life (but before infirmity through old age). As I get older I may be less sure on my feet, so the probability goes up but the consequence remains the same. If I start wearing glasses then the consequence may get worse – I break them as well as the teeth – but the probability will not change

Probability is easily expressed as a numerical term. Consequence is normally descriptive and less amenable to being associated with numbers. So to obtain a numerical value for consequence there has to be another approach.

As risk is a function of frequency (or probability) and severity, then

$$R = f(F, N)$$

where R = risk, F = frequency, and N = severity.

It can be seen that risk can be the same value for a severe event that is rare or a minor event that is frequent.

To take this further, let us assume that the risk is not a single one, but that there are various degrees of accidental damage. For the nuclear industry, which initiated the application of this technique, the concern was with possible fatalities. This makes for an easy analysis as the end result is not marginal; people are either alive or dead. A particular accident, say, the release of radioactive material, might produce x deaths from cancer in a twenty year period. We then need to estimate the number of times that particular type of accident might happen. If the event were of the magnitude of the Chernobyl accident, the number of

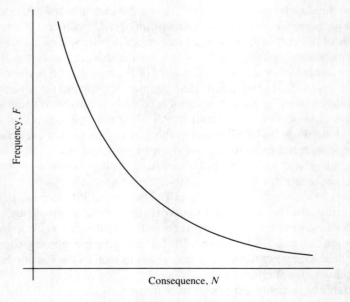

Fig 15   *F/N* curve

deaths would be high, but the frequency is low. At the other end of the scale there might only be the risk of perhaps one death in the population for that period if there was a small leak from a broken valve. By examining this range of possibilities were can construct a *F/N* curve. (Fig. 15.) If we wish to compare the installation of a reactor with that of a coal-fired power station we construct curves for both. If the curves are the same then the risks are also identical. (Fig. 16.) Life being what it is the curves are probably quite different and indeed may cross at some point. (Fig. 17.) We will now have to choose between two systems one of which is best under some circumstances and the other under a different set

As is shown later, we do not have to use death as criterion but could select any other type of event, such as days off work, financial loss, delays in journey time, or whatever. The choice of application is much wider than engineering – it could be damage to the environment, with such components as the loss of trees, the killing of wildlife, or the spread of disease.

It is, however, the human fatality aspect that has caused the most interest and this is often divided into two areas: the risk to a person – the Individual risk, and the risk to groups – the Societal risk

The nuclear and chemical industries have been pioneers in the evaluation field, largely because of the emotional impact of, as well as their actual potential for causing, damage. With these industries it is common to divide the Individual risk into several sub-divisions: the workers engaged on operating the plant; ancillary workers, perhaps in offices or other areas removed from the immediate vicinity of the work proper; and the population at large, perhaps passing the plant or living or working nearby.

The criteria for Individual risk are usually divided into bands. For example, with the minimum of two bands, above a certain level risk is unacceptable; below that figure it is considered tolerable. It is more common to use three bands, in which case the middle band is one where, although tolerable, either something needs to be done to improve the situation, or a close watch needs to be kept on it to ensure it does not deteriorate. The risk with the latter is that, to be effective, there must be some sort of monitoring system. If the plant is in existence for many years the monitoring arrangements must be very strong to ensure they do not deteriorate over time. Complacency and familiarity can allow a gradual deterioration to occur without anyone appreciating the consequent increase in risk.

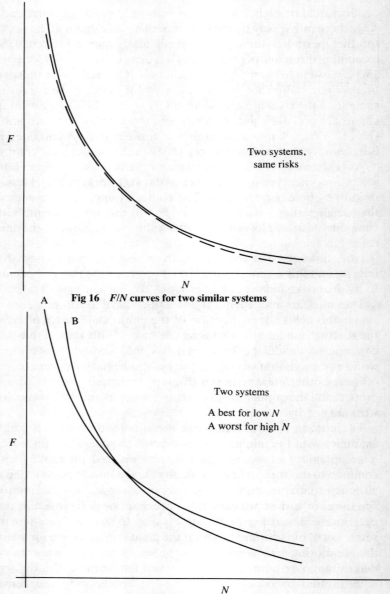

Fig 16   *F/N* curves for two similar systems

Fig 17   *F/N* curves for two dissimilar systems

Individual risk is conventionally measured by the Fatal Accident Rate (FAR), although any feature of interest can be used, such as the chance of serious injury, vulnerability to illness, or similar. Risk can be found by considering the following.

(1) How often is the accident likely to occur?
(2) Assuming the accident has occurred, what is the likelihood of the person being killed?
(3) Where there are a number of alternative risks present in one location/ situation they must be aggregated to obtain the overall risk.

Societal risk is effectively determined in the same way but only one set of criteria is used. Societal risk is concerned with the number of fatalities, that is, 'how many' is more important than 'who'. Thus, twenty workers or twenty passers-by are usually regarded with equal concern. Care must be taken in using this criteria that all persons are not always perceived as equal by the public. Twenty men lost at sea is probably more acceptable to the population as a whole than twenty children killed in something like the Aberfan disaster.

In assessing Societal risk it is essential to consider the exposure of the relevant population. In the case of an earthquake, those in the open are probably at less risk than those in some buildings. However, if there is an explosion, buildings may offer some protection – unless they are glass-walled, in which case they may make things worse.

Whilst the risk analysis techniques are primarily used for the determination of human casualties, the basic techniques have wider application. They can be used to evaluate the worth of protecting assets. For example, a particularly valuable painting or ancient archaeological site may be at risk from some industrial or even natural disaster.

The analysis work is time- and cost-consuming, so the decision to initiate it has to be justified. There may be a statutory or similar requirement, in which case there is no doubt as to the need. Where this incentive does not exist the reason may be that the organization concerned wishes to gain the approval of the public by reasoned argument. Alternatively it may be that the study will make not only for a safer system but also protect the capital assets of the organization. The employer may also wish to reassure his labour force that the system is safe.

During a system's design and development programme there should be reviews of progress and an evaluation of the safety information gained at each step. Frequently safety is regarded as a fall-out from the design process. It may well be that there is a sudden realization the the design is a 'no hope' system and there needs to be a radical rethink. On the other hand it may well be that it is suddenly clear that the risk is going to be so small that in-depth investigations are not warranted.

There are no universally accepted risk levels and, indeed, within a single field there are often anomalies. It is usual to concentrate on the major, but remote, events where a large number of people might be killed, yet of the some 20 000 accidental deaths a year, most arise due to 'small' accidents. For example, some 5000 people are killed on the roads each year, yet it is uncommon to have an accident causing more than a few fatalities. The worst recorded motorway accident caused less than 20 deaths. It is worth considering whether the money spent on pursuing the major events would not be more effectively redistributed toward examining the minor ones.

For our three groups of people, the operators, the ancillaries, and the public, it is necessary to decide on the acceptable risk level. Let us take the public as a baseline, as a figure for the risk of everyday life might be assumed to be a good starting point. Even this is not simple, however, as some groups of the public are at more natural risk than others. People living in areas of high radon emissions are more at risk from cancer than those in other areas. Smoking, overeating, and alcohol are all factors which make the determination of a realistic baseline risk very difficult. It would be difficult indeed to convince a smoker that he should work on a dangerous industrial process, because his everyday life risk is higher, rather than the nonsmoker who, using his own lower-risk standards, should not work on it! A further twist to taking the median for the population is that it means a plant in one country might not be acceptable in another. As a rule, however, people expect an artificial and imposed risk to be significantly lower than a natural or voluntary one.

If the study shows the risk to the individual to be above that for the public, then it is clear his work puts him at a disadvantage. Normally steps should be taken to reduce the risky activity (or activities). In some instances this may not be possible – for example, agriculture, deep sea diving, and mining. In traditional fields of work the individual can be expected to understand which of those are more risky than normal. In the case of new plant, processes, or operations it is unlikely that this risk will be clearly understood. Indeed, if it has taken a detailed scientific analysis to find the risk, then the individual is certainly not likely to know of it, or if he does know, he is not capable of quantifying it.

To assume a person has knowingly accepted an above-norm risk two factors have to be determined. Firstly, has he had full information presented in an intelligible manner? In other words, has the information been supplied in a form that he might reasonably be expected to understand. Secondly, has he been informed of the alternatives that exist? These may or may not be acceptable, and could range from a change of job within the organization to the lack of a job at all.

The FAR value naturally varies from industry to industry, and to assess a new system it is obviously desirable to use figures from a similar field of work. One problem in determining a realistic FAR is that the data is sparse. Not many people get killed in most industries, and when they do quite often the cause is something commonplace, like being run over or falling off a roof. In other words the fatalities are not so much specifically industry related as 'general activities' accidents. Because of this, data on industrial accidents must be treated with great care.

The chemical industry FAR is around one death for every 25 000 years of work. This needs translating into hours and shifts – it is not calendar years. Looking at it another way, in a workforce of 25 000 there should be 1 death a year, if work is at the rather high rate of about 2500 hours a year.

It has been suggested that a trivial risk is one in which there is one death in 10 000 000 exposure years. Whether this type of statistic really means much in quantitative terms is debatable, but it has the merit of providing a yardstick for comparison. If a system is shown to be twice as good as this figure, then considerable comfort is felt. If it is twice as bad, then, whilst not a cause for complacency, at least it is not that catastrophically bad.

These figures are for the death of a person in the group, and not for any one individual, which is an entirely different matter. As with so many of these types of figures, the vital answer that is missing is 'When?'. Although the likelihood is remote, there is no reason not to expect the accident to happen almost immediately. Indeed, to maintain the statistical value, there could be two deaths in a short period, followed by a very long gap to the next casualty, just to average out the figures.

Public concern is not a linear response, nor is it a very tangible one. For one thing, the public has a relatively short attention span. For example, the outrage caused by the Zeebrugge ferry disaster, whilst laying the ground for long term improvements, has not really changed the situation by a significant amount. Ferries are still able to sail with their bow doors open with no additional 'fail safe' engineering measures to prevent water getting in. It is expected (hoped) that operator discipline has now been improved.

We are now in a much better position to understand and evaluate risk, but on the other hand, the advances of engineering and science mean that we are creating more systems with the potential for generating a major accident. We are, however, probably getting better at eliminating the smaller industrial accidents, as well as naturally occurring risks, such as disease.

6

Assessment Techniques

To determine risk there are a number of techniques or methods that assist in the logical evaluation of what is likely to happen and when. The field of reliability studies has been the basis for the assessment technology, as the need to present reliability in quantitative terms was established long before the similar need for safety. The nuclear industry provided the initial impetus for the technology and it has been applied to an ever-increasing number of activities across the whole range of industry. Risk analysis can be more appropriately described as technology than science, as the need to provide both a quantitative and qualitative judgement means that many decisions and conclusions are only valid because they have been based on experience and not on arbitrary values.

As the essential mechanics of risk analysis are comparatively simple it is not difficult to train engineers and scientists to undertake this type of work. The real expertise and specialization lies with the interpretation of data and the determination of the likely frequency of very rare events, often when the database on which such judgements are to be made is somewhat lacking. On the negative side, and this is a matter that must be taken into account, too often the teams task is seen as detailed criticism by people who have little responsibility for getting the project completed. This impression is particularly relevant where the design is fundamentally a sound one and no 'discoveries' are made, as it all seems to be a waste of time; hence the criticism can be that a lot of effort was spent on discovering the obvious..

Whilst the assessment of risk can be, and indeed at times is, a full-time job, there is the possibility of tedium setting in and people working on 'automatic pilot'; they may well begin to ask the questions in a routine manner and loose some of the 'inquiring mind' attitude that is essential for success.

One obvious problem is the recording of the information, as the charts can become quite large if the information is to be legible. Computer aided recording can, of course, accommodate what is effectively a very large sheet of paper, although this is not quite as helpful as it might seem as only a small portion can be viewed at one time.

Because it is often preferable to use staff not directly connected with the design team for safety analysis, for the smaller organization there is considerable merit in placing such work to a specialist contractor. Should this route be adopted frequent reviews of progress are well worthwhile to avoid the chance of missing the opportunity to cut short the investigation; if only for the fact that the contractor has a vested interest in expanding the task rather than concluding it.

The common feature of all of these techniques is that for a system of any significant complexity they are very time consuming and require the most careful management. As the methods can be used to analyse a system at different levels, spanning the broad concept to literally the last nut and bolt, it is relatively easy to finish up with a monumental task plunging deeper and deeper into the design. However, the dilemma is that it is often the small component failure that leads to a major accident so the need to become engrossed in detail is sometimes unavoidable.

Even with computer technology an analysis can get unwieldy and it becomes difficult for any one person to be able to grasp the whole system. The problem with comprehensive and very detailed results is that people come to accept them without question, as the amount of work seems of such a magnitude that it must surely have been done thoroughly. When an analysis demonstrates that the chance of a hazard occurring is exceedingly remote, there is probably a greater risk of some outside factor being overlooked than there is of the identified accident happening.

There is no guarantee that a systematic risk analysis will be 100 percent effective, but it is, nonetheless, very worthwhile, provided a false sense of security is not built up. For potentially very dangerous systems there is no alternative to undertaking the full analysis, as we cannot rely on 'back of envelope' assessments made in good faith.

One of the most important features of Probability Risk Assessment (PRA) is that it enables comparisons to be made between various activities that each carry some form of risk; we can then decide if we wish to pursue one or other of a choice of alternative designs. On the other hand we may use the figures to compare these activities with some acceptable figure, say the risk of everyday life, to judge if that activity is acceptable.

To identify the possible hazards of a system the HAZard and OPerability (HAZOP) study technique can be used. Properly applied this will identify what might happen; in common with Value Engineering and similar techniques the success depends on the user being able to ask the 'supposing/if' question.

The questioning might well follow the 'more of/less of' routine. For this purpose it is the practice to use key words or phases to provide mental triggers as to what might happen if certain parameters are changed. Experience has shown that, in most industries, the following phases serve the purpose

NONE
MORE OF
LESS OF
PART OF
MORE THAN
LESS THAN
WRONG ADDRESS
OTHER

In some instances it may be confusing to apply the whole list and in others it may well be that some other word is more appropriate to the particular industry. The principle to be followed is that of assuming a change has taken place and evaluating the consequences, deliberately changing things to enquire into what might happen. The procedure follows a routine such as is shown in the following example.

Typical activities for a HAZOP examination.
- (a) Identify general condition, feature, function, and so on.
- (b) Narrow the field to concentrate on smallest handleable unit of interest.
- (c) Analyse – by applying systematic criteria, for example, a 'what if' type list.
- (d) Chart the variations of condition from (c), for example, power failure, power surge, and so on.
- (e) Examine the various reasons for each, both general and specific.
- (f) Determine consequences.
- (g) Determine action required, if any, to make the consequence acceptable.
- (h) Select next subsystem, unit, feature, to study and go round again.

Note that it is probable that the above series of activities will have to be a cyclic process dealing with the reasons and consequences of various failure modes for a single unit; in other words, loop (d) to (g)

As the starting point is the selection of an activity or subsystem it can readily be appreciated that the opportunities for making deeper and deeper investigations can grow at an ever increasing rate. This is where the judgement enters the management side of the activity. It is sometimes necessary to make an arbitrary decision to finish the work at some partially completed stage to avoid the whole exercise getting out of hand.

If, for example, the method were applied to a vehicle brake system dealing with the wheel cylinder unit, the questioning might well be 'What happens if?':

More of = an excess of fluid pressure is applied;
       = wheel locks;
       = loss of control.
Even more pressure
       = damage to cylinder and or disc.
Less of = reduced/zero pressure;
       = reduced breaking;
       = loss of control.

and so on.

But this is not the end, because by understanding the brake cylinder and pad assembly function it can be seen that, when not operated, the pressure must be zero (or thereabouts); so

More than zero
       = rubbing of the brakes;
       = undue wear;
       = probable loss of breaking in long term.

The HAZOP method can, of course, be computer aided, but it is essentially an expert-driven method and cannot be a rigid questionnaire routine. Whilst check lists may act as an aid, it must be appreciated that they can channel thinking.

HAZOP is time consuming and tedious, but it is very effective. Its main values are that it:

(a) is systematic and recorded and is reasonably intelligible to people from a wide range of abilities and backgrounds;

(b) forces an examination of the obvious and expected but does not permit the focussing on those aspects at the expense of the obscure the unexpected – it therefore encourages/demands breadth of thought;

(c) makes people think of what can go wrong, rather than pursue the more comfortable line of what will go right;

(d) gives a fall-out benefit in that it displays the system's functions in a logical manner.

Its disadvantage are:

(a) it is labour intensive and usually involves design staff who need to get on with the design work;

(b) it can become an end in itself if not properly managed;

(c) if the system has been properly (safely) designed it seems, to those undertaking the analysis, to be a waste of time, as they do not appear to make any changes to justify their work.

For very complex systems Failure Modes and Effects Analysis (FMEA) is particularly useful. The process is one of defining faults or failures and then determining what might have caused them. This is unlike the HAZOP study, which takes the system as a whole and then explores changes to it. For FMEA the system is divided into convenient units; these may be engineering sub-systems existing in their own right, or they could be functional ones.

The size of the unit can either be as big or as small as seems appropriate. It is essentially a 'what if' process. Assumptions on failures are made and their escalating effect (if any) traced up though the system; it is also extended down the system into the particular unit under consideration. For example, if we consider an engine in an aircraft the upward consequence could be a crash; the downward line would take us to, say, the failure of the magneto or fuel pump, and so on.

FMEA is complementary to Fault Tree Analysis (FTA) and it can be used as an input to the latter. As FMEA involves very detailed work absorbing considerable effort it should be applied where the need is greatest rather than as a matter of routine. Having identified critical items by other means FMEA is best applied after the detail design has been done. (Fig. 18.)

The method of analysis for FMEA would normally be as follows:

(a) select unit (subsystem) to be examined;

FMEA for car brake pipe					
Unit	*Mode*	*Unit effects*	*System effects*	*Characteristics*	*Counter measure/ Remedial action*
Pipe	Crack	Leak	Loss of braking	Oil expelled and visual	Stronger pipe, protect pipe, sleeve pipe, etc.
Pipe	Bend, kink	Stop flow	Loss of braking	Visual only	Protect pipe, clamp pipe
	As above		Brakes jam on	Visual only	As above
Pipe	Corrode, external	Leak	Loss of braking	Oil expelled and visual	Protective finish
	Corrode, internal	Stop flow	Loss of braking	Failure	Change fluid/ change pipe material, protect pipe
	Corrode, internal	Stop flow	Brakes jam on	Failure	Change fluid/ change pipe material, protect pipe
and so on . . .					

Fig 18   FMEA chart

(b) select/devise a failure;

(c) derive the cause;

(d) determine the effect on the whole system and identify actions, consequential effects, and so on;

(e) determine the effect within the subsystem and identify actions, consequential effects, and so on;

(f) note and analyse safety implications, counter measures, and the like, for (d) and (e);

(g) loop as required.

As with so many non-specific techniques the effectiveness is dependent on the imagination of the analyst. The FMEA prime requirement is that the system should be adequately defined down to the level of study required. This means the interdependency of each unit and its companion must be defined. Having described the system in adequate depth the operator than needs to identify failure modes. Supposing a car were being examined and the lowest level which was initially chosen was that of components. Therefore a typical item would be the brake pipe which might be considered to fail. Failure could be caused by over-pressure, corrosion, physical damage, or even obstruction. It might however be worth considering an even lower level of model of perhaps the surface finish of the pipe, where failure could be identified as corrosion, physical damage, poor quality control, or something similar.

The danger is, of course, that the FMEA method can get unwieldy, and it is necessary to use a considerable amount of judgement in deciding the level of detail. Quantification normally requires not only knowing how vulnerable a component is but also how likely it is that the contributing event (environmental, for example) is going to occur. As with all of the analytical techniques, judgement, experience, and technical knowledge are the essential ingredients.

It is not unreasonable to extend the study to the man/machine interface. The 1989 Kegworth air crash was mainly caused by the crew mis-interpreting the instruments and shutting down the wrong engine. An FMEA would have revealed that failure to fully understand the reading of the instruments could in turn cause this catastrophic failure.

FTA may be used for a variety of purposes, although the most common use is for reliability and safety studies. Fault trees are simple to construct and are essentially a building block system using a few conventional symbols to show the interrelationship of events.

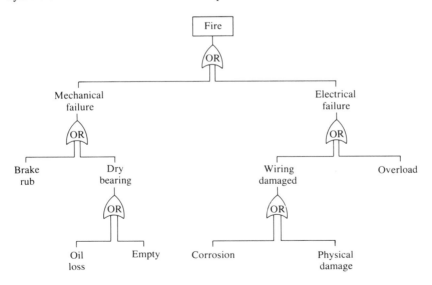

Fig 19   FTA chart

FTA involves the systematic search for the cause of a preconceived failure. Supposing the failure selected was the one needed to initiate a fire in a railway coach due to a mechanical or electrical fault.

To give a pictorial illustration of how a fault (or hazard) might develop, the diagram showing the links between the final fault event and those leading up to it is constructed. (Fig. 19.) By inserting probabilities at each node it is possible to estimate the probability of the fault developing.

By convention, and for no other reason, the end event, the fault, is either placed at the top or left hand side of the sheet. The events likely to lead to this end fault are linked by lines which form branches of the tree. If there is more than one event that can lead to the fault these are connected by 'And' or 'Or' gates. The gates' titles describe their function exactly. An 'And' gate means the the events leading into it both have to occur whilst the 'Or' gate means either one can cause the fault event.

Using the simple 'And'/'Or' blocks we can follow even the quite complex systems through to their basic parts. For the more elaborate analysis there are other symbols covering such variations as 'Inhibit', 'Not', and so on. (Fig. 20.) We stop expanding the tree when all of the input ends (at the bottom of the tree) can be allocated probabilities. If the probabilities of a part (or even the whole) of a tree cannot be derived, the system is still of considerable help in appreciating where weak points might exist, and it can be used for sensitivity studies if rough estimates are used for the lack of firm data on probabilities.

To illustrate FTA, and as a change from engineering, let us assume we wish to evaluate the choice between eating from the delicatessen across the road or the *Greasy Spoon* cafe next door to the office. Both carry degrees of risk. Food poisoning is possible from either place. Fiona at the delicatessen is quite hygienic but is inclined to use high risk foods such as eggs, shellfish, and, because she holidayed in Italy, wild fungi in season. On the other hand, Bert at the *Greasy Spoon* is a great one for cooking at high temperatures, but his washing up water is somewhat dubious, and the family pet rotweiler has the free run of the kitchen. To add to the problem the route to Fiona is via a very busy road, so there is the risk of being knocked down, whilst the steps down to Berts are worn and slippery.

If using Fiona's delicatessen we can judge that, to get food poisoning, we need for the mushrooms to be on the menu and for Fiona to pick the wrong ones. This is shown by putting the fault – poisoning – at the top (or left-hand side). There are two inputs to the fault: that mushrooms are on

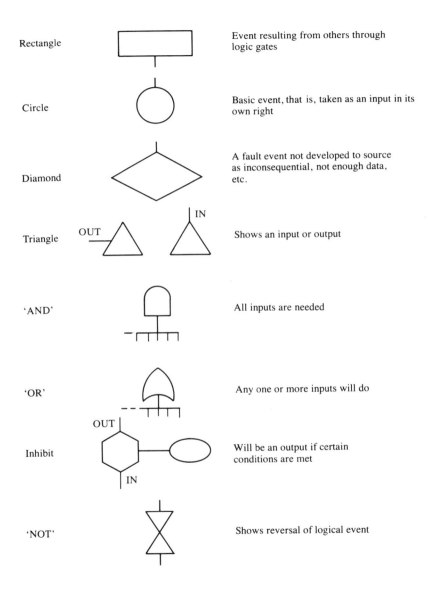

Rectangle		Event resulting from others through logic gates
Circle		Basic event, that is, taken as an input in its own right
Diamond		A fault event not developed to source as inconsequential, not enough data, etc.
Triangle	OUT / IN	Shows an input or output
'AND'		All inputs are needed
'OR'		Any one or more inputs will do
Inhibit	OUT / IN	Will be an output if certain conditions are met
'NOT'		Shows reversal of logical event

Fig 20   FTA symbols

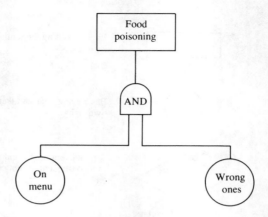

Fig 21   FTA example 1

the menu, and that Fiona picks the wrong ones. If we know the probabilities for these events we need go no further. (Fig. 21.)

We can show more complications if we assume Fiona's friend Gerald helps with the picking and he can also collect the wrong ones. Now we can use an 'Or' gate. Indeed we may think Gerald is less knowledgeable than Fiona and when it comes to the final analysis we may put his probability of a mistake as greater than hers. There is, however, a further complication in that mushrooms do not grow all the year round, and whilst the good ones grow for a two-month season the poisonous ones only grow for one month. We therefore need another branch to the tree. (Fig. 22.)

We stop expanding the tree when all the inputs can be allocated probabilities. To show this let us consider we do not know the probability of Fiona picking the wrong mushroom, but we can say that for her to do so there must be two other inputs: that it must be the season for the poisonous mushrooms to be growing, and that they must be growing in that location.

What we need, however, is some means of *comparing* risks. The risks themselves first need defining and as well as food poisoning there are traffic and walking accidents. What we need is a measuring device to enable us to put values against the risks. We can choose days off work as our units. A bad case of poisoning can be fatal so that becomes infinity unless we believe in reincarnation. At the other extreme a very mild upset may just give us a headache and we take the afternoon off. The old

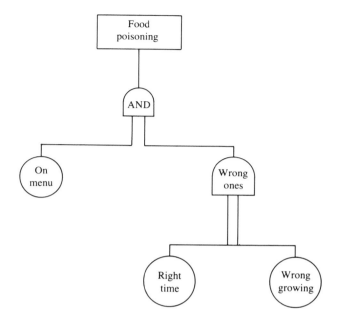

Fig 22   FTA example 1 expanded

toasted egg sandwich with fresh egg mayonnaise might warrant two days as would the dirty plate. Something more severe, caused by Fiona's mixed wild mushroom and shrimp roll might be a ten day affair, as would Bert's Steak Tartare, which he learnt to make from his friend who works as a cleaner in a big hotel in London.

For either choice of eating there are a range of possibilities which can span from the half-day loss of work to the total lack of activity in the office. If we select one of the suggested incidents we have a measure of its severity – that is, days off work – and we can also decide the frequency of its occurrence. Assuming we work at the office for ten years (before the Fraud Squad strikes!) we might assume we have Fiona's mushrooms twice a year, and of those twenty portions only one might be the wrong fungus, giving a frequency of 0.005/year. (Fig. 23.)

If we work out all the different ways in which the owners can damage or kill the customers we can obtain a series of figures of severity and probability. If we wish to think of this as risk, then

$$R = \mathrm{f}(\,F,\,N\,)$$

where R = risk, F = frequency, and N = severity

We can substitute whatever we wish for Fiona and Bert. The shops can be installations, systems, such as transport, or any other activity base.

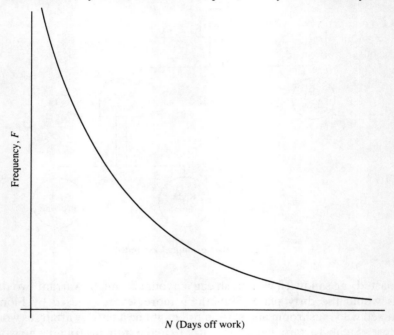

Fig 23   *F/N* curve for Fiona's food

The risks can range from toxic chemicals to mechanical injuries. We might wish to compare the *F/N* curves to determine which is the best option. Bearing in mind the inherent inaccuracy of obtaining reliable data on the probability of rare events, unless the curves are markedly different the judgement as to which is best must be made with great caution.

Assuming it is possible to agree a figure for risk, then one has to examine the results of the study to decide first whether the risk is acceptable and if not what can be done about it. Let us assume that Fiona's insurance company decides one case of poisoning a year is the absolute limit.

However, Fiona's risk may be greater than this, so she must solve the problem by perhaps only serving mushroom dishes on half the number of days that she used to; or even dumping Gerald and going out with daddy's nice farmhand Jed.

The very simple examples of Fiona and Bert can be expanded, and the principle will encompass even the most complex system. What will change apart from the scale is the complexity and quality of the data and the various options that are available. In many instances the data will be nonlinear and more difficult to handle. It is recommended the reader explores a few domestic or similar examples to judge some of the complications in using the above techniques, and it should not be a surprise if some quite anomalous and confusing answers emerge.

7

Evidence and Assessments

It is unlikely that purely physical evidence will be sufficient to form a case for determining a design is safe. There will be a need to put various trial results into perspective and to convince people that what has been achieved is both accurate and credible. To construct a good case it will be necessary to examine historical evidence as well as gather new material. It is unfortunate that history, although alleged to repeat itself, rarely does so under exactly the same conditions. Similarly, trials aimed at ensuring that equipment will behave in a safe and predictable manner will inevitably have grey areas and inconsistencies.

The designer will often have to seek advice from others more knowledgeable than himself on certain aspects. He will have to weigh and balance the information he has gained to present a coherent picture. Unless these tasks are approached in a fairly orderly manner the end result will be a fragmented story that is likely to lead to prolonged debate which obscures the real purpose.

Whether one starts with a historical search or whether one initiates trials from scratch is very much dependent on the particular circumstance. Historical information is rarely as complete as one would wish, neither is it likely to be recorded in a convenient manner for comparison with current and future events. On the other hand, to obtain fresh data is not only expensive and time consuming but also inefficient.

The first and most important step to take when looking at historical information is to determine how comparable the information really is with the current situation. It is likely that human error information is more comparable than equipment failures. The early caveman probably mistook the instruction to turn right and fell into the hole on the left just as often as his modern counterpart. The tremendous change in materials and their properties ensures that engineering history is riddled with uncomparable equivalents. For example, modern controls on cranes are much more sensitive than in the past so failures of lifting cables should now be much rarer.

Probably one of the biggest advances in safety has been achieved through increased reliability. The modern test pilot has far less to worry about in terms of safety than his equal even twenty years earlier. Paradoxically, the increasing use of less skilled labour, or indeed no labour at all, has led to the elimination of many sources of error. Whilst the craftsman was able to make a good job of an assembly, each one could vary in some way from the other. Aircraft are 'repaired' by changing the black boxes, and there is a much better chance of getting a fully serviceable replacement than a repair standard. There is also a reduced chance of tools being left inside aircraft to jam the controls, for not only are there fewer on-aircraft repairs, but the control systems are far less vulnerable to obstruction; indeed, the fly-by-wire aircraft has no moving parts until the control surfaces are reached.

When relying on history to provide experience the immediate problem is that it is rarely recorded in sufficient detail at the time. Certainly significant accidents and failures are recorded, debated, and judged in considerable depth. However, it is the bulk of past experience, rather than the 'high spots', that provides the most significant information. The number of failures that did not occur and what had been done to bring about this quiescent state of affairs is not going to be the subject of detailed reporting. The reason for this is that, almost by definition, management is the control of crises. Thus only the activities that lessen success are taken note of. For example, there are probably fully detailed accounts of the numbers of accidents caused by the site workers who are wearing safety helmets. It is less likely that there is a record of the number of hours spent on site by workers wearing helmets who do not have accidents.

The first step is to compare the designs in considerable depth. This means it must be established with a high degree of confidence that not only was the design accurately specified but also that it was actually built that way. What materials were used and were they specified or just bought as propriety items? Some companies, perhaps the majority, have no mechanism for keeping the user informed as to variations (improvements) in their products. As long as the interface and general performance is to specification events inside the suppliers' interface are often judged to be of no concern to the purchaser

It might be thought that an improved product is bound to be superior to the earlier version. This is not necessarily so. If an electric motor has more power available even though it is the same design designation it may well be that over-speeding can result. Where the old design kept the machinery running below some critical failure speed the new one might allow it to exceed it. Structures that are more rigid than earlier ones may distribute the load in a different manner and cause a completely different failure elsewhere.

A careful examination of earlier designs might show features which ought to have failed but did not. It is as important to find out why a failure did not occur as it is to examine why it did.

Having examined the design it is also necessary to compare situations. As with the design itself, it is the ordinary and unreported that might be of interest. For example, the modern office, workplace, or storage area is likely to be much warmer and drier than twenty years ago. Some materials rely upon a certain amount of moisture to retain their properties. The excessive dryness in some locations causes a build-up of static electricity, as does the use of insulating materials such as plastic sheets and nylon carpets.

As well as comparing the similarity of situations there is the comparability of people. Are the operators and users more or less skilled? Are they subjected to the same discipline? Is there an effective hand-on of information when staff change? On the latter point, in many areas staff are very mobile, and ten years experience in the same field may be rare.

For new and novel systems it is at times difficult to establish the safety by reference to past practice and historical information. The solution to this might be the use of experts to examine the design and make recommendations. Unlike investigating boards, courts of enquiry, and so on, these experts should be expected not only to make a contribution to the design but also accept some responsibility. Too often the expert, or consultant, called in to help the designer hedges his contribution with so many conditions that, in the end, although he has raised positive points, there is no feeling that he is part of the design team.

When seeking advice, the expert's contract must clearly set out his remit and responsibilities. The problem that occurs so often is that someone brought in to examine and comment on a design can quite easily find all manner of things that can go wrong, but does not evaluate the likelihood of it happening. This attitude is frequently seen in politics and in the press, where all manner of red herrings are raised no matter how remote the chance of their occurring. The contract with the expert adviser, then, must require him not only to investigate potential problem areas but also to evaluate them and give a firm view as to their probability of occurrence. Another limitation that must defined is the extent of the work. It is not unknown for someone charged with looking at a particular part of a system to gradually expand this remit until he has investigated and perhaps turned upside down all manner of areas which there was never any thought of him approaching. Frequently the expert or consultant feels he can only justify his position by either making a large and significant discovery or, failing that, a lot of small ones. It should be clear from the outset that to agree there is no problem is just as much an achievement as finding that there is one.

In summary the use of expert advisers needs to be approached with some caution, although frequently they make very worthwhile contributions, especially as they often bring a breadth of experience that may not be available in-house. These comments apply equally well to both the individual consultant and the specialist company. There is no doubt that in a great many ways the use of specialists is well worthwhile. They do not have the same vested interest in a design as the originator and can view things from a different angle. Many specialist organizations have access to large quantities of data which the individual company may not have. Thus, providing everyone knows their responsibilities, limitations, and objectives, the use of experts can be worthwhile, especially as so much of safety depends on imagination and analysis of non specific matters.

If the appointment of experts is not considered to be justified by management they frequently decide to form a committee to look at the design instead. Indeed, if the organization is large enough, there may be a standing committee or committees to undertake such tasks as a matter of routine. It is important to distinguish between the body set up to examine the design to agree, or otherwise, if it is satisfactory, and the committee charged with contributing to the design. The former should not offer design solutions but should seek to set the requirements and determine if the design meets it. The committee formed to assist the designer should do just that.

Design committees, if unavoidable, need to be made up of staff who have a positive contribution to make. Not only do they need to have members who are technically qualified but also, on many occasions, the broader aspects of management, sales, accounting, contacts, and so on, can be helpful. It may be that a particularly thorny safety problem is difficult to solve by means of design features alone, and the sales representative could well point out a way forward through changing customers' requirements and practices. Similarly, if the accountant understands the implications, additional funding to solve the problem may be more forthcoming than if he were left in isolation.

The running of committees to help the designer should do just that. Occasionally committees or groups are set up to solve a particular problem and to avoid these gatherings becoming self-perpetuating, the designer should be in a position to control their activities. If this is not done, then the tail is wagging the dog. Management should regularly review the work of the committee, and once it has ceased to contribute in a fully effective manner it should be disbanded. The committee must not be allowed to make demands on the designer without accepting the responsibility for its action. If the committee demands additional trials and tests, it must take the responsibility for assisting in obtaining the funding. Likewise care must be taken that the designer does not use the committee as a devious means of expanding the work. It is relatively easy for a designer to invite the committee to support additional trials and then turn this round to make it look as if the committee asked him to do it.

Trials and assessments are the mainstay of safety assurance. To demonstrate a system works is, of course, far more convincing that a paper analysis. But it is also two-edged in that on some – usually particularly inconvenient – occasions, the trial shows just the opposite result to that desired. It is, therefore, important to be very careful in both deciding what trial or demonstration to give and to whom to show it.

Before deciding on a trial or test it is worthwhile deciding the real purpose of the exercise. Quite amazingly trials are often embarked on without this essential decision being made. A corollary to this is the need to define what will be regarded as success and what will be regarded as failure. It is often through debating the latter that the former becomes much clearer. Life being what it is, partial success, or failure, is a frequent result, so it must be recognised that, in the end, judgement will be needed

A frequently overlooked point is that of build standard. The final production equipment may not be available and some intermediate design might have to be used. In this case the build standard must be recorded by every means available, especially if the trial might result in the loss of material. Intermediate designs are often produced to less than perfect drawings and specifications. This, coupled with a certain amount of 'hand crafting', can completely devalue the results of the trial.

The generous use of photography, especially colour, and video, can save many hours of argument as to the condition things were in before the trial. If, for example, containers were being tested, then the photographic record of the real condition of all surfaces before the trial may enable damage during the trial to be more accurately assessed. It may well be that the test container has already had some previous testing experience, or has suffered some damage during the preparations for the trial. Unless this is recorded the damage may be allocated to the wrong event.

In dynamic trials, shock, vibration, and the like, and the condition of parts prior to the trial is of crucial importance. The recording of surface blemishes pre-trial is essential to enable determination of any rubbing or deflections during the test. The photographic evidence is also very useful and convincing in post-trial debates and often can be used to reinforce the designers opinions and assurances in the 'inquest' that follows.

Written procedures for the conduct of trials are a necessity, not an optional extra. Too often the failure to properly start a recorder or camera loses vital data and, should one be working away from base, a list of materials is absolutely necessary. It is surprising how often even well-equipped trial sites and test houses do not have available the simple devices such a the right sized socket key or roll of temperature recorder paper. Lifting attachments frequently do not match and the site crane hook is just often too big for the shackle provided.

When embarking on a trials programme, especially one which includes both safety and performance trials, some form of ranking is useful. Supposing there are a number of safety trials leading to the launch of a missile. There are, no doubt, a number of trials which, although important to the overall programme, are not essential at a particular point in the programme. For example, if there is to be a trial firing from a ground range it may well be that trials such as container waterproofing, transport shock, and so on, are not essential precursors. What is required is an 'essential trials logic'; this will show at each stage of the programme those trials that have to be completed before the next step can be taken. It will also identify trials that can be done on an 'as and when basis'. (Fig. 24.)

Having completed the trial the next milestone is the report. There are many sources of information on different aspects of report writing, so the following only addresses points that are particularly important for the safety field. It cannot be emphasised too much that a good report is vital. The acceptance of a design as safe depends upon confidence. With performance there is usually something positive to report, such as power attained, velocity, temperature, and so on; with safety the report is often negative in that something did not happen, and people need to be assured

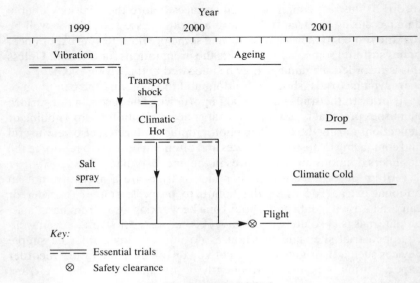

Fig 24   **Essential trials logic**

that in everyday life it will still not happen. Safety reports are often studied by lay people who for their own reasons may be determined to show that something is wrong.

The format and style of a report will depend upon the parent organizations 'house style'. Whatever this style may be, it is crucial that the objectives of the trial are stated, and the evidence of success or failure. Great care must be taken with the language, and every sentence should be positive and unambiguous. This may seem obvious, but experience shows that reports, even by official bodies and organizations of high standing, often lack these attributes. Whilst a report may be clear when it is written, because a particular topic is relevant at that time, some five to ten years later it may well be almost incomprehensible. It is necessary to be sure that reports are complete in themselves, and where they cross refer to other sources of information arrangements should be made to ensure those other sources remain viable.

The layout of the report should reflect a positive attitude. It should come to the critical point early, with the background and detailed information following in a clear and logical manner. The aim of the report is to quickly establish confidence and authority. It is not helpful if the report grinds through every action until the conclusion is reached on the last page. The reason for this is that if the positive result is not shown at the beginning the reader is left to form his own conclusions as he goes along, and these conclusions may be wrong.

Although the overall style of a report depends on the parent organization, the first page should state the objective and the result. As much detail as possible should be consigned to annexes. If the trial is a very large one with information covering many pages it is helpful to issue a management summary provided there are adequate cross references to the body of the main report. An important detail that is frequently missed even in the most competent of organizations is the need for comprehensive paragraph numbering. There is nothing more confusing than a group of people talking or writing about two different paragraphs but thinking they are both addressing the same one. The aim is to get the reader on the side of the designer and the easier the reading, the more likely the success.

The *Concise Oxford Dictionary* defines 'assessment' as having to do with the establishment of the monetary worth of something. In safety the object of an assessment is to examine information and draw conclusions. The reason for using assessments is usually either because it is not possible to demonstrate by trial and test that a certain thing will happen, or that the information obtained from trials and tests is not as complete as one would wish.

An assessment differs from a trials or test report in that it represents a gathering of information, perhaps from various sources, and uses this to make a case for what is the likely outcome of certain events. Assessments are used where it is not possible to carry out a totally realistic trial.

For example, if it was necessary to agree that a container could survive a crash in an aircraft it is unlikely that resources would be available to actually fly an aircraft, with the container, into the ground to see what happens. In any case there are a number of ways in which an aircraft can crash: head on into a hillside, a glancing collision with the ground followed by hitting a building, and so on. The normal arrangement is for a specification to be agreed as representative of the crash – perhaps a drop of the container from a certain height followed by a fire trial of agreed duration. The compilation of the trial environment is an assessment of the representative conditions of a crash manipulated to encompass a range of crash conditions.

In constructing an assessment there is a need to draw upon a variety of sources of information and ideas, thus building up a logical argument as to why a system should be considered to be adequately safe, even though this has not been directly demonstrated. Assuming some trials data of similar systems is available, it is necessary to establish the link between those systems and the one being evaluated. This comparison can be positive: there is a direct read across between the new system and the associated one. Thus one would argue that, because A was safe, then B will also be safe under the same conditions. Alternatively there are the negative points: A might have been unsafe under certain circumstances, but B will be safe because its design is different and avoids the unsatisfactory features of A. If at all possible it is important to avoid the optimistic approach. To say we have never had an accident of that type is a fairly weak method of assessing the probability of such an event occurring. If the argument for safety of a system is to be based on the premise that the event will not occur it must be backed by the appropriate theoretical study such as would be produced by a Probabilistic Risk Assessment.

Assessments stand or fall by the confidence they engender. In something as simple as a fire or drop trial the evidence of survival is there to be seen and it is often backed up by instrument readings. With an assessment no such concrete evidence exists, and what theoretical evidence is offered still remains a paper study.

There is no perfect way to assemble an assessment. Inevitably there will be an iterative process. Some of the key points involve determining that the actual scenarios are realistic. Is the available data truly relevant? Are Failure Mode and Effect Assessments needed? Can a Probabilistic Risk Assessment be made? What level of assurance is required from the assessment? Is it to make a legal comparison, or should it be 'beyond reasonable doubt' or 'on the balance of evidence'?

On some occasions assessments will be needed to bridge the results between two similar trials. In the case of equipment using hazardous materials it may be necessary to have two trials which each have active materials replaced by inert ones. A rocket containing fuel and an oxidant could be tested under, say, vibration conditions with the vehicle containing fuel and an inert oxidant substitute, and vice versa. The two results could then be combined. It might, however, be necessary to assess the representative nature of the results. For example, the cooling effect of liquid oxygen, which was not present in one trial, may or may not be judged to affect the validity of the trial.

A further example of the need to make a reasoned judgement is when the environment to be represented is that of vibration combined with a steady *G* load. The assembly may be tested on a vibrator and the steady *G* simulated by applying loads by a tensioning system. The latter is, of course, liable to error; no matter how the loading is applied it will only simulate *G* at isolated points and not as a uniform distribution. Mounting a vibrator on a centrifuge also introduces errors due to the *G* gradient along the axes.

On occasions there will be a need to mount what might be called the 'Grand Trial'. This event is usually staged to demonstrate the likely outcome of some particularly disastrous accident and involves the possible loss of expensive or scarce equipment. One such trial was held by British Nuclear Fuels Limited and the Central Electricity Generating Board to demonstrate the effects of a railway locomotive and carriages hitting a Magnox spent nuclear fuel container.

Quite often these trials add very little to the information already held against a particular design. They present a considerable risk in that they usually cost a lot of money and are carried out in front of a critical audience. Thus, the margin for error is small and the adverse reaction can be large. One such trial was mounted in the USA to demonstrate the reduction in fire risk to an aircraft by the introduction of a change to the fuel. The aircraft was radio controlled and an error led to the aircraft crashing at the wrong point of the trial range and the trial failed.

A problem with these large demonstrations is that they are frequently over-ambitious. Pressure is put on the sponsors to have worse and worse scenarios. If a certain standard has been agreed for a trial there is the difficult decision by the organizer as to whether to aim to add a bit extra to be sure the objectives are covered, or whether to aim directly for the target and stand the chance of just failing to met it. An additional problem, and this is common to any trial, is that the build standard of the equipment can be affected by instrumentation. In addition, it is usually undertaken with 'as manufactured' equipment, rather than with used equipment which has suffered the usual wear and tear.

The Magnox spent nuclear fuel container trial is an example of the dilemma faced by organizers. Critics complained afterwards that the train was made up of old coaches which might have affected the impact, and it was not agreed that the container was placed at the worst angle to the impact point. At times the only realistic achievement that should be expected is a demonstration that the item under test withstood something that *might just* be like a bad accident. A one-off trial is a poor statistic, and a complicated one is even worse. The demonstration for fitness is best achieved by a series of trials which gradually build up knowledge.

With any trial it is advisable to decide in advance what is to be regarded as a success; this saves a lot of post-trial argument. With the large, one-off, trial agreement on what will be considered a success is essential. Take a simple example of a container designed to protect the contents against a drop of one metre. Is the trial successful if the container is damaged but the contents survive? If the container is supposed to survive, then is it to be fit to be used again? If so, how many times? Should the contents be new each time if there are to be a series of trials? If not, how many trials should they survive?

If trials represent a series of environments there is the need to decide when to examine the test system for damage. It may well be that waiting until the end means that the particular environmental factor that caused the damage cannot be identified; on the other hand, breaking down assemblies at each stage carries the risk that the subsequent re-builds will add a degree of uncertainty to the assembly build standard.

In summary, an assessment is the argument one presents to convince others to agree a decision that the design is safe. It must, therefore, be not only soundly based but also inspire confidence. In addition, recognition must be given to the needs of the reader and the argument should, therefore, be presented in his terms. Any errors, evasions, or omissions are likely to devalue the whole document, and the subsequent effort needed to regain credibility will be quite significant.

8

Causes and Compromises

Accidents occur for one fundamental reason – there has been a mistake. The mistakes take many forms and occur at various times, but in the end it all comes down to the fact that something happened that was not identified and dealt with. There are very few accidents that could not have been predicted before they occurred. The fields where unforeseen events can cause harm tend to be ones involved with chemical or radiation effects on life. The complexity and possible long term nature of reactions makes prediction difficult for both the phenomena and their magnitude. Among engineering systems there are much fewer opportunities for surprises.

Breaches of safety are usually caused by:

– not realising it could happen;
– knowing it could, but not believing it would, happen;
– knowing it would, but not considering the consequences to merit prevention on economic, social, or other grounds;
– knowing it could happen, but underestimating the size of the event.

Generally speaking designers, managers, and politicians are optimists. They have to be as their aim in life is to make things happen, and unless they have a fundamental belief in success they are unlikely to achieve anything. It is, therefore, rather against their nature to think of accidents and safety generally, as these normally impede progress. The discipline required to reduce performance to enhance safety is a hard one and requires a considerable amount of mental juggling. Every pound or dollar spent on safety adds to the cost and not to the performance. We are, then, starting off with an inbuilt reluctance to really explore what might go wrong with a system.

There are three basic areas where the necessary standard and activities toward a safe system might fail. The 'inception', where the design is being produced and specified. The 'execution', where the system is constructed and commissioned. And, finally, the period of 'use' – which is what it is all about. The first area requires imagination and decision, the second, discipline and understanding, and the third competence.

The designer of a system often has certain safety standards laid down for him to meet. These might be comprehensive and legally binding requirements, or they may just be informal codes of practice or even company standards. In these cases the layman may well expect safety to be absolute, with any chances of significant accidents being so remote as to be disregarded; this view is clearly inaccurate.

Firm requirements, at whatever level of authority, are often a great contribution to safety, but there are serious limitations, especially in the long term. The most authoritative requirements forming part of the law are usually, indeed almost invariably, the result of the experience of a number of serious accidents. Being instruments of statute they are almost always compromises between the needs of safety, the practicalities of life, commercial interests, and the tolerance of the user – or the public.

Legal requirements can make for some strange decisions. It is legal to mine uranium ore but not to dispose of it by burial as the radiation level of the ore is too high.

As usual transport, because of its involvement with everyday life, provides the best examples of compromise. In the UK seat belts were introduced as compulsory for the front passengers in cars, yet passengers in the rear seats were exempt from the need to wear them for a long time afterwards. In fact rear seat passengers are not only at risk themselves, but are a danger to the front seat passengers as well. Not only was the law inconsistent in this respect but it also still allows other factors to come into account. Front seat passengers may be exempt from wearing belts if they have an adverse medical condition. Why, one might ask, is the requirement not that the seat belts, or other forms of restraint, must be made tolerable to the medically exempt classes?. It is almost certain that the reason for this anomaly is one of cost. It is relatively cheap to produce a simple standard belt. Therefore governments must believe that the cost of protecting certain classes of individual is either not sound economically or of no real concern.

The occurrence of accidents, or their consequences, is not always to be laid at the door of the regulators. Crash helmets are recognised as a significant means of reducing head injuries to motor cyclists. There is, therefore, a requirement in the UK that crash helmets shall be worn by those using motorcycles – except for members of the Sikh community. Here, then, is a conscious decision by authority to allow a certain element of the public to put themselves at risk because they belong to a religious group, and yet forbid people whom might judge they are able to take the risk from taking it.

At times commercial needs prevail in setting standards. To some extent this is not only practicable but justifiable. In recent years this economic influence has reduced, with the additional cost resulting from increased regulation being accepted. It was a great shock to many people to learn at the time of the *Titanic* disaster that the shipping regulations did not require the ship to carry enough lifeboat accommodation for the complete compliment of passengers and crew. The current parallel with the *Titanic* is the use of Roll-On, Roll-Off ferries. It is known these ships are vulnerable if a hole is made in the side; without internal compartments there is an extremely high risk of a rapid capsize. Perfectly sound technical solutions to this problem are available, yet there is no regulation requiring the remedy to be fitted to ships in current use.

We have, therefore, a cause-of-accident category where social and economic factors influence the level of safety.

Another cause of accidents is progress. Regulations are, as has been stated, largely followers of accidents and, as such, tend to prevent a recurrence of a class of accident that has already been experienced. In very many instances there is no continuing review of state-of-the-art changes in designs and fields of activity. For many years road passenger coaches in the UK were treated as cars for the purposes of many road regulations, and were subject to the same speed limits and so on. In recent years the power-to-weight ratio of coaches has increased dramatically, as has their size and carrying capacity. At one time the coach was regarded as a struggling vehicle which was by its nature limited in speed. The modern coach now has power to spare, with a top speed capability of the order of 90 mile/h or more. After a long series of accidents, largely attributable to the increased performance of these vehicles the regulations were changed. The applicability of the changes was, however, spread over a number of years, although technically all could have been implemented in a short time. Thus we have both a change of situation and an economic factor affecting the safety standard recognised as necessary.

There are strong arguments for increasing the UK speed limit on some roads to avoid 'bunching', and to recognise that the law is flouted almost with impunity. At the same time it is recognised that, whilst many *cars* are capable of over 100 mile/h, there are far fewer *drivers* capable of driving at that speed.

A general sense of optimism among designers and managers at times leads to the 'well it could happen but I do not believe it will' syndrome. This tendency is reinforced by at least two influences. Firstly, the need to spend time and money on safety studies when there are perhaps more interesting things to be done. Secondly, the person who goes round the project casting doubts on safety tends to be lower down the popularity list than the optimist.

In the 'knowing it could but not believing it would' category, the R101 airship and the US space shuttle *Challenger* are classics of their type. To fly a new airship in bad weather on a long maiden flight was, to say the least, risky, and even irresponsible. By all accounts politics prevailed over engineering, and the accident did more than any other event to remove lighter-than-air transport from the scene for many years. The *Challenger* was an accident waiting to happen. Space flight is, by its very nature, a relatively risky business, for at the start and finish of each flight there are significant periods where the machine functions completely outside human control, and is committed, with no options of a second chance. The design contains some 700 items, any one of which is critical to a successful flight, yet which have no back-up or redundancy features. Whilst this may seem to be unsatisfactory, it is not unreasonable, as to increase the safety margin would impose either design or weight penalties which would probably prevent the vehicle ever lifting off. Perhaps the prime example of this is the fact that the return flight is unpowered, and there is only one chance at touching down. To provide flight power would either mean installing engines or adding some means of using the main rocket motor.

It was recognised that the first shuttle launch was a pioneering adventure, and yet all subsequent launches were no less risky. Admittedly the equipment was more proven with each launch, but, by the same token, it was also wearing out. By obtaining a series of successes the authorities convinced themselves that the system was reliable enough to introduce publicity events into the programme. The introduction of a female school teacher was hardly the basis for a scientific experiment, although it was justified on those lines. Another flight contained a politician, and one was planned for a journalist.

It is difficult to eliminate the 'knowing it could but not believing it would' type of accident, even when the number of victims is likely to be large or significant from some other point of view. There are usually one or two reasons for this regrettable inevitability. In many instances the success stakes are high: 'New airship flies to India' headlines for the R101, and 'School teacher in space' for the *Challenger* were probably factors that affected the decision process. Coupled with these needs the importance of maintaining programmes plays an important role. If there have not been any accidents, then the enthusiasts who are prepared to take the risk usually hold the upper hand, and the voices of caution are ignored. However, it is important to realise the person taking the decision may not have the background knowledge that enables him to really understand the probability of an accident occurring.

This apparently reckless decision making attitude is, in part, a result of the growth of the size and/or importance of projects. In general, the unusual is more risky than the routine. The designer of a chemical plant is more likely to put a greater value on safety than the equivalent manager of a politically sensitive project, such as in the space field. One has to beware, therefore, of high-profile pioneering projects. It is clear that for the correct amount of caution to be introduced into the management process, two conditions must exist. Firstly, there must be recognition of the risk, and, secondly, there must be a means of introducing it into the decision-making process.

There are adequate techniques for evaluating most risks, even in the most complex system. It is generally only a limitation of resources to apply the methods, or a reluctance to accept the need, that opens the way to accidents. Provided the risks have been evaluated, the next barrier is the introduction of the correct judgement into the management chain. Normally the management structure of a project takes account of the needs of safety to the extent that the senior manager *listens to the views* of the safety managers. After a significant disaster the system is likely to be changed so that senior management *cannot proceed without the approval* of the safety authority.

The Channel Tunnel is an interesting example of a project going ahead before safety has been agreed. At the point where the completion of the tunnel bores was imminent, the design of the signalling system, as well as other matters affecting safety, had not been finalised. There is, therefore, a pressure on the safety authorities, in that they could hold up the project to the point where financial support collapses, as the technical aspects of safety have not been cleared. As in the case of the Channel Tunnel, the setting up of a safety authority with mandatory powers does not remove from that authority the pressure to consider the implications of their veto on a successful completion.

The Channel Tunnel example is an extreme one in that there are pressures from two countries and major financial implications. On a smaller scale this type of pressure exists right down the the small product and system. The careers of the designers are greatly affected by the completion of their work in a timely and cost effective manner. The safety analyst who has to give his advice, or even authority, for the advance of the work, is still a human being, with career and domestic pressures. If senior management are 'know it could but do not believing it would' philosophisers, the safety adviser may face the difficulty of knowing just how far to go in making his point. It is relatively easy to argue he should stand his ground, but, with a career and mortgage, how far is it realistic for someone to do this? If the accident can be shown to be highly likely, then the task is relatively easy, but if it is remote, but, nonetheless, possible, then the difficulties increase.

The reality of life is that, in many instances, the policy of 'knowing it will but not considering the consequences merit prevention on economic, social, or other grounds' is often justified. All transport works on this basis. It is clear that, now and again, a passenger will fall out of a train, but, short of sealing the doors, it is a risk that has to be accepted. Similarly, road and air travel both carry their inherent risks. To make this policy acceptable there has to be a fine judgement not only on when something will go wrong but also on the likely reaction to the consequences. The problem is that the acceptability of accidents is based neither on logic nor on numbers. Indeed, having correctly assessed the right 'casualty rate', for want of a better description, the whole judgement based on this can go badly wrong over time.

It is, in fact, unfair to always blame people who judge the prevention of a particular accident as not being worth the cost. Trying to establish what the public will pay for safety is almost impossible. Very few goods are sold on their increased safety over their competitors. Safety is often a question of judgement; weighing up the risks and consequences and then, most difficult of all, determining the worth of prevention. It is interesting that passenger transport will often offer increased comfort at high premiums, but never offers increased safety in exchange for money. One can cross the Atlantic extra quickly by Concorde, but no one offers an extra safe aircraft, with rear facing seats, non-combustible cabin materials, adequate gangways, and the like, and yet many people are afraid of flying.

Underestimating the size of an event is usually due to inadequate study. It has long been recognised that clouds of combustible material (usually vapours) can burn in a fairly energetic manner. What was not understood for a long time was that, given a big enough cloud and the right conditions, one could actually achieve detonation which turned a major fire into a particularly nasty type of explosion. This fact is now the basis of some modern explosive weapons.

In examining a potential accident the important extra question to ask is 'is there anything else that could contribute to this event'. Take a fire in an oil tank – a fairly simple scenario. However, if their is a layer of water in the bottom the situation may be quite different. Water may seem to be a fairly innocuous substance, engendering no additional safety risk, but if, during the fire, hot residues or perhaps material from the tank sink to the bottom, then the water may suddenly boil. The result will be a sudden generation of steam, and the oil will 'erupt'.

Taking a potential dust explosion, it may be judged that, because the amount of dust in the area is small, the explosion will be limited and contained in a small area. One result of the explosion will be an air wave which, a short distance from the point of explosion, may not necessarily be of sufficient intensity to cause structural damage, but a secondary effect may be the stirring-up of dust in adjacent areas, which in turn could explode.

There are, in fact, very few accidents that cannot be avoided, and the majority of those occurring are due to the recognised boundaries of safety being crossed, either deliberately or inadvertently.

Safety is almost always achieved at the expense of reliability, and may even require the removal of performance features which, paradoxically, may seem to degrade safety. Suggesting to a motorist that a safety mechanism will relieve some of the forces applying his brakes might meet with incredulity, but the Antilock Braking Systems (ABS) being fitted to many new vehicles works by reducing the braking force applied to a wheel that is skidding, thus ensuring maximum braking effort is available. The overall effect is to produce cars that can stop in a shorter distance. This is a splendid means of enabling the driver to retain control under heavy braking, and avoid or reduce the impact of a frontal collision. There is, however, a penalty in that, if the driver with anti-lock brakes has another car close behind fitted with conventional brakes, the chance of a rear-end collision is probably increased.

Anti-lock braking systems are a prime example of the achievement of safety through the apparent reduction of performance. To ensure safety the authorities require that such braking systems shall switch off in the event of failure, with the system automatically reverting to conventional braking. At the same time a warning indicator must show the change over has occurred. The way in which these requirements are met varies from manufacturer to manufacturer as each solves the dual technical problems of performance and safety in their own way. The regulations give neither a requirement nor any guidance on the criteria affecting safety. How long a time interval is allowed before a failure is detected and what system monitoring (testing) is required are left unspecified. Thus, whilst a requirement for safety has been specified, the interpretation of this is left to the individual manufacturer, so it is possible to have differing standards of safety all meeting the same specification.

As an anti-lock braking system will normally only show a failure when it is needed (that is, when the brakes are applied), manufactures build in a self-test facility which monitors the health of the system when it is not in use. This may take the form of an automatic test when the engine is started. The ability to design ABS units has only been achieved through electronics, so the safety is achieved by the addition of new technology and complexity.

Because the systems have been 'sold' on increased safety the public has accepted them without the need for comprehensive and technical explanation. The same public would probably not accept a new chemical plant with the same degree of confidence. It is perception that is the key to this acceptance, and this is coupled with the feeling that the driver, and not someone else, is in control.

In the altogether more dangerous field of parachuting, the acceptance of an 'anti' safety feature is based on two concepts. Firstly, the wearer believes he is well enough trained not to make a mistake and, secondly, he believes (probably correctly) that the feature prevents a greater risk of injury occurring. The quick-release buckle on a parachute is, in essence, operated when the wearer judges the parachute has become a liability rather than an asset. There is no safety stop in that the release is achieved by a simple one-handed action (turning the buckle and hitting it). This action should only, of course, be taken after the parachutist has reached a point of safety, that is, firm ground – *not* hung in a tree. This is an extreme example of procedure being the only safety feature, and training being relied on in a stressful situation. It is interesting that the same technique is not applied to hot air baloon baskets, where dragging along the ground is a similar hazard.

The majority of large aircraft are unable to land at their full take off weight, and it is practise to provide a fuel dump system to enable a rapid loss of weight to be achieved. The preferred routine is to burn off the fuel rather than jettison it. As neither procedure is a quick solution in an emergency, it is clear that a balance has been struck between commercial needs and safety; the commercial requirement is to carry the maximum load at take off, whilst the safety requirement is to be able to land at all times.

The use of ejector seats on military aircraft demonstrates not only the calculated risk element that is balanced against safety but also the differing logic for similar situations. Ejector seats have proved themselves very reliable and have saved many lives. The risk element is twofold. Firstly, there is a relatively small margin between a slight injury and a serious one caused by the ejection process. The ejection process itself, therefore, carries a significant risk, although it is obviously the best choice. There is at least one recently recorded incident of an accidental ejection thought to have been caused by the seat being lowered in flight and a foreign object damaging the ejection system such that it fired inadvertently.

A double standard is evidenced by the provision of ejection seats for combat aircraft but not for others operating in combat zones – heavier aircraft such as tankers and bombers. There is also no provision for helicopter escape, even though these are front line aircraft. In these instances it is a case of the user deciding the safety level to be achieved, although due account has to be taken of public opinion if too many casualties result from the set standards.

The realities of life are clearly demonstrated by the introduction of features that contribute to safety only by degrading some other part of the system. The majority of train doors in the UK are opened by lowering the window and working the handle from the outside. Thus it is necessary for a member of the public to lean out of the window of a door to open it, perhaps when the train is still moving. What is more the doors are hinged alternately left and right, so the slowing of the train is helping 50 percent of the doors to open and the other 50 percent to close. This risky procedure does not seem to be too dangerous in practice, although it is only necessary through lack of a better design. The doors on some trains are locked and released according to the actions of the crew. The London Underground is an example of doors totally controlled by the crew, yet it is deemed unnecessary on many surface trains. The main reason for making doors open from the outside is to prevent accidental opening from the inside. This, then, is a choice between two risks, both of which are difficult to evaluate, and which could both be avoided by a relatively simple design change.

On a more technical level, it is a frequent requirement to monitor a system to establish whether or not it is in a safe condition. Taking the simple case of pressure or liquid-level gauges, these often require additional penetrations of the container to gain access for the monitoring pipe or wires. These penetrations are extra weak points in the container and need to be carefully designed. Similarly the use of additional wiring in electrical systems can provide additional conduction paths into the equipment in the event of lightning strike, RF pick up, and so on.

Attempts to increase safety associated with cars has at times proved a mixed blessing. Some years ago manufacturers in the USA fitted a monitoring system to seat belts which prevented the driver moving away until the belt had been fastened. The first result of this was that a number of drivers started leaving the seat belt fastened to enable them to drive off quickly. It was soon realized that an even greater hazard existed: it was reported, on a number of occasions, that women, on being approached by undesirable characters, were unable to drive away from the danger without first fastening their seat belts. The industry soon discarded the belt inhibiting system and relied on a warning light and buzzer instead. The introduction of centralized locking creates a similar risk; anyone wishing to gain the safety of a car automatically unlocks all of the doors, thus enabling someone else to get in as well.

The use of tempered safety glass has produced a major reduction in the number of injuries caused by broken glass, yet it has presented other problems for the engineer. A British Rail sleeper train caught fire in the night and, because the guard had locked the corridor doors for security, some passengers were unable to escape – the windows proved too difficult to break without special tools. A similar thing happened in coach crashes; rescuers were unable to break in to help passengers, and the passengers were similarly unable to get out. As a result of these incidents special 'hammers' are fitted adjacent to the windows; but not until the need had been proved by accidents. If tempered glass is replaced by laminated glass,there will be a need to rethink this solution as laminated glass cannot be easily broken with a simple tool under most circumstances. In some cases where laminated glass is fitted to coaches the design is such that the window can be released from the frame from the inside.

The provision of doors and windows in aircraft weakens the hull structure. Obviously doors are necessary to allow the passengers to board the aircraft, but it is arguable if the number of doors provided for evacuation in an emergency has been weighed against the number of accidents caused by failures of those doors precipitating an accident. Windows are provided at a normal spacing of two per row of seats, yet on most long flights the passengers cannot see the ground, it is dark, or the blinds are down to allow films to be shown. So what real purpose do the windows serve? In the British Royal Navy's nuclear submarine messes there are curtains where windows might be to give the impression of being in a normal room and not well below the surface of the sea. This idea could well be acceptable to passenger in civil aircraft, especially if the windows were replaced with suitable pictures.

There is a continual search for a compromise between the remedies that could be employed to deal with accidents and those that people wish to employ. The fact that many safety features are, in effect, creating fresh problems means that we are transferring the critical features from one part of the system to another. In addition, as with the policy of making holes in the pressure hull of an aircraft to give people windows that they cannot use, logic and safety do not necessarily go hand in hand.

9

Scenarios

The major input to many safety studies is the specification of what accidents are to be considered. Unless it is agreed as to what possible events could occur to cause an accident then the work will be based on very uncertain foundations. Surprisingly often studies are carried out without any real consideration of the initiating event or events.

The nuclear industry in particular has suffered from continual movement of the goal posts. Objectors to reactors and nuclear processing are adept at raising new issues. The protagonists and antagonists follow each other round in what seems to be an increasing spiral as the targets set by the 'anti's' keep moving on. This process is incredibly time consuming and makes the task of the safety analyst very difficult.

When any safety study is undertaken there is not only a natural increase of knowledge, with a consequent need to move the targets, but also considerable merit in doing so. What must be achieved is not only to make the targets more realistic in what may be called the 'plus' direction (that is, more stringent) but also to move them the other way (relaxation).

Having agreed a set of conditions that must be met then it is prudent management to arrange to formally review these at different stages of the project. If this decision to review the criteria at certain points is made clear from the outset, then there are a number of benefits in the long term. Firstly, there is the obvious economy of saving unnecessary work. There is the consideration implanted in the analysts' (and others') minds that everything is not cast in concrete, but is open to review. This will lead to a more questioning approach. An important point is that, when the review time comes and a change of target is justified, the proposal does not look like an excuse to get out of a tight corner. If reviews of objectives are not scheduled, not only is there a problem of finding the opportunity to make the change but also it looks expedient rather than planned.

Deciding what is the worst that can happen is not too difficult if all of the things that can go wrong are just added together. Unfortunately that is likely to kill any design. It must, however, be admitted that, in the real world, problems do seem to come all at once: 'they come not in their single spies but in their legions'. It is prudent to cater for several things going wrong at the same time, but judgement must be exercised as to how many and in what combination.

It is always helpful to look back and analyse what has gone wrong in the past with similar systems. In the UK the source of much of this information in the chemical industry is supplied by the *Loss Prevention Bulletins* issued by the Institution of Chemical Engineers. There are many sources of information available for other fields. Some of the best collections of data are within insurance companies who use the information to set their premiums. Unfortunately these are not normally made available to outsiders.

There is a surprising lack of data on the causes and consequences of road accidents. The statistics for these normally concentrate on fatal accidents. Anyone wishing to determine the risk of carrying goods by road will find that the information on damage to vehicles is confined to those where a fatality occurred.

When considering a combination of events it is helpful to ask if any single one of them is survivable on its own; if it is not then the other events are fairly irrelevant. If an aircraft is going to fly into a mountainside at 500 mile/h it is not very relevant if the fuel tanks leak or not. On the other hand, if it is going to crash onto flat ground, then integrity of the tanks may be vital to the final outcome.

In endeavouring to describe the worst possible accident it is tempting to have a brainstorming session and accumulate a list of possible candidates. Indeed, this is very worthwhile, but it is possible to be rather more logical and start with a credible accident and ask what would make it worse, followed by 'and worse than that', and so on.

Assuming, for example, one were designing a road tanker to carry inflammable liquids and the requirement was to survive a motorway crash. As a first accident one could postulate a burst tyre causing the vehicle to swerve off the carriageway onto the hard shoulder. Worse than that would be for it to hit a bridge support; even worse, the bridge could collapse onto the vehicle. This could be worsened further by a petrol tanker on the bridge falling onto the original vehicle. And the escalation can continue. Having reached a point where it is all getting rather ridiculous, it is possible to back-track and find a realistic stopping point. Firstly, what are the chances of a second tanker being on the bridge at all? It is not uncommon to see tankers crossing bridges, so it is not a factor that

can be ruled out. Consider the bridge falling down. Here a fairly short
piece of research may well show that motorway bridges have never fallen
down. This, then, is getting to be a remote possibility. Would the vehicle
actually hit the bridge support? If bridges are, on average, five miles apart
and fifty feet wide then

$$\frac{5280(\text{feet}) \times 5(\text{miles})}{50} = 528{:}1$$

anyway. If we assume only one in a hundred bridges are likely to fall (a
very generous estimate) we have a roughly 50 000 to one chance.

By rapidly analysing the 'wild' scenarios it is possible to start to weed
them out. It does not need very accurate information in the first place.
Some people may say 'why bother to go through the analysis?', after all it
is fairly obvious that the probability will be a very remote one. However,
unless the exercise is undertaken, the question will keep coming up and
the same arguments will ensue. It is far better to be able to say it has been
thoroughly examined rather than just respond that it is an irrelevant
scenario. Convincing people that a system is safe depends just as much on
the approach to both the problem and the critics as is does on the
technical analysis.

Setting up the worst credible accident is, of course, the mainstay of
protest groups and similarly minded people. From the point of view of the
system designer there is a need to treat such aims as, at the very least,
meriting serious attention, but *not* to the extent of ignoring mundane and
minor possibilities. Nearly all major accidents – even worst case scenarios
– have their origin in the lower order events. Taking the example of the
road tanker with the burst tyre, the real effort should go into ensuring the
tyre does not burst.

As well as major systems and serious accidents, the problem of
unrealistic targets exists even in very small areas of design. Taking the
domestic iron as an example, it is the practice of consumer associations to
subject these to a drop test, simulating a fall from an ironing table. It is
reasonable to expect a user to drop an iron once or twice in its lifetime,
but how many times it should survive is a debatable point. The trap is
that, with such tests, the manufacturer of an iron that survived, say, three
times as many drops as other makes would score more points for good
design, but one could argue that, above a certain number of drops, the
figures become unrealistic.

There is a similar over-specification where safety and tools and equipment are concerned. Just how much should skill and training be taken into account? The requirement to take safety precautions can be carried to extremes, the consequence being that the precautions become so obstructive that they are ignored. It used to be a well-known practice for guards to be hurriedly fitted to machine tools as the Factory Inspector entered the gates. Better guard design has reduced this considerably.

It is an important point that, given extreme accidents to guard against, if the precautions are excessively onerous they may not be implemented. This in turn may lead to smaller accidents occurring that would not have done had the requirements been less strict. Safeguarding against the very remote accident by complicated arrangements may make the lower level risk more likely. The Three Mile Island reactor accident was really due to people believing that the safety systems were so complex and perfect that they only had to follow the instructions, and not think things through.

In the process of considering extreme scenarios – the worst of worst cases – inevitably the value of a life becomes a major factor. Society is not very good at deciding the value to be placed on human life, as not only is there an inherent difficulty in finding acceptable factors to take into account but also the manner of death also affects the thinking. Generally speaking the killing of one or two people does not merit much discussion amongst the public at large unless it happens to be particularly newsworthy, or unless there is some personal connection.

The approximately 25000 accidental deaths a year in the UK average out at about 120 a week, or nearly 20 a day. Given suitable adverse publicity the costs of saving a life can be quite high. British Rail manages to kill only a few people each year (say 25) which is about 0.1 percent of total accident casualties. To cut this already low figure tens of millions of pounds are spent on additional safeguards, which could work out at between £500 000 and £1000 000 each. To transfer this to road casualties would mean a minimum expenditure of about £2500 000 000 (5000 fatalities annually). Clearly the value for a life is not constant, but dependent upon the circumstances.

Faced with the almost impossibly remote scenarios which can be generated the system designer cannot possibly provide remedial action and still keep within normal economic constraints. It is under these circumstances that the solution must by to 'live with the problem' by the employment of educational and other means to reduce opposition to a reasonable level. Management must recognise at what point extreme requirements must be countered by social, political, and educational means, rather than by technical solutions.

After the *Challenger* accident there were extensive technical investigations, design changes, and additional systems employed. In the end, despite all of the work, the fact remains that at certain, indeed, the majority of, times, in the event of a major failure there is no suitable means of saving the crew. This 'living with the probability of an (almost) unacceptable accident' applies right across the spectrum, from systems as large as the *Challenger* and the Channel Tunnel, right down to the domestic appliance.

The average electric hedge trimmer is hazardous if the cable is severed. Three solutions to this problem are available. One route is the provision of a cable that cannot be cut. This can be achieved either by making the cable too large to go in the blades or too strong to be cut. Alternatively a circuit breaker could be built into the plug – rather than relying on the owner to fit one to his socket. The third answer is to fit a transformer to reduce the voltage to a none hazardous level. Society accepts none of these as mandatory solutions but relies on the user being careful. As a consequence deaths from this source are far from uncommon.

We are, therefore, back to the concept that safety precautions and the acceptability of risk are not so much the actual risk levels as the social view. This rule applies at any level of safety on large or small systems.

Optimism and enthusiasm commonly exist together. There is, of course, a need for a strong dose of each in any successful project. At times there may be a requirement to take an overly optimistic approach rather than a cautious one; indeed, it may be unavoidable. It must be accepted that,under these conditions, accidents and failures are more likely to occur. To counter the increased risk the approach must be to try and identify features, events, or other monitoring points that will give a warning of pending problems.

The aeronautical field lives with an optimistic approach both with the equipment (aircraft) and the operating conditions (air traffic control). Excessive risk is countered by setting up a monitoring service that identifies, records, and broadcasts the occurrence of faults. If, for example, it is noticed that a particular type of component regularly experiences small cracks, which in themselves are innocuous, the database of information is widened by alerting all users to monitor this feature. Warning is thus obtained about a weak area which is not at that time critical but which could become so. Were this system not in existence, a single operator might well consider his experience to be an isolated one not requiring action. The cautionary approach would be to ground all aircraft until the cause and significance of the cracks had been identified and a solution to the failure obtained.

On the operational side there is a system for recording potentially dangerous incidents that in themselves are not worthy of a formal report. The system allows anonymous comments to be gathered, thus building up a picture of the grey area between really hazardous conditions and completely safe ones. There are many instances where this type of information can alert those responsible to trends which might, at some later date, cause a real problem.

Safety may, therefore, be achieved by observing, recording, and analysing small defects or deviations that are not significant in isolation. The key to achieving this forewarning of serious trouble is the setting up and maintaining of a monitoring service. It is, in fact, another part of obtaining reliability data. It is important to be selective in choosing the boundaries of the data collection system. It may be that, for reliability data, only failures are noted, whereas for safety it will probably be necessary to collect information on *all* deviations from normal behaviour, even though failure does not occur. It should not be automatically assumed that reliability data is exactly what is required for safety.

Wear and tear is a source of degraded performance, and if one includes corrosion here, then a prime source of failure is described. When studies are undertaken into safety it is usual to make the not unreasonable assumption that all parts are to specification. Yet we know that there is always a deterioration with time. Problems usually occur due to a small incremental growth of the deterioration rather that a rapid and marked change that is easily identified. This is particularly noticeable with cars where, as the miles accumulate, the ride gradually gets worse, the engine and transmission get noisier, and the bodywork corrodes. It is never possible to identify the point where this deterioration becomes marked – it is a gradual change.

Just how much allowance to make for wear and tear is a particular problem with new designs. One of the difficulties is setting the criteria. Are maintenance schedules, inspections, and the like to be time-based or operation-based? For wear of mechanical parts operational life would seem to be the criteria, but there are not necessarily any simple answers. In some cases non-operating machinery is more likely to deteriorate than systems which are kept running at a steady rate. Certain types of bearings, for example, ball and roller bearings, may 'Brinell' if kept stationary under heavy loads. A similar problem exists with liquid and gas seals, where permanent deformation may occur which would have been avoided if the rubbing surfaces were moved at intervals.

Corrosion prevention is a well advanced art these days, and the problem in this area is not so likely to be an under-estimation of the effects but the recognition that corrosion is occurring at all.

Malicious acts are usually considered to be security problems rather than safety problems, although the incident at Bhopal appears to have been a case where the system could have been improved by safety precautions. Particularly in the chemical industry, there are many instances where good design for safety could be of use to security. As an example, consider the possibility of unauthorized discharge of noxious substances into a river; if a plant can operate with a small diameter discharge pipe, then there will be good chance of detecting any unauthorized discharge at an early stage. Quantities of stored material, especially at an intermediate stage of manufacture can be minimized – again, in the Bhopal incident, this would have saved many lives.

British Rail's design of coach coupling and the general dynamics of the coaches has eliminated much of the risk of derailment. Thus, the placing of obstructions on the track has lost much of the hazard potential that existed at one time.

The majority of malicious acts are either by disgruntled employees or ex-employees, or by strangers bent on mischief or with a grudge against the organization or industry; if safety can be compromised by deliberate actions, then there is a strong possibility that the same event could be caused by human error. It is often useful to consider not only what might go wrong with a system but also what could be done to *make* it go wrong – perhaps from misuse or physical damage.

Ignorance means lack of knowledge, but people often think of it as a deficiency in the mental process. Accidents can and do happen as the result of competent people being unaware of a situation or the behaviour of a system. In designing any system with the potential for causing a breach of safety care must be taken to ensure that assumptions about the knowledge of those associated with it are valid throughout the system's life. Indeed, the essential knowledge must be maintained right through the disposal process. This is illustrated by the existence of asbestos in buildings, which is often discovered quite unexpectedly when demolition is underway. The frequent discovery of old mine workings and hazardous materials are examples of, albeit unforeseen, ignorance. All energy sources, hazardous materials, and the like, should be clearly and permanently identified. When fluorescent light tubes were first manufactured a number of them were filled with a beryllium powder which was highly injurious if inhaled, yet there was no indication of this for the user. At the time of manufacture the toxicity of beryllium was not widely known, but this is just another demonstration that great efforts must *always* be made to examine all materials for unacceptable properties.

Quite frequently ignorance is the fault of neither the user nor operator. If equipment is of a design similar to an existing system, then care should be taken that controls, for example, are only similar if their functions are similar. An easy illustration of this not being done is where one car has turn indicators on one side of the steering wheel, and they are reversed on another model, not necessarily of a different make.

Clarity of instruction is a key to avoiding breaches of safety through ignorance. It should never be assumed that material will always be read as the author intended unless it is crystal clear. There is the apocryphal story of the engineer who sent plans for wells to a somewhat low technology island. When he arrived to inspect the work he found the landscape covered with narrow chimneys. Enquiries showed that the workmen had held the plans upside down.

10

Review Bodies and the Like

It is quite common, and indeed often essential, for safety matters to be dealt with by a person or persons other than the direct designer or manager. This does not mean that the latter have no responsibility, but rather that their safety activities are subject to scrutiny by an independent person or body. This independent element can be in place before a design is completed, as an ongoing review or as an investigation after some untoward event such as an accident. The key elements to success in any of these activities are comprehensive terms of reference and competent participants.

Terms of reference should be short, to the point, and generated before any activity starts. It is a common fault for terms of reference to be far too long. Whilst it is not possible to be dogmatic, half to one page should be adequate for most purposes. They might well be set out in the following manner.

(1) To inquire into the causes of the accident at [place] on the [date] and make such recommendations as are deemed appropriate.

(2) A Board, reporting to the Managing Director, has been formed and will require members of staff to provide information, both written and oral, in aid of the investigation. The Board is authorised to make such investigations as they think necessary. They may co-opt specialist advice. The Board has no managerial responsibilities within the organization, but may make recommendations direct to the appropriate managers. A list of members is at Appendix A.

(3) A preliminary report shall be issued by [date] and the final report should be available by [date]. The Board may issue such intermediate reports as they consider necessary.

Note the use of the words shall and should; also the use of an end date.

(4) The Board will make recommendations and advise on any remedial steps they consider appropriate. The Board will not recommend actions against individuals, but will apportion blame.

Note that they are told what is expected. If this is not done there is a risk that all that will emerge is that there has been an accident and why.

The above gives a wide ranging brief to the Board, but limits the extent to which they can affect the workings of the organization. On the other hand, there is a communication line for the issuing of advice or recommendations, the implementation of which is at the discretion of the management concerned. Too often there is the temptation to tell a Board or an individual how to go about the task in detail. A similar temptation exists to ask for reports at regular and frequent intervals. This is unwise as progress is rarely uniform and the group eventually spends time trying to think what to say each week rather than getting on with the task.

An additional important piece of information is the use of an end date. There must always be some form of termination specified otherwise there is the risk of the exercise continuing *ad infinitum*. If a termination date is not obvious, because it is an ongoing project or because there are too many unknowns, then some arbitrary date should be fixed. Failing to put in a limit will offer the opportunity to carry on just that bit longer before the exercise is completed.

If a person or body has been charged with working with designers and managers on the safety aspects of a system, it is important that the right relationship is decided at an early stage. There are two parties to all these types of arrangement, the 'askers' and the 'answerers', and it must be appreciated that the latter probably have the most work and also shoulder the burden of all the normal management responsibilities. The 'asker' can easily fall into the trap of either sitting back and making more and more demands, or, alternatively, trying to join in with the designers' or managers' work. The latter practice will lessen independence, while the former may create significant management problems, as well as cause ill feeling.

Clear objectives should be specified at an early stage of either consideration of a design or investigation of an event. Investigations or examinations are frequently started without any very clear idea of what is to be achieved. Worse, unless the aims are spelt out it is quite probable that different people will have different views of what is required and by whom. Specifying the requirements also eliminates unnecessary work – for example, seeking unnecessary information or conducting pointless trials.

In selecting an individual to investigate a problem or to comment on or examine a design, choosing the right person is clearly very important.

Who to choose depends very much on the circumstances, for not only are there technical considerations but also those of personality. Investigating an accident may well require a strong character to cut through the fog of information that may be created by people with something real or imaginary to hide. On the other hand, in analysing a design as it progresses, a personality that is not going to rock the boat is very valuable.

Where technical subjects are involved there is a temptation to appoint a specialist to undertake investigations, or to form a group composed of experts in the field of activity being considered. There is no doubt that the use of specialists does have many advantages, but there are also severe drawbacks. There is always a tendency for the system to be viewed not only with the wisdom of experience but also with considerable suspicion if it is different from the norm. In such a situation it is difficult to get a truly independent view as opposed to a critical one, and there is the problem of peer group association, with a reluctance to criticise colleagues or those of a similar profession.

When it is considered appropriate to select one person as opposed to a group to investigate an accident and examine a system for potential hazards, the individual concerned has a particularly difficult task. Not only is there a high degree of responsibility but there is also the difficulty of working alone, or with strangers who have little to gain by one's efforts, and maybe quite a lot to loose.

For the individual there is a need to plan the investigation. The first thing is to ensure everybody concerned is quite clear about the objective; like most obvious things, this is frequently forgotten or ignored. Unless the individual is completely familiar with the organization, the next step is to establish who is involved, their responsibilities, and to whom they report. The temptation to get involved in the technical data straight away should be resisted. By understanding the staff hierarchy it is possible to avoid treading on people's toes or forming inappropriate information routes; if this happens it can sour the whole exercise.

If working away from base it is essential for the individual to set up a proper working environment. The too-frequent suggestion to 'use x's desk while he's on holiday' is just not good enough. There must be a recognised area, with permanent allocation of a telephone and the like, plus any clerical support that is required. However, arrogance when 'lodging' in other people's departments is to be avoided, and the aim must be to establish amicable working relationships.

The typing and holding of confidential papers may be necessary. It is extremely undesirable, for example, for reports to reach senior management by unauthorised routes – it is always possible that new information will lead to the re-interpretation of such reports – and it is in the individual's own interest to ensure that the right information is transmitted at the right time. Some level of secrecy is inevitable in such a situation, where careers may be at risk, but unnecessary secrecy can be destructive. It should be possible, and is advisable, to keep senior management informed of the direction an inquiry is going so that they do not have any nasty surprises. It is a common problem for senior management that people are often afraid to tell them all the bad news, and when things really do go wrong they are then unable to admit that they withheld information. However, there is a danger, if a senior manager is too well briefed, that he will pre-empt the report. A simple one or two line note once a week should be sufficient to keep senior management informed of progress, unless, of course, there is something substantial to report.

Once settled into the organization, the investigator needs to establish some ground rules. The things to be determined will include the following. Will work be on a one-to-one basis or via group discussion? Will written submissions need to be backed up by verbal explanations? How will people be informed? How much information will be made available? And any timetable requirements or critical dates will also have to be made known.

The starting and finishing of any investigation are usually the difficult parts. Work in the middle tends to generate and steer itself, although there is a constant need to keep to the prime objectives; it is relatively easy to go down a path that deviates from the main purpose. The form of an investigation is almost entirely dependent on its type and scope. There is no 'correct' way to undertake the task, but there are a few simple guidelines.

Apart from the obvious initial briefings and questioning it is a useful to obtain copies of all relevant papers such as instructions, specifications, regulations, and so on, as soon as possible. It is also useful to establish how these documents are generated and distributed, and the means of control and implementation.

The report itself is, of course, of crucial importance. It should open with a statement of the mandate for undertaking the work, and should then outline the problem or purpose, to ensure that every reader starts from the same point and is clear about the purpose. Limitations, either external or self-imposed, on the way in which the task was discharged should also be explained at the beginning. As with all reports, the main body of text should be as short as possible, with generous use of Appendices to carry the detail, and any conclusions or recommendations should round it off. The content of the appendices is very dependent on the nature and size of the task, but the following should be considered: a diary of major dates if the investigation took a long time; a list of people contacted; a description of any equipment and a description of damage, if appropriate; a bibliography.

The distribution of the document should be agreed with the commissioning authority. This will depend very much on the sensitivity of the information, but it should always be remembered that if there is anything like a story the media will be keen to get a copy by one means or other. It is good practice to limit the number of distributed copies, but to hold enough extras to ensure that people who are entitled to can borrow one.

A Board, Committee, or other assembly has three main elements in its composition: the Chairman who may or may not be a specialist, the Secretary, and the members. Whether or not the group is called a Board, a Committee, or something else is of no real significance; for simplicity the following refers to a Board, but is equally applicable to other groups be they Committees, Working Parties, or whatever.

It is obviously best if a totally independent Chairman can be found. The Chairman may select the rest of the Board. The choice is dependent on the task. For an important enquiry, where the findings will have a significant effect on an organization or externally, there must be recognizable competence and authority. There is obviously a need for specialist advice on a Board, and arrangements should be made to co-opt such expertise as necessary. It is always helpful to have at least one person from a different discipline to the topic under consideration. It is too easy for a group of like-minded people, either by discipline or association, to get too concerned with the interesting aspects of the task rather than standing back and taking a broader view.

The Chairman has the difficult task of balancing the views of different members of the group and trying to obtain a consensus opinion. This is particularly important either when the personalities vary a lot or when there is a wide difference in seniority. In highly technical investigations the expert in a particular field may well be quite junior to other members, which can cause difficulties.

In large organizations, or where there is a mix of people from several bodies, the Chairman may find that, if travel is involved, say to visit a plant, then the group may be split up due to the different travel regulations of the parent bodies. It is most annoying for all concerned, and certainly bad for morale, if some of the party travel First Class and others do not. It is not unknown for a group of just a few people to be split this way and, for example, end up sitting in different sections of the same aircraft. The Chairman should guard against this type of discrimination for he has to create a harmonious group, without rank order, if he is to obtain a balanced conclusion.

The appointment of an effective Secretary, preferably with a technical background, who can work closely with the Chairman is a necessity. A good Secretary can save a lot of time by obtaining, sifting, and processing information, as well as supporting the Board's technical activities. The Secretary can also greatly influence both the effectiveness and decision making process of the Board.

The duties of the Secretary should be laid down so that there is no misunderstanding about his role. First and foremost, he should *not* be at everyone's beck and call, and he should be provided with adequate clerical assistance to ensure that papers and the like are generated and distributed quickly.

Board members are likely to be chosen for a particular expertise or for their independence; if the former, this expertise should be made clear to the rest of the Board. The activities of the Board is no different from other types of Committee, although the problem of agreement of the final report may give rise to difficulties. By its nature a Board will probably have been charged with producing some conclusions. It is an advantage from the beginning to decide whether or not the majority decision will prevail, and, if there is disagreement, if the majority will be identified only numerically or by name.

Public Enquiries and similar formal bodies are usually organized by government departments, which are well practised in setting them up. Some such bodies have impressive credentials, and costs to match: in the UK the Sizewell B Reactor Enquiry was a planning enquiry with the additional task of considering safety, and is estimated to have cost some £20 million. The precise conduct of such events is dependent upon the legal system which means that procedures may vary from country to country. The UK Legal system is adversarial, and so Public Enquiries are similarly organized. The difficulty with this system is that experts never talk to experts but have to communicate with each other through Barristers, and the whole business relies on one side scoring points off the other. In engineering the decision-making process, especially between experts, relies on the proving of a point, rather than just winning an argument, the important difference being that expert talks directly to expert.

The major Public Enquiry, although theoretically allowing for the involvement of the public themselves, rarely fulfils this aim properly because the method of working and the huge financial burdens cannot be supported by even small groups, let alone individuals. Safety matters in particular, with their requirement for experts in risk assessment and the like, are not really best resolved in such a forum.

Anyone charged with setting up an enquiry or participating in one should be aware of the problem of cost. In most big organizations costs can be readily absorbed in the overheads. Apart from the loss of useful working time, travel and accommodation costs can often be significant, and anything to do with Public Enquiries is likely to involve significant legal costs.

If a Board, in investigating a problem or examining a proposal, requires additional work to be done, then the cost of this should not fall on the department involved. Trials required by the Board can only reasonably be charged to a body if that body were remiss in not anticipating the requirement. Funding a Board to enable it to have its own trials and tests conducted independently is far fairer than expecting a design or production facility to carry the burden. Allowing any committee to have a free hand to demand additional work, without the financial responsibility, is a recipe for disaster.

The setting up of Standing Committees to review designs and systems on a regular basis is a good idea, provided the organization is large enough to support it. There are a few pitfalls, but with a well-run Committee these are outweighed by the advantages. The most important point is to ensure that the Committee does not end up carrying out the design. This requires discipline and tact. The Committee should never be asked how they would like to see a design; rather, what approach they might look upon in a favourable light. In other words, the Committee might either be asked to set the policy or invited to endorse it. A second pitfall is the possibility of the existence of the Committee inhibiting innovation and progress – the Committee is always on safer ground agreeing a design that has already proved to be satisfactory. A third problem is that the designer may be less careful than he should be and rely on the Committee to find the problems – something that the Committee will need to guard against.

11

Attitudes

In matters of safety, engineers and scientists, in common with Politicians, are often not held in much respect by members of the public. The public view with some suspicion assurances that all will be well and serious accidents will not happen. As an essential matter of good communication the engineer or scientist must understand the cause of this scepticism and distrust.

It is increasingly well known that attitudes to safety are neither rational nor consistent, although this lack of rationality is usually not recognised by the person concerned. From an industrial point of view this multi-valued attitude can be expensive in both money and time. Indeed, on occasions it is a barrier to progress and may be used as a factor to barter for higher pay or changes to working conditions.

The most obvious difference in attitude is the fact that people will willingly accept greater risks in sport and other personal activities than they will at work or public life. Self-imposed risk is seen as acceptable whilst imposed risk is viewed with greater concern. The problem is compounded by a difference of perception between the engineering and academic worlds and the public. To the public risk is something that might happen, and, not unreasonably, they do not grasp the importance of tying it to frequency.

The 'not invented here' syndrome is as prevalent with safety as it is with any new ideas. The prejudice is fostered by reticence or secrecy which some organizations and people seem to impose with no good reason. On the other hand the adverse reaction of pressure groups and individuals has the opposite effect to that intended, as the 'authorities' find that every piece of information is minutely examined. Thus, secrecy encourages opposition and in the end the genuine and valid concern is lost in a welter of mis-information and rhetoric.

The opposite to the negative attitude is sometimes seen in a drive for novelty, in a 'pioneering spirit', or in simple over-enthusiasm. It is not only confined to those directly involved but also involves those who consider they have an association with what is new. Faced with the rush of enthusiasm, the voice of caution is often lost in the general urge to make progress or achieve some objective. In recent years there is a greater element of caution creeping into new ventures, although the ability and determination to examine existing systems is less pronounced.

The designer or manager responsible for a new system needs to weigh very carefully the value of discussing safety with a broader audience. Very few designs are sold primarily on safety as opposed to performance or economy. Where the type of engineering system – for example, a chemical plant or method of transport – is fairly well established, the best starting point is probably to compare new with old, which may well give the reassurance that things will be no worse and, indeed, may even be better.

The first step is to establish how safe the existing system is; the next requirement is to identify the differences, both positive and negative. For example, a faster train may have better brakes, a plus, but there is a negative in that there is less time for the driver to react. To the public the idea that the brakes are better, especially if expressed in the time to stop from a nominal speed, will be reassuring; driver reaction time will probably not be considered.

The technical critic or assessor will wish to take a total view rather than concentrate, as the public is likely to, on the interesting and recognisable parts. This is not an unreasonable difference. Nor is the public likely to be able to assess the probability of the event as opposed to the consequences. Consequences are of the greatest concern to the layman as he usually takes the view that what could happen will do so within his timeframe. The designer/manager must therefore appreciate that consequence is more important than frequency to the public.

By and large the public wants a no-risk situation for any system that it has to use or live with. It has been shown many times that the reassurance that an accident will be no more likely or severe than many everyday risks will probably not be acceptable. There are many people who consider the proposed Channel Tunnel to be unsafe, yet it is quite unlikely to be even a tenth as hazardous as a similar length of road, especially on a dark wet night.

However, negative reactions to even low-risk situations can readily be overcome, often by financial inducement. If the Channel Tunnel were to offer fares at, say, a tenth of the cost of other means of crossing the Channel, then it is probable that the number who would not travel because they considered it unsafe would be infinitesimally small. At the launch of a publicity campaign to restore air travel after the Gulf Crisis in 1991, Lord King, the Chairman of British Airways, when challenged that people were still afraid to fly, commented 'not when there are free seats'.

A similar situation exists at factory floor level, although slightly different criteria apply. There will be suspicion of the new as opposed to the old and familiar, but there will also be greater scope for 'buying' a way out of the problem, provided any risk can be kept to reasonable levels. At what stage in the design the workforce should be encouraged to participate or be informed is very much a matter to be decided by the circumstances and attitudes within the organization.

The subject of risk within a workforce has assumed new dimensions with the growth of equality between the sexes. Tasks that were considered too risky for women are having to be re-assessed as pressure is applied to allow them greater opportunities. Indeed, one might ask, if risks are too great for women, why should men be expected to take them? Risk at work is almost as confused as risk in everyday activities. Coal mining is considered to be a relatively high risk activity, yet the number of fatal accidents in agriculture is much higher. In the UK the Health and Safety Executive has an annual budget approaching a £100 million to ensure safety at work is maintained, or rather to ensure that safety regulations are enforced, which is not quite the same thing. Everybody would agree that this is money well spent. However, roughly ten times more people die from accidents in the home than at work, partly because there are far more people at home than at work, but how can a similar amount of money be spent to prevent accidents in the home? No Government department is responsible for money spent on home accident prevention, and the reason for this apparent lack of logic is that people perceive home as being safe and have no wish for it to become monitored and 'policed', as the factory is. The whole safety scene is therefore completely irrational, and whilst the engineer may consider this unreasonable, it remains a fact of life that designers of system have to take account of and the public has to pay for.

In trying to convince a lay or even a technical group of the merits of a design it is important to put the explanation in their field of understanding. An expert extolling the safety virtues of design and quoting risk probabilities, frequency of accident rate, and so forth is unlikely to influence the nonexpert. This need to translate to the audiences level of understanding applies even with a group that has a modicum of technological knowledge. For example, a new missile fuel tank made from aluminium alloy was presented by the designer to an audience with a good knowledge of military equipment but not of the subtleties of metallurgy. An opponent of the proposal remarked that an Izod test of the alloy showed it to be as brittle as cast iron. The fact that the Izod test was completely irrelevant to the circumstances was not accepted. The tank designer won the day in the end by demonstrating his tank was of the same type of material used for domestic pressure cookers; the audience then felt that the tank was not susceptible to brittle fracture after all.

It is a common failing of experts that they are astonished when, on occasion, their statements are not accepted without question. At one time there was a prevailing attitude that problems were 'best left to the experts'. This was symptomatic of the fact that society in the industrial nations at that time was strongly hierarchical; it was commonly accepted that everyone 'knew their place'. Political and social changes, particularly since the 1950s has meant that not only is authority now often challenged but also that it has come to be distrusted. Accidents that at one time were accepted as part of everyday life – as 'acts of God' – are no longer viewed in that light. As the authorities and bureaucracy have become more involved in the details of everyday living, so the 'ivory castle' stance that they enjoyed has been lost.

For engineers this apparent lack of faith is a problem that has to be accepted. As a consequence, the ability to communicate not only with one's peers but also with the layman is now more important than ever. The problem has been compounded by advances in theoretical knowledge which enable assessments and calculations to be undertaken which were just not possible not many years ago.

Largely driven by the concern over nuclear power, the policy of determining safety before a major accident occurs has become routine. At the start of the Industrial Revolution, when energy became available in large quantities, spectacular accidents were experienced in many industrial societies. Natural disasters generally caused the biggest accidents until the mass use of chemicals and fuels became significant. Even today the likelihood of dying from an accident it much less than from disease, even with the advances of medical science.

In the early days the policy, probably unwritten, was to learn from the accident. Once there had been a large explosion at an ammunition site, regulations would be revised and changes made. This 'don't do it again' approach has now been superseded by the 'determine the problem first' philosophy.

In line with all matters relating to safety, the investigative approach is not applied in a uniform manner. The transport industry, as ever, tends to provide the worst examples of the 'wait and see' rule. It takes accidents such as the Zebrugge ferry disaster and the Clapham rail crash in the UK to initiate investigations. Both accidents were well within the capability of modern hazard analysis, but as the systems were ones with a long tradition of self control, no one challenged their way of working.

The dilemma to be faced is that, given a system that has not experienced significant accidents over many years can the cost and disruption of a reexamination be justified on either political, consumer, or cost grounds. After the accident has occurred there seems no doubt that the analysis would have been justified. However, prior to the event, would it really have been acceptable to spend time and effort on looking into a system that was essential to daily life and was, apparently, safe?

Once an examination of a system has been carried out, or an accident occurred, the consequences may spread across other industries and fields of activity. Systems that have proved themselves satisfactory by being accident free may be viewed with suspicion because of events that have occurred elsewhere. The lack of common standards between countries means industries are at risk when political alliances, and what in industry would be called mergers, are effected. The advent of the European Community free trading policy in 1992 meant that whilst goods could be moved from country to country without restraint the safety of those goods was not necessarily uniform.

To some extent people's readiness to accept risk is tied to their ability, real or imaginary, to exert control over a situation. This may be the reason why 5000 road deaths a year are acceptable but a hundredth of that number on the railways would cause a storm of protest. More people are killed on motorway hard shoulders than on the motorway itself, yet the strategy of most stranded people waiting for help on the motorway is to stay on the hard shoulder in the car rather than stand away from the traffic. Part of the reason for this is probably due to the feeling that the familiar is safe. The inside of the car is an extension of home and provides protection from the weather, the noise and the sight of passing traffic – like a horse with blinkers. If the car were facing the other way, so that the passengers could see the traffic approaching and rushing past a few feet away they would probably feel most unsafe.

It is, then, the *illusion* of safety that gives confidence, rather than the calculated assessment. The engineering lesson is that unless it looks safe it will not be trusted to be safe. People judge structural strength by bulk and deflection. Indeed it is difficult to find any other parameters that can easily be observed. Thus walkways, handrails, and supports have to have reassuring dimensions rather than optimised engineering ones. Almost any average person can walk along a six-inch wide, ten-foot long plank placed on the ground; raise the plank three feet off the ground and a substantial number of people will not even attempt to use it. Many non-swimmers will not enter a waist deep pool even to rescue a child in difficulties. It is confidence that is important rather than substance. Given the difficulties people experience in situations which can be tested (for example, the plank), it is not surprising that they are often quite unable to comprehend safety arguments offered verbally or in writing

The realization that in many areas of the UK the levels of radon gas in the home are significant has not yet provoked an outcry for action. It is estimated that lung cancer deaths from radon are likely to be about 2000 a year, which is equal to half the number of people killed on the road. The problem with obtaining statistics on such risks as radon-induced fatalities is that the exposure is part of every day life and cannot easily be identified against other cancer causes. The removal of most of the risk could be achieved by spending about £750 on changes to houses, which is probably about a hundredth of the cost of the house. People do not, however, perceive it as a significant risk, and very few undertake the modifications. Yet if a chemical plant discharged waste matter which would produce only a hundredth of this number of cancers it would not be allowed to operate.

It is clear that endeavouring to convince the public that a process or facility only marginally adds to the community risk is likely to be an unsuccessful exercise. It has to be accepted that equipment imposed on the public must, to all intents and purposes, be completely safe. Complete safety is an almost impossible standard to reach, and in the end the compromise is a that it is safe in the eyes of the public against what they see as a credible accident.

The lay person is unlikely to be able to grasp that a very low level of risk is substantially the same as completely safe. They will wish to be given the assurance that there is a zero chance of an accident. The engineer, on the other hand, knows that he can never guarantee 100 percent safety, but he can accept that, say, a probability of one in 10^8 is sufficiently remote to be treated as zero for all practical purposes. However, he cannot honestly say it *is* zero, and when faced by the press or a critical audience is bound to say there is some risk.

The acceptance or rejection of risk depends not only on the situation – whether or not the risk is imposed by someone else – but also on another very important factor; the majority of people do not like to disagree with others in the same group. The group can range from a few friends to the population of a whole community – a sort of tribal support feeling, which can be used to good effect by pressure groups and can be quite formidable. Pressure groups will often form when there is a lack of information, as uncertainty tends to bring people together.

The engineer should aim to make as much information as possible available from an early stage of the design of a system. However, at times, for commercial or similar reasons, information is restricted, or it may simply not exist. The British Nuclear Fuels permanent exhibition on radioactive material processing is an excellent example of the endeavour to change attitudes toward nuclear power. The similar exhibition on the Channel Tunnel is another example of investment in educating the concerned public.

The issuing of detailed information does not guarantee acceptance as there may be other motives driving the resistance to proposals. Safety is often a convenient topic to affect a project when the real objection lies in other areas. Information issued in good faith is frequently used by pressure groups to raise fears and gain support. It is, therefore, another reason for issuing information in a manner and style that will be understood by the potential recipients. We are again back to the situation where the expert can no longer say 'believe me I am right'; it must be 'believe me because . . . '.

It is well established that people will accept the risk of natural disasters far more readily than artificial and imposed ones. The number of people voluntary living in earthquake zones and on flood plains is quite significant, Similarly, housing estates in line with airport runways are fully occupied by people who judge the risk is small compared with the benefits of cost or convenience. The number of deaths from heart disease which could be avoided at no cost or great inconvenience is quite staggering, and if the equivalent number of deaths was in some other field there would probably be strong demands for action

The antinuclear lobby in the UK is strongly against the addition to, and continued use of, nuclear power stations, yet quite close by the French nuclear industry has quite a large number of nuclear plants. No attempt is made to change that situation, probably because it is recognised that the UK population is usually fairly indifferent to anything on the other of side of the English Channel, which is seen as a significant barrier

Thus it can be seen that trying to predict people's reactions to proposals is not just uncertain: it is almost impossible. There must, therefore, be a recognition, not only of the inconsistencies but also of the need to approach those concerned in a way that they can understand.

12

Human Interfaces

The source of the majority of accidents is a failing in the performance of a person associated with the system or activity. At times people of widely varying levels of intelligence and ability can perform the most complex tasks in a highly competent manner. At the same time the reverse is true and simple tasks are not carried out correctly

Before the car was invented anyone suggesting that almost every member of the adult population could work a complicated machine would be derided. Yet the car requires the use of both feet, performing highly coordinated movements, plus totally different actions of the hands. In addition the driver is required to maintain a lookout, often in the dark and in rain, whilst reading instruments and deciding which route to take. All of this whilst travelling at up to 70 mile/h between other vehicles. And on a purely physical level, the ability to ride a bicycle shows that the coordination of movement and mental activity can be remarkably effective.

It is clear, therefore, that complicated patterns of activity and thought are within the ability of most people. We are, then, starting with a system (the human being) that is very effective in dealing with complex physical and mental processes, but which we know can be subject to very simple errors

The contributions of human error can, for convenience, be split into a number of categories.

(1) Knowledge.
(2) Observation.
(3) Interpretation.
(4) Decision.
(5) Action.
(6) Achievement.

In the operation and usage of engineering plant, equipment and systems generally the commonest way of imparting knowledge is either by training or by written instructions. For particularly complex systems there may be additional training facilities in the way of simulators and dummy equipment. Knowledge must, for the purposes of safety in particular, be regarded as the resource that enables the right decisions to be made and the right actions to be taken. It is not a neat package that can be passed to those concerned with the expectation that from then on all will be well. Where operational safety can be defined by absolute instructions, with no significant need for interpretation and judgement, then this can be equally, or better, performed by automatic systems. Where the speed of response is critical automation is essential; the launch of the US space shuttle and other systems is better performed by computer. However, the take off and landing of aircraft, although capable of automation, is still better under manual control.

The use of written instructions is unreliable unless they are compiled in such a way as to be readily understood and easily accessed. It is surprising how often instruction manuals are deficient in many respects and not infrequently this is the result of the author being familiar with the system and not being able to see it as a non-expert. As a starting point for learning about a system and ensuring the safety of its operation, the manual or other publication is not as good as it is written but only as good as it is understood.

It has been the practice of many organizations to issue instructions, particularly in the form of leaflets and bulletins, concerning safe practices to be used for various activities. The common error in many of these cases is the temptation to keep issuing fresh papers as additional requirements are recognised. Unfortunately this causes an accumulation of documents that is suddenly presented to a newcomer to the organization. Unless particular care has been taken to create the documents in a systematic manner and to index and structure them logically it is very difficult for the reader to obtain an accurate picture of the information. To compound this problem there is often no system of priority, so the essential, the routine and the background become mixed up in a mass of documents.

Safety information should be clearly identified, preferably in a separate document. If there is no use of a dedicated document, then there should be a recognisable format within the main document showing which information is safety related. The use of a different typeface or 'boxing' of the relevant passages is relatively simple. The use of coloured printing to pick out the essential text is not a particularly good practice as the identifying feature is lost if the document is photocopied.

For any publication containing safety information the issue of amendments and updates must be clearly and effectively controlled. In many organizations minor amendments are listed on a sheet which is circulated to the document holders who then have to copy this to the main text. Not only is there a risk of error in the transcription but also there is the temptation to stick the amendment sheet in the front of the existing document and hope people will refer to it. The minimum acceptable practice, which is barely satisfactory, is to print the amendment so that it can be pasted in. If the document is important and is related to safety the only really acceptable change is to replace pages. Needless to say whatever method is used there should be a record amendment sheet in the front of the document listing the changes, their date of embodiment and the person responsible for the alteration.

Frequently manuals and the like are used where lighting and general conditions are poor. Material must be printed in a legible manner and, in particular, diagrams (especially for wiring and pipework) need to be easily handled. If procedures are such that an error can lead to a hazard arising, then check lists should be either embodied in the document or supplied as supplementary sheets. The use of colour to identify information on diagrams or drawings, as well as the limitations mentioned above, is also not satisfactory under adverse lighting conditions, where available light may be far from white.

It is particularly important where large or complicated diagrams are used to provide grid references. If text cannot be kept on the same or opposite page to the relevant diagrams, then the sheet size should be such that the diagram can be opened out to lay alongside the text. A frequent error is for documents to be printed on high quality glossy paper, the reflections from which can make reading difficult. The person working in a duct or underneath machinery cannot always select the best lighting.

Training is an essential element of safety and can range from the on-the-job to long and complex courses. Obviously the end product of a training course should either be a specialist for a particular system or a person of wide knowledge who can adapt to demand. The critical feature is the ability to determine if the trainee has achieved the intended standard. For large and complex courses there are usually the resources available to establish the standard, but this is not necessarily the case for short courses and on-the-job training.

Training and discipline go hand in hand, and there have been a number of significant accidents where apparently well-trained individuals have not responded correctly. In the USA the Three Mile Island reactor failure was due to incorrect responses to a situation rather than equipment malfunction. In the USSR the same applied in the Chenobyl accident, where trained personnel did not follow the guide lines. We are then faced with the question as to whether the training or discipline were inadequate. Whilst blame might well be attributed to those at the 'sharp end', it is much more important to determine if training and discipline should be regarded as a complete package instead of treating them separately; neither is effective without the other, and both form part of the essential knowledge bank.

Where the potential for a significant accident is recognised, the responsible organization will endeavour not only to ensure people know *what* to do but will also regularly test their ability to *do* so. On the other hand, where training is necessary but the resources do not permit regular reassessment, then the equipment should be designed to act as an *aide memoire*. The average factory or office worker should, in a large organization, be shown how to work a fire extinguisher; it is not otherwise likely that they will use one regularly enough to become proficient. It is a failing of many extinguishers to show their method of working clearly. Instructions are often printed in small type, requiring a significant number of people to use spectacles. In addition some extinguishers have to be inverted to function properly, and the instructions are either printed upside down when stowed or, if printed the other way up, cannot then be read in the functioning mode. A simple policy of printing both ways would ensure that reading was possible at all times.

The safety of many systems depends on the acceptance of certain familiar standards and conventions. In the UK the fact that light switches are down for 'on' is widely accepted, although the US practice of up for 'on' is rather safer as an accidental blow is more likely to turn the current off. The convention in the UK that circuit breakers are up for 'on' was fine when these devices were confined to substantial ironclad housings, but the advent of miniaturized circuit breakers has meant they can be confused with switches, and the 'on' position is now by no means clear.

It is generally accepted for electrical systems that rotation in a clockwise direction increases the function under control, yet hydraulic and gas valves shut off with a clockwise movement.

It cannot be a surprise to anyone that a high proportion of accidents are attributable to errors in observation. Engineers should take count of the specialist knowledge that exists on presentation and interpretation of

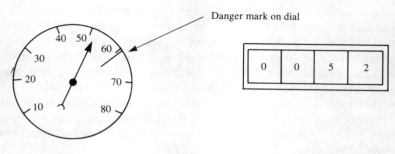

Fig 25

visual information. There is still a tendency in many areas to regard the design of controls and instruments as a nonspecialist task.

There are a number of widely recognised conventions such as the general practice of instruments indicating an increase by a movement of, say, a needle from left to right. The increasing use of digital readouts means the facility for judging not only position but also trend and proximity to a limit, offered by a needle and dial gauge, is no longer available. (Fig. 25.) Another advantage of dial gauges is that an array of them can form a recognised pattern when all is operating normally, and any unusual position would easily be noticed. The bank of digital instruments offers no easy reference points, and each one has to be read and considered.

Fitting gauges with a very wide range may mean that very low readings of, say, pressures are not detectable. Similarly, a digital gauge with only units displayed will not record below 1. In the Kegworth air crash in the UK it was judged that the modern instrument displays were less easy to read than earlier ones and were contributory to the accident.

Visual observation is at times extremely unreliable. There is always a tendency for people to see what they expect to see. This is especially so under boring or routine conditions. Notices and coloured markers have a relatively limited effect as once they become familiar as part of the every day routine they get ignored. A frequent error is for warnings and instructions to be too long or to be written in a complicated manner. With the increase of mixed racial and cultural societies the choice of words is particularly important, and they should be short and well known. If multilanguage signs are supplied, care should be taken that the person installing them is given some indication as to which way up they should be fitted. To a westerner the correct orientation of some Middle and Far Eastern scripts is by no means clear

Even quite commonly accepted Western pictograms have been devised without any thought to the international population; for example, women are portrayed with skirts and men with trousers, but this is hardly appropriate for Arab states.

The number of people unable to read even quite short sentences is quite high – the very young (to some extent the most vulnerable), people with poor eyesight, and those who are dyslexic or illiterate. Added to this is the problem of colour blindness, which is especially common as far as red is concerned.

Warnings should be written in letters that most of the population can read without glasses and should be on a contrasting background; signs should be consistent and unambiguous. (Fig. 26.) Many building lifts passenger control panels are poorly designed, in that style is given a greater priority than efficiency. The button for the emergency bell is often mounted along with other operating buttons and without distinctive labelling. Even worse are the flush touch pads that are sometimes mounted low down (for children or wheelchair users?) where, in a crowded lift, there is not enough room to see the panel clearly. Such problems can be solved with only a little thought and almost no cost. For example, if a low-mounted control panel were titled out by about 10 degrees it could be easily read from above.

Emergency telephones in buildings often have the instructions, including the number to dial, in faded lettering behind a highly reflective transparent panel and, for good measure, hidden in a dark corner.

Fig 26

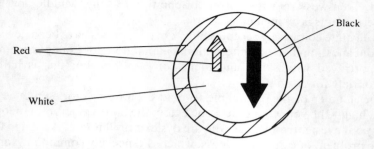

Fig 27

Direction notices should be clear in their meaning. It is quite common for instructions to be given by points of the compass; for example 'on leaving the building assemble in the West car park', or 'the first aid kit is in the North entrance foyer'. None of these directions are necessarily clear.

There is an increasing use of symbols and pictograms to convey safety information. Provided they are unambiguous these devices are usually better than written notices. It is, however, all too easy to produce misleading signs, as the 'experts' do not appreciate the average person's concept of pictorial representation. One of the earliest signs to fail in this way was the traditional skull and crossbones representing poison or death. Whilst this was adequate for most adults it meant little to children. The standard UK road sign for priority traffic is entirely unclear to most people. (Fig. 27.) It has no real analogy to the situation and relies on the observer remembering which arrow has priority. The problem is compounded by the fact that the interpretation depends partly on colour, which is unsatisfactory. A UK survey of passengers' understanding of cross-Channel ferry signs showed only about 60 percent understood the sign for a 'muster station' with a third being nowhere near correct. A similar figure was obtained for the evacuation slide. The very use of the words 'muster station' shows a complete lack of appreciation as to what lay passengers might understand. Similarly, the use of the 'port' and 'starboard' is unsatisfactory. (Fig. 28.)

A number of universally-recognised symbols are quite incomprehensible and inconsistent to the untrained. For example, the variations in emergency exit signs must have been compiled by a bureaucrat who had no knowledge at all of human perception. Similarly, 'way in/out' signs are hardly self explanatory. (Fig. 29.)

Muster stations

Evacuation slide

Fig 28

Emergency exit

Exit

Way in

Fig 29

One of the worst example of all on roads in the UK is the commonly experienced de-restriction sign. This does not mean that any speed is permitted, but that the limits are 60 mile/h on single carriageways and 70 mile/h on dual carriageways. This is quite misleading to foreign drivers, especially as the transition from, say 30 to 40 or 40 to 50 is not marked in the same way. Officially the sign is used to denote 'National speed limits apply'.

An important feature about warnings is that they should be realistic. If a risk is not present, then the sign should be removed. A simple example of the consequences of leaving signs when they are not required is the use of temporary speed limits on motorways in the UK by illuminating a sign that reads, say, 50 mile/h. The driver then finds there is no obstruction for the next five miles and decides that this type of sign is best ignored. Thus, when it *is* necessary it has lost its value. Frequently warning signs are installed to protect management rather than the worker, and using devalued signs means that the important ones will probably be ignored.

In many cases the colour red is used to indicate danger, or the control to operate when a dangerous situation is likely. Aside from the problems of colour blindness, many machine tool starter units use the red button to start the machine rather than stop it, whereas on other equipment the red button is used as the emergency stop. In the UK British Rail has used considerable quantities of red paint to modernise the stations yet, as the staff have pointed out, red lights and the like are being lost against a background of red paint.

Noise prevention and abatement techniques mean that early faults in machinery are less easy to detect. In a similar vein the production of quieter transport means that such vehicles as fork lift trucks need warning lights and buzzers. Noise generated warnings should be distinctive not only from background noises but also from each other if there are several sources. A problem is deciding at what point a warning noise can be switched off. Whilst noise can be used to attract attention it can become not only a source of annoyance but also a real hindrance to people taking actions in stressful situations. By fitting a cut-off device there is the risk that it will be switched off either by accident or deliberately. The latter is particularly likely if there are frequent false alarms. One solution is to have an automatic cut off after a set period, provided some recognised action has been taken; and then perhaps re-alarm after a further period. The risk here is that there may be the time when operators just clear the system automatically, without really thinking what action they should be taking. A safer system would be a combined sound and light alarm, with the latter remaining on until the fault has been cleared.

The use of bells and the like as fire alarms is a common practice for areas where there are numbers of people who need to be evacuated. The system looses much of its effectiveness if there are frequent fire drills. The use of a set time for a fire drill is less likely to create an air of indifference than initiating them at random times, especially without warning. Having experienced a few drill alarms the tendency will be to treat all alarms as drills, and either ignore them or take a leisurely approach to responding.

Sirens and similar devices are often used to warn the workforce or the public of a risk situation. The limitation of these devices is that they are not very good for conveying anything other than simple information. In attempts to improve the information conveyed, codes such as short blasts meaning X, long blasts meaning Y, and so on, can be used. The problem is that it is unlikely that many people will remember the code, and unless the difference in pattern is particularly distinct they will not be sure what alarm they have heard. There is the same disadvantage as fire drills if the system is regularly exercised.

Little use is made of physical alarms, though some aircraft have been fitted with 'stick shakers' to warn the pilot when he is approaching stall speed by vibrating the control column. The Honda anti-lock motorcycle brake system is designed so that the rider experiences a vibration of the brake lever or brake pedal to enable him to judge how close he is to the friction limit between the tyre and road surface.

Smell can be used as a warning system, although there are relatively few examples. In the UK the provision of North Sea gas meant that the traditional smell associated with coal gas leaks no longer existed. To combat this an artificial smell was added as an identifier. Many people suffer from defective 'smelling ability' either as a permanent feature or temporarily due to, say, a cold. This means of warning is, therefore, rather unreliable.

An important, indeed essential, feature of all alarm systems is that they should have some form of priority grading. It is unhelpful to an operator trying to deal with a crisis to be presented with a number of flashing lights all of the same colour backed up by several alarms sounding. If priority cannot be achieved by colour and sound difference, then every attempt should be made to layout the control or indicator panels in a priority order. It might be possible to rank the lights in order of importance from, say, top to bottom or left to right. As it is not easy to indicate priority with more than about three sounds, such as high note continuous, low note continuous, and intermittent, then consideration should given to parallelling them with lights or some other visual indicator.

The effectiveness of the human decision making process is dependent on a wide range of factors and conditions thus performance is probably as much to do with the environment as with mental ability. For safety it is obvious that the fewer decisions and the better the environment, the more likely it is the correct decision will be made. It is also obvious that the less pressure there is to reach a quick decision the more likely it is to be correct. There is, however, an optimum time for decision making: many people will avoid making a decision until the last moment, and become confused in the process.

Decision making for safety divides into three areas. The initial decisions on the design of the system, the decision during normal operations, and the decisions in the event of an emergency.

The technical and managerial decisions during the design of the system are frequently influenced by commercial and political pressures. These in turn affect the thinking activity of the designers and managers to such an extent that decisions are sometimes taken that, in retrospect, are not only unwise but are even admitted by those concerned to be decisions they would not have arrived at under normal circumstances.

A major problem with many decisions regarding safety is that they are based on something that might happen, and the chance of it happening is not only remote but also unquantifiable, even with the best technological facilities. An additional and important point is that safety usually costs money and reduces performance, neither of which commends itself to the economic management of an organization.

It is possible to hypothesize that the designers of the *Herald of Free Enterprise* involved in the Zeebrugge disaster could have foreseen that it was possible for the ship to go to sea with the bow doors open. Given the commercial climate that probably existed at the design stage it would have been difficult for the designer to insist on a complicated control system to ensure the accident did not occur. It is likely that had he suggested a complex system he would have been told there was no case to answer as the procedures were adequate.

Whilst one would like to think the decision making process is based on competence, integrity, and a social conscience, in reality there are pressures that, although undesirable, are real and significant to the people involved. The decision process at design and later stages is bound to be influenced by the effects decisions might have on the future of those concerned. There is a limit to the integrity and principle that a normal person can apply; most staff have a great interest in keeping their job.

The manager is concerned with progress and cost, and allowing the designer to add safety feature after safety feature is not supportable unless there is fairly firm evidence that the requirements are real and not just the worries of an overcautious engineer. The designer might believe he will not be considered suitable for, say, promotion if he raises too many difficulties. Other members of staff may be concerned that if the design is not economic then not only will the design not be marketable but also the Company may fail.

Right down at the personal level, the 'junior' of a group headed by an overbearing and critical manager will hesitate to raise matters which, although worthy of concern, will not be received in a tolerant manner. This attitude is likely to prevail when it is found out late in the day that something has been overlooked; not only will there be criticism of the additional requirement but also blame for the original error.

The decision making process cannot be isolated from the pressures of everyday life. To avoid this type of problem wherever possible safety should be the responsibility of the designer in the first place, but overseen quite separately by another person or body of equal or greater status.

The existence of a separate authority brings its own problems in that there may be a view that its special safety role has to be justified by finding things the designer has missed.

During normal operational activities the same pressures, but often in a slightly different form, are applied to those concerned with the system. In a production plant or with a form of transport there is great pressure to keep things running. The person who finds, for example, an undesirable practice, has to determine whether he is justified in perhaps creating a stoppage or loss of production. He has to judge if he will get support or criticism, or if he will even be treated seriously. As a simple example, the road-tanker driver or ship's captain has to decide, if the weather is bad, whether to continue the journey, and risk an accident, or to wait until it clears; he will depend very much on the support of the traffic manager if the delivery is late.

The existence of regulations helps to avoid some of the pressures on the individual in that if, say, the minimum visibility for an operation is specified, then it is a simple case of stopping if the limit is exceeded. Most decisions are easier to take if there is a 'peg' to hang them on, and the correct safety decision is often aided by this type of backup; even if there are choices at least the person making the decision does not feel quite so isolated.

Decision making for most people tends to be a sequential process, and they normally identify one problem and solve it before proceeding to the next one. This single route approach is rather different from that required for many safety activities, where the 'width' and combination of problems has to be put in perspective, often in a relatively short period. For that reason the usefulness of exercises cannot be over emphasised. When an emergency occurs there is a need to switch from the routine to the specific and unusual.It has to be recognised that some people are better at handling emergencies than others, and for this reason the provision of controls, information, and plans of action should be carefully thought through.

The optimum grouping of controls and instruments may not be the same for the normal running of a system as for an emergency. Computer controlled systems may work well under standard conditions but under stress the keying in of an incorrect number to control a valve may shut or open the wrong one. This can readily be seen on a switch panel, but is not so easily identified on a screen, especially if the display is moving. If at all feasible it should be made possible to put the system into an automatic mode where all keyboard instructions are printed out as they are entered. Tape recordings, although useful for record purposes, are not as satisfactory as a print-out, which can be studied by several people and have written notes added.

Many of the processes and functions of even quite complex engineering systems are under the control of a human operator. The tasks may be large, such as landing an aircraft, or small but highly significant, such as the handling of chemicals. In the UK the introduction of an aluminium compound into the Camelford drinking water supply resulted from a simple human interface error causing the delivery of the wrong substance to the wrong tank.

Human errors are not always related by their size to that of the eventual outcome. Proper analysis should identify those areas for error where the eventual output is significant either in the damage it causes – for example, the toxic or similar effect – or the monetary loss.

It is sometimes thought that human error is reduced or eliminated by computer control or automation; this is not true. All that the introduction of other control systems does is to put the human interface further back down the line of construction or operation. A full computer control of a system is only as good as the people who write and qualify the program. The automated system is only as good as the designers and installers have made it. Indeed, the more a system is committed to 'hands off' control the greater the likelihood that, if something goes wrong, the machine or the control system will not have the flexibility to cope with the unexpected situation.

Systems should be designed to support human control when operating normally and provide additional support when an accident occurs. Unless the designer has been particularly good at anticipating every possibility and every action required under all circumstances there is a need for human monitoring and action at frequent intervals.

Specialist organizations have banks of data on the probability of human errors occurring during operations, including mental tasks. Provided a systematic study is undertaken of the tasks and their consequences, after both correct and incorrect actions have occurred, then a good assessment can be made of the likelihood of errors.

The Systematic Human Error Reduction and Prediction Approach (SHERPA) was developed in the USA and, like so many of these systems, such as Problem Analysis By Logical Approach (PABLA) for design in the UK, has its origins in method study techniques.

SHERPA requires the system to be illustrated by a network of tasks, their objectives, and their end results. An analysis of the actions and their consequences enables priorities to be established and, in particular, errors identified which are likely to go undetected and those with the greatest impact. The human error data can be used to build up an assessment of the likelihood of errors and, as a consequence, the appropriate action can be taken to reduce or eliminate the risk areas. Of particular importance is the identification of errors that may go undetected in the first instance, and from which subsequent recovery is difficult.

13

Evidence and Presentations

Selling safety is an important task for the designer or manager of a system. He has to convince other people that the system is safe not just to his standards but also to theirs. As engineers are notorious for being poor at both verbal and written communications there are, in many instances, fundamental problems to be overcome in the process of assuring people that all is well.

The following applies to a wide spectrum of designs, operating systems, plant, and so on, as, in the end, the objective is the same; to get someone else to agree with what is proposed. At times people are inclined to regard safety organizations as an interfering group who do not trust them to do a proper job. This may be so, but they are, increasingly, a fact of life which has to be dealt with.

Depending on the importance and complexity of the system, the process of gaining confidence and acceptance may range from informal discussion amongst colleagues to a full scale Public Enquiry. The important thing to remember is the purpose of the exercise, namely to sell safety and generate enthusiasm for the new system. To achieve this there must be confidence: in the accuracy of the data presented; in the soundness of any arguments; in the judgements made, and, overall, a belief that any conclusions are soundly based and are not likely to cause problems.

Generally speaking when people are associated with the *performance* of a system they wish it to succeed and take an optimistic view of data – provided it is reasonably based. With *safety* the situation is different. They know that if there is a mistake there could be unpleasant consequences which, in an extreme case, may result in a court appearance or in some direct loss especially, if they are personally involved in an accident.

Safety committees and organizations are usually experienced people with a good deal of sympathy with the designer or manager. At the same time they tend to be independently minded and not greatly moved by arguments about cost, delay, or the like.

The type of organization likely to be encountered is dependent on the project or system and on the potential problems that might arise. Not only are the likely interested parties going to vary with what is being planned and where, but also the popularity of the topic at the time will be a factor. To propose the construction of a sewage plant discharging onto a beach near a seaside resort after there has just been an outbreak of typhoid is going to attract more attention than if nothing untoward had happened.

The designer, having the potential to create a system that might cause accidents or some other untoward effect, must be prepared to optimize the design to take account of non-engineering influences. The current trend is to be concerned not only with the traditional worries about death and injury but also about the wider environmental impact.

The term 'safety' is, therefore, being applied in a broader manner. In particular, the eventual disposal of materials which, even only a few years ago, would have been discarded without thought, is becoming increasingly important. The safety scene must, therefore, be expanded to cover not only construction and use but also disposal as well. An illustration of the detail of this concern are the questions raised over the fumes from crematoriums containing mercury vapour from the fillings of teeth.

The first step in obtaining the endorsement or agreement of any body is a tactical one: how to go about it. For a well-organised group, or for one of long standing, there are probably established procedural guidelines. There is little point in simply giving a superficial description of a new design and expecting everyone to just accept it at face value.

It is sometimes necessary to involve safety authorities before a design has crystalized, with many important details still unsettled. There is a considerable advantage in going to a safety organization at the earliest possible stage as it gives them the opportunity to make a contribution and it gives some warning of what they might want whilst there is still an opportunity to provide it.

In making such an early approach the temptation is often to gloss over the uncertain areas. This is likely to cause problems as the safety authority is likely to find the uncertain areas of riveting interest. To overcome such a problem it can be advisable to break the submission into various stages.

The first stage could be an outline of the concepts, the design objectives, and the policy being adopted toward safety. At this time it is crucial to identify known hazards and uncertainties. The committee will need some clear explanatory documentation, and for anything other than the most simple of systems, special drawings highlighting the potential hazardous features are a good investment. Also of help is a set of notes about the design. If the design is portable and a prototype exists, then it saves a lot of problems if it is made available to the meeting. For systems that are large a visit does wonders to clarify the situation. If nothing yet exists, then a visit to something similar can be useful, as long as the differences are pointed out.

A timetable of when information is likely to become available is a great help and often staves off pressure for progress. If there are trials of equipment associated with safety, the committee should be encouraged to attend or be represented. It is very important that neither the safety committee nor individuals on it attempt to inject their own design ideas into the project. Not only does this cause confusion but it also tends to destroy the committee's independence.

The middle phase of the submission should cover the completed, or almost completed design, and at the time of submission should contain associated specifications, operating procedures, and the like. The final phase may well be at the commissioning stage of the system or some equally late date, and should tie-up any loose ends and provide answers to all questions raised. Also available should be the infrastructure supporting the design, such as maintenance proposals, inspections, record keeping for performance data, and so on.

There is one final thing to be achieved from all of this, hopefully successful, activity, and that is agreement that the system meets the safety requirements. Sometimes a formal document or certificate will automatically be issued covering the design. If this is not the case, then some written statement must be obtained; otherwise, at a later date, there will be long arguments as to what had been agreed.

To many people approaching a committee of potential critics is a worrying experience, especially if it is their first time. Again, depending on the scale of the enquiry, the committee may be a few people of slight seniority, or a group of learned experts. A carefully thought out approach will be an advantage to all as it will save time, avoid confusion and make the whole business more bearable.

Except for the most simple of enquiries there will be a need to create or compile a set of documents. In the following list a number may be part of normal project practice rather than specially compiled for safety. If the safety authority has not stated a preference the following package might well be suitable.

(1) *A Safety Policy Document.*
   (a) A very brief outline of the design or system
   (b) The configuration control system.
   (c) Sponsoring authorities and their responsibility.
   (d) The persons/departments responsible for interfacing with the safety authorities.
   (e) The policy toward commercial materials and equipment embodied in the design – that is, will it be assumed fit for the purpose?
   (f) The policy regarding subcontractors – for example, will they be responsible for obtaining the safety approval for their subsystem?
   (g) The role of Quality Assurance.
   (h) Safety responsibilities during construction.
   (i) Safety responsibilities during operation.
   (j) Safety responsibilities for disposal.
   (k) Management and responsibility organization trees.

(2) *Design Definition Document.*
   (a) A description of the design.
   (b) A technical specification.
   (c) An environmental or similar specification.
   (d) Identification of the potentially hazardous features – for example, stored energy or toxic materials.
   (e) A description of the safety features.
   (f) Drawings and specifications as required.

(3) *Trials Technical Summary.*
   (a) A descriptive list, including objectives, of trials planned to demonstrate safety features.
   (b) A trials programme.
   (c) An essential trials list to clear certain stages of the project or work.
   (d) The intended build standards of trial assemblies, test configurations, and the like.

(4) *A Documentation Summary.*
   A list of project documents, such as specifications, certificates, and reports that are relevant to the project, which should show their interrelationships and the issuing authorities.

Engineering System Safety

The above suite of documents would probably be appropriate for a fairly large project, but it is surprising how much is needed for quite small tasks if one wishes to proceed in an orderly manner. The normal practice is to gather together the information in dribs and drabs, and only later is it clear how much effort has been required.

One major advantage in producing a package such as the above is that it means everyone concerned has a clear picture of the total scope of the activities aimed at ensuring that a satisfactory standard of safety is achieved. Too often safety information is a byproduct of the drive to establish performance and, as such, assumes a secondary role. This is unfortunate as while the product might be accepted with a shortfall in performance, a shortfall in safety is less likely to be satisfactory.

Trials form a major part of the evidence required by safety authorities and can be very expensive as equipment is often lost beyond recovery. There is a temptation to economize by using assemblies which have survived other tests. This is quite satisfactory provided care is taken to have the assembly's condition thoroughly and formally assessed. It is then possible to determine if the failure of such an assembly during a safety test is actually due to the effects of previous trials. Economy always carries a risk and it should always be minimized.

With safety a trial failure always leave a doubt at the back of people's minds; having demonstrated a weakness there is always the possibility that it could happen again, even if by a slightly different route. This is not generally true of performance trials, but such views are not uncommon.

The bane of every designer's life is the 'grand trial'. This is often arranged not so much as a technical necessity but as a demonstration. The problem is that such trials are often expensive to mount and, because they have to have a very high chance of success, are usually preceded by numerous smaller trials to gain confidence. The result is that so much data has already been accumulated that there is no real need for the final trial at all.

As part of the evidence required by safety authorities trial and test reports are a major contribution. Safety is achieved by meticulous attention to detail, and the same care that is taken over design must be applied to the writing of reports. Apart from the obvious need to include a full account of the subject, great care must be taken over the wording. Where the project is divided into subsystems the manager must ensure that reports on each subsystem or by a subcontractor stick rigidly to the area of responsibility of the organization. Gratuitous comments about interfacing equipment and associated systems must be avoided, firstly because they are out of place, and secondly because there may be a perfectly acceptable explanation for the performance that the writer is unaware of.

Whilst this is not the place to enter into great detail on report writing, it is appropriate to emphasise that any doubts raised with safety authorities are difficult to erase. Reports must, therefore, be unambiguous. For example, the phrase 'it appeared to be undamaged' is unacceptable; either it was damaged or it was not – any doubt should be resolved. Again 'no problems were found with . . .' leaves doubt as to whether or not some would have been found upon further investigation. A report which stated that a relay 'failed at 60g' resulted in considerable transatlantic correspondence before it was confirmed that it should have read 'failed at 60g and above up to the limit of the test'.

Verbal presentations require equal care and attention. Whilst one is not expected to give a prize winning lecture there is every reason to expect the speaker to know what he is talking about. The presenter should also be aware that many committees are composed of people from different disciplines and backgrounds. It is important in this type of mixed assembly to avoid using specialist terms or acronyms which may not be widely understood; the vast number of such acronyms in use and the popularity of creating more is an area of some concern.

The presentation of a difficult and controversial case is often best left to a competent junior designer. This enables the senior members of the design team to join in any discussion from a different angle whilst still allowing the main flow to continue. Interruptions are to be avoided unless vital as they will cause confusion and open up the discussion as well as damaging the confidence of the speaker. The key to a successful presentation is ensuring that all concerned are completely clear about who is going to say what and, in particular, how questions will be answered.

During technical presentations there is frequently a need to refer to other documents for detailed information. If files and documents are to be taken to a meeting the relevant parts must be clearly 'tagged' for easy reference. Loose 'bookmarks' are unsatisfactory as they can easily slip out, and asking people to wait whilst a reference is found is a guaranteed way of loosing the case.

Legitimate behind the scene lobbying can be rewarding at times, and briefing the chairman on the background and finer points can often be useful to all concerned. It is also possible to pass the chairman information in confidence. However, there are two things to be aware of: firstly, a chairman who limits discussion on the basis of confidential information; and, secondly, the formation of factions – committees take a dislike to people 'ganging up' and are inclined to become difficult.

A good presentation is like a good speech – it should know when to stop. Very often prolonging a debate will spark off doubts, and before long the topic is wide open again.

In presenting a safety case it is often helpful to provide comparisons that are within the knowledge of the committee members, although this is not necessarily an easy option as accident figures are often very dependent upon the particular parameters of the statistics.

If engaged in a transport study comparisons between different forms of transport are fraught with difficulties. It might be that an accident rate for air travel is given in terms of passenger miles flown, accidents per passenger, accidents per hour of travel, or accidents per landing and/or take off. Clearly, if arguing the case for rail travel there are some statistics under these headings that are inappropriate and others that are very dubious, but appear to be solidly based.

As air travel usually involves longer distances than rail it is possible that it is attractive for railway organizations to relate to air passengers flown as there will possibly be more passengers on the rail than in the air; accidents per passenger mile might paint a different picture.

The comparisons of the characteristics of materials are useful especially when comparatively new ones are involved. People obtain a 'feel' for materials and with the widespread use of wood, aluminium, and steel, can better appreciate the likely strength of a structure than if it were made from, say, carbon fibre. A ladder made of carbon fibre is likely to appear weak compared with its aluminium counterpart as its strength will probably be judged on the dimensions of the treads and rails. As an aside, it will be interesting to observe if children brought up with high strength materials will have the same reservations as their parents, who gained early experience with wood.

It is possible to use the idea of equal to or better than some existing similar system. However, the use of 'equal to' is liable to raise problems, and it is, therefore, probably wiser to use 'not less safe than'. One of the greatest difficulties is that it is often very difficult to determine what the standard was, or is, for another system.

Comparison should be appropriate to the case and supportable in logical argument. There is little benefit in telling a group of Muslims that a product is less harmful than alcohol, or vegetarians that a new food contains less fat than beef. Nor is it sensible to argue that a proposed chemical works will be less hazardous than a rubbish dump as people will point out that they were not going to have a rubbish dump anyway. It is also inappropriate to argue that a new system will be no less safe than an existing one which it is installed alongside; it will not take long for someone to point out that this doubles the risk.

Comparisons between artificial accident risks, natural ones, and voluntary ones are not always meaningful. People tolerate natural disasters such as earthquakes and floods much more readily than they do industrial risks. The inhabitants of San Fransisco quite happily live in an active earthquake belt, yet are extremely concerned about their local industry. In the UK, many inhabitants of Cornwall would object to a nuclear power station although they live with a high level of radon in their houses and do not take any precautions. Comparisons with self-imposed risks such as swimming or fishing (the latter causing about 50 deaths a year) are not particularly persuasive as people will accept self-imposed risks far more readily than those wished upon them.

In arguing the validity of trials to demonstrate that a system is safe the question is sometimes raised about the effects of aging, wear and tear, and corrosion, as well as engineering tolerances. It is usual to construct trial assemblies using nominal material and machining or drawing tolerances without trying to produce, say, the weakest components. Machine shops tend to set their tools to leave maximum metal when making small numbers of components and to work the other way for long runs to cater for tool wear. This means there can be some surprising variations in weight, although not necessarily in strength.

It is almost impossible to cater for all of the permutations of dimensional and material tolerances, and the argument to cover these variations usually has to rely on allowing either a greater safety factor in the design, or on increasing the test conditions to compensate.

With nonmetallic materials the effect of aging can be quite marked, and some effort should be made to reproduce this effect. Subjecting materials to storage at above ambient temperature can significantly effect the aging process by an order of magnitude or so. It might, therefore, be necessary, in some instances, to reproduce the effect of age on seals or electrical insulation.

For critical assemblies it might be possible to operate a surveillance system, and withdraw from service aged units well before their expected life expiry date and check their condition. The safety authorities could be presented with such a plan to reassure them on the problem of long term deterioration.

Safety authorities are likely to be concerned with both the long and short term suitability of a system. In the long term there will be a need to safeguard against modifications to the system, not only directly affecting the equipment but also the procedures and the like. With the increasing use of computer control there will also be the problem of changes to software; safety requirements must cover the management of such changes. The Flixborough disaster in the UK in 1974 is a case in point; temporary changes were made to the facility which departed from the approved design. One problem of long term usage is that the original concepts and intents get forgotten with changing staff, and alterations are made which remove or alter parts whose function has been forgotten; when an accident occurs part of the counter activity supplied by these changed units is no longer available.

For long term stability the liberal use of labels and the orderly control of documents is essential. At the end of commissioning or development all temporary labels and markings must be replaced by permanent ones. Where these affect safety arrangements must be made for the safety authorities to be made aware of their importance.

On occasions the designer/manager will find he has to deal with more than one safety authority. It is not unknown for these to have, if not actually conflicting and incompatible requirements, at least an overlap of interests. Each organization can be dealt with as appropriate, but if a lot of work is involved there is considerable merit in trying to make special arrangements. It might just be possible to arrange that group A agrees to take those parts that group B have looked at 'as read' and vice versa. This is most likely where the different parties have the same sort of interests, but have to report to different authorities.

As an alternative the setting up of a combined committee has considerable merit, provided arguments over status and administration can be resolved. There is no reason for members of such a gathering to loose their independence or allegiance, they certainly do not have to agree with each other, and they can issue separate reports. A further alternative is for each body to have observers at each other's meetings; indeed, such observers could also express their parent committees' views or likely reaction to proposals. From the designer/manager's point of view almost any arrangement is better than having to deal with separate bodies working in isolation, and it is worth a considerable amount of effort to try and make suitable arrangements from the beginning.

Index